Problem Drinkers: Guided Self-Change Treatment

TREATMENT MANUALS FOR PRACTITIONERS
David H. Barlow, *Editor*

PROBLEM DRINKERS
GUIDED SELF-CHANGE TREATMENT
Mark B. Sobell and Linda C. Sobell

INSOMNIA
PSYCHOLOGICAL ASSESSMENT AND MANAGEMENT
Charles M. Morin

PSYCHOLOGICAL MANAGEMENT OF
CHRONIC HEADACHES
Paul R. Martin

TREATING PTSD
COGNITIVE-BEHAVIORAL STRATEGIES
David W. Foy, *Editor*

PREVENTING PHYSICAL AND EMOTIONAL
ABUSE OF CHILDREN
David A. Wolfe

SEXUAL DYSFUNCTION
A GUIDE FOR ASSESSMENT AND TREATMENT
John P. Wincze and Michael P. Carey

SEVERE BEHAVIOR PROBLEMS
A FUNCTIONAL COMMUNICATION TRAINING APPROACH
V. Mark Durand

DEPRESSION IN MARRIAGE
A MODEL FOR ETIOLOGY AND TREATMENT
Steven R. H. Beach, Evelyn E. Sandeen,
and K. Daniel O'Leary

TREATING ALCOHOL DEPENDENCE
A COPING SKILLS TRAINING GUIDE
Peter M. Monti, David B. Abrams,
Ronald M. Kadden, and Ned L. Cooney

SELF-MANAGEMENT FOR ADOLESCENTS
A SKILLS-TRAINING PROGRAM
MANAGING EVERYDAY PROBLEMS
Thomas A. Brigham

PSYCHOLOGICAL TREATMENT OF PANIC
David H. Barlow and Jerome A. Cerny

Problem Drinkers
Guided Self-Change Treatment

MARK B. SOBELL
LINDA C. SOBELL
Addiction Research Foundation, Toronto

Series Editor's Note by David H. Barlow

THE GUILFORD PRESS
New York   London

© 1993 The Guilford Press
A Division of Guilford Publications, Inc.
72 Spring Street, New York, NY 10012

Printed in the United States of America

This book is printed on acid-free paper.

Last digit is print number: 9 8 7 6 5 4 3 2 1

Library of Congress Cataloging-in-Publication Data

Sobell, Mark B.
    Problem drinkers : guided self-change treatment / Mark B. Sobell,
  Linda C. Sobell.
        p.   cm. —(Treatment manuals for practitioners)
    Includes bibliographical references and index.
    ISBN 0-89862-212-3
      1. Alcoholism—Treatment. 2. Self-management (Psychology)
  3. Alcoholics—Counseling of.   I. Sobell, Linda C. II. Title.
  III. Series.
      [DNLM: 1. Alcoholism—rehabilitation. 2. Self Care—methods.   WM
  274 S677p 1993]
  RC565.S62   1993
  616.86'10651—dc20
  DNLM/DLC   92-48479
  for Library of Congress   CIP

About the Authors

Mark B. Sobell received his Ph.D. in psychology from the University of California at Riverside in 1970. He is currently a Senior Scientist and Associate Director for Treatment Research and Development at the Clinical Research and Treatment Institute of the Addiction Research Foundation in Toronto, Canada, and Professor in the Departments of Psychology and Behavioural Science at the University of Toronto.

Linda C. Sobell received her Ph.D. in psychology from the University of California at Irvine in 1976. She is currently a Senior Scientist, Assistant Director for Research and Clinical Training, and Chief of the Guided Self-Change Unit at the Clinical Research and Treatment Institute of the Addiction Research Foundation in Toronto, Canada. In addition, she is Professor in the Departments of Psychology and Behavioural Science at the University of Toronto, and is currently President-Elect of the Association for Advancement of Behavior Therapy.

Together, the Sobells have authored/edited five books, written more than 100 journal articles and 35 book chapters, been members of several journal editorial boards, led many workshops, and consulted widely. They are nationally and internationally recognized for their work in the area of addictive behaviors.

*This book is dedicated to E. Mansell Pattison, MD,
our mentor, teacher, colleague,
and, best of all, our friend.*

Before his life ended in a tragic traffic accident,
Mansell's contributions to the field of alcohol studies
were manifold and well ahead of their time. It is not
just for his contributions to the field that we pay tribute,
however. This is a personal tribute, one we never had
a chance to convey fully while he was alive.

We had the privilege of working with Mansell for
2 years very early in our careers. This was an exciting
experience. He was always full of life, energetic,
informal, and able to hold your attention with his
magnetic personality. Above all, he was willing to spend
time helping others. We did not realize, some 20 years
ago, how unusual it was for such a prominent and busy
individual to pay attention to the little things that
really matter and how rare it was for a physician to
mentor psychologists. To discuss an idea with Mansell
was an exciting experience, for he was always well versed
in the current literature and could see both the big
issues and the small. Best of all he spewed forth idea
after idea, many of which have influenced our thinking
and our research.

Like an adult looking back on childhood, we now
treasure the memories of what we then took for granted.
We are grateful that we had the opportunity to be
among the cadre of people who were influenced not just
by Mansell's writings but by the experience of working
with him. The alcohol studies field has lost one of its
most advanced thinkers. What makes the tragedy worse
is that much of what Mansell championed is now
reaching fruition, and he is not here to witness this
field's emergence. He is dearly missed.

Preface

Three major research areas greatly influenced the formulation of the treatment approach for alcohol problems described in this guidebook for clinical practitioners. In the late 1970s treatment trials began to be published that reported beneficial effects from very limited interventions, the best known of which was a study by Edwards and his colleagues (Edwards, Orford, et al., 1977). These researchers found that a single session of advice/counseling was associated with treatment outcomes comparable to those associated with intensive treatment (see Chapters 1 and 2). The second influential area of research was a growing literature on natural recoveries from alcohol problems (e.g., Tuchfeld, 1981). It was becoming clear that many individuals were able to overcome their alcohol problems on their own. Finally, the conceptualization of motivation as a state that could be influenced and the development of motivational interventions (Miller, 1983, 1985) suggested a possible explanation for how brief treatments might work and how natural recoveries might come about.

The treatment described here is a motivational intervention. However, guided self-management (or self-change) extends the way motivational interventions have been used. Rather than being employed as a means to gain compliance with treatment, in guided self-management *the motivational intervention is the treatment.* This approach is based on the idea that a sizable proportion of individuals with alcohol problems can solve their problems on their own if they are sufficiently motivated and are provided with some guidance and support.

The guided self-management approach is best understood as one of many approaches that can help people with drinking problems. The first few chapters provide a context within which the guided self-management approach fits in the alcohol studies field. In succeeding chapters we discuss the rationale, the methods, and procedures in some detail. Since this book was written for practicing clinicians, we emphasize the clinical utility and applicability of the procedures. For example, when we discuss assessment instruments, we explain how they can be of value in treatment. When we discuss selected treatment findings, we emphasize what they tell us about how to do the treatment or about how the treatment might work. Finally, we go to some length to emphasize the need for flexibility in adapting research treatment procedures to clinical settings. While adherence to a protocol is essential when conducting a research study, in clinical practice one is free of research constraints (e.g., the amount of treatment can be determined on an individual case basis), and one has to deal with a wider range of clients (unlike research studies, which involve volunteers who usually must satisfy a set of screening criteria). The results and clinical examples presented in this book are from the major evaluative study of the treatment (Sobell, Sobell, & Leo, 1990). The version of guided self-management used in that study involved an assessment plus two 90-minute structured treatment sessions.

Our primary goal in writing this book was to increase the consciousness and knowledge of service providers about *how to identify problem drinkers* and about *what types of treatment approaches make sense for such individuals.* We hope clinicians will find this book helpful and will use the treatment principles and procedures in their practice.

Acknowledgments

We are very grateful to Wayne Skinner, Joanne Spratt, Julie Henderson, and Simonne LeBreton, who were therapists in the evaluation of the guided self-management treatment and who enthusiastically and meticulously followed the study protocol. Also, we appreciate the assistance of the Assessment Unit, medical, and other staff at the Addiction Research Foundation, who helped in the evaluation of the treatment. Lastly, the evaluation was greatly aided by the invaluable research assistance of Gloria Leo.

MARK B. SOBELL
LINDA C. SOBELL

Series Editor's Note

Advances in scientific understanding and treatment are hard won and always controversial. Few individuals have made more substantial contributions or have had to endure more controversy along the way than Mark and Linda Sobell. Working at one of the leading centers on research in addictive disorders, the Addiction Research Foundation in Toronto, the Sobells have developed a new treatment protocol for clinicians that takes advantage of findings on natural recovery from alcohol problems. This program capitalizes on the ability of many individuals with alcohol problems to help themselves when provided with a proper program and support. Written in a way that facilitates ready integration into clinical practice, this latest important contribution represents a state-of-the-art protocol for dealing with problem drinking and is a text no clinician working with alcohol-related problems will want to be without.

DAVID H. BARLOW
University at Albany
State University of New York

Contents

NOTE ABOUT PHOTOCOPY RIGHTS

The publisher grants book purchasers permission to reproduce handouts and
forms in this book for professional use with their clients.

Problem Drinkers: Guided Self-Change Treatment

1

Treatment Approaches to Alcohol Problems

This book is intended for clinicians wishing to use a self-management approach in the treatment of persons who have nonsevere alcohol problems. The approach is largely motivational and cognitive-behavioral. It is directed toward helping people help themselves. While the nature of the target population—persons whose alcohol problems are not severe, whom we will define as "problem drinkers"—is discussed at length in this book, an understanding of this treatment approach is enhanced by viewing the alcohol field in perspective. Self-management approaches have been a part of an evolution of treatment approaches within the alcohol field. In a broader context, this evolution is consistent with changes occurring in other health-related fields, where there has been a growing acceptance of brief treatments and self-help based interventions for many health and mental health problems (Mahalik & Kivlighan, 1988; Scogin, Bynum, Stephens, & Calhoon, 1990). For this book, however, consideration of these issues will be restricted to the alcohol field.

The Evolution of Approaches to the Treatment of Alcohol Problems

It is now widely acknowledged that treatment for alcohol problems has developed in and continues to be practiced in the relative absence of integration of scientific knowledge about the nature of the disorder (Gordis, 1987; Heather & Robertson, 1983; Pattison, Sobell, & Sobell, 1977). One reason for this state of affairs is that treatments for alcohol problems were not initially based on scientifically derived knowledge about the disorder but rather on anecdotal and subjective impressions. Another reason is that although considerable scientific knowledge about alcohol problems has accumulated over the past 30 to 40 years, the treatments most widely available in North America are

1

remarkably similar to those used several decades ago (Cook, 1988a, 1988b; Fingarette, 1988; Hill, 1985; Peele, 1990). These treatments either lack research support or are contraindicated by research evidence (Fingarette, 1988; Hill, 1985; Miller & Hester, 1986a; Peele, 1989; Shaffer, 1985).

In what follows, we will call "belief based" those treatments that have been developed without a research basis. Most often these are 12-step treatments based on the Alcoholics Anonymous literature (Nowinski, Baker, & Carroll, 1992). Treatments that have been empirically evaluated and have a scientific basis will be referred to as research based.

In light of how the alcohol treatment field has evolved, an interesting question is why treatments should be research based. If one considers treatments for other health problems, the answer, reflected in the words of Enoch Gordis, a physician and director of the National Institute on Alcohol Abuse and Alcoholism, is obvious:

> It would be unthinkable, for instance, to unleash a new drug therapy for cancer, a new antibiotic for kidney disease, a new medicine for the prevention of second heart attacks or even a new flavoring agent for foods without careful evaluation and planning. . . . Yet in the case of alcoholism, our whole treatment system, with its innumerable therapies, armies of therapists, large and expensive programs, endless conferences, innovation and public relations activities is founded on hunch, not evidence, and not on science. . . . [T]he history of medicine demonstrates repeatedly that unevaluated treatment, no matter how compassionately administered, is frequently useless and wasteful and sometimes dangerous or harmful. (Gordis, 1987, p. 582)

In spite of Gordis's admonition, the most common treatment programs in the alcohol field, the Minnesota Model programs (Cook, 1988a, 1988b), are 28-day intensive inpatient programs. These and most traditional alcohol treatment programs have not been evaluated in the kinds of controlled trials that would support their widespread acceptance. In addition, there has been no research showing that these approaches are more effective than alternative, less intrusive, and less costly approaches. Much of what is taken for granted about the nature of alcohol problems and its treatment is based on beliefs rather than research. Unfortunately, while research-based treatments can and have changed to accommodate new research findings, belief-based treatments have changed very little despite contradictory evidence.

Some Key Issues

While it is not our purpose in this book to present an in-depth review of conventional notions about alcohol problems and treatment approaches, certain aspects of alcohol problems and treatment are important to the understanding of self-management treatments. One point we wish to emphasize is that conventional treatments were developed to treat *chronic* alcoholics. The program we present in this book is intended for persons who are *problem drinkers* (see Chapter 3).

There is considerable disagreement in the alcohol field about what constitutes alcohol problems and who has them. For example, what are the differences between those labeled as alcoholic and those we call problem drinkers? More specifically, what are the defining features of alcoholism versus heavy drinking? Is alcohol dependence a better term than alcoholism? These and dozens of definitional questions cannot be answered, for there is no consensus on terminology in the alcohol field.

Consideration of some recent definitions will illustrate these difficulties. In the *Seventh Special Report to the U.S. Congress on Alcohol and Health* (National Institute on Alcohol Abuse and Alcoholism, 1990), the National Institute on Alcohol Abuse and Alcoholism (NIAAA) divides the drinker population into three groups: (1) persons who drink with few, if any, problems; (2) nondependent problem drinkers who have difficulties secondary to alcohol consumption; and (3) persons who are dependent on alcohol and who suffer from the disease called alcoholism or alcohol dependence. The latter individuals are characterized by (a) tolerance, (b) physical dependence, (c) impaired control over regulating drinking, and (d) the discomfort of abstinence, or craving. The report goes on to assert that "an estimated 10.5 million U.S. adults exhibit some symptoms of alcoholism or alcohol dependence and an additional 7.2 million abuse alcohol, but do not yet show symptoms of dependence" (National Institute on Alcohol Abuse and Alcoholism, 1990, p. ix). Based on this, the NIAAA defines two types of alcohol problems—alcohol dependence (which is referred to as alcoholism) and alcohol abuse (which is referred to as nondependent problem drinking)—and they assert that the population of dependent persons is approximately 45% larger than that of alcohol abusers. This classification, however, relies upon the difficult-to-define and even more difficult-to-measure characteristic of "impaired control over regulating drinking."

In contrast to the NIAAA estimate, a recent report to the NIAAA by the Institute of Medicine (IOM) of the U.S. National Academy of Sciences states that "Approximately one-fifth [of the population of the United States] consumes substantial amounts of alcohol, and approximately 5 per cent drink heavily" (Institute of Medicine, 1990, pp. 30–31). The IOM report defines the former group as "problem drinkers" and the latter group as "alcoholics" or "dependent drinkers." The findings are summarized as "most people have no alcohol problems, many people have some alcohol problems, and a few people have many alcohol problems" (Institute of Medicine, 1990, p. 214). According to the IOM report, there are four times as many problem drinkers as there are alcohol-dependent individuals.

To complicate matters, consider definitional changes that have occurred in the *Diagnostic and Statistical Manual* (DSM) of the American Psychiatric Association. Whereas the Institute of Medicine report (1990) cites references in support of its classifications, the DSM diagnoses are based on consensus by a panel of professional consultants. The third edition of the manual, revised in the mid-1980s (DSM-III-R; American Psychiatric Association, 1987), includes categories of alcohol abuse and alcohol dependence, with definitions relatively consistent with those used by the Institute of Medicine. However, a fourth edition of the manual, which is intended to serve as the mainstay for psychiatric diagnoses for the 1990s, may change these definitions so that most of what has been considered alcohol abuse in the DSM-III-R will now be considered low-level dependence (Nathan, 1991), thereby blurring the definitional distinction introduced by the IOM (1990) report.

Obviously, there are many classifications and definitions of alcohol problems. However, since this book is intended as a guidebook for practitioners, we will use definitions that have practical value. Thus, when we refer to chronic alcoholics, we mean the stereotypical image of the alcoholic, the image often portrayed in the media. Chronic alcoholics are individuals whose life is centered around procuring and consuming alcohol and who, upon stopping drinking, suffer severe withdrawal symptoms (e.g., severe tremors, hallucinations, seizures, delirium tremens). Some chronic alcoholics will experience significant brain and other end organ damage (e.g., cirrhosis) as a result of their drinking. Usually there is extensive social impairment, for example, few meaningful relationships with family members, vocational problems, and a history of alcohol-related arrests.

Historically (i.e., 1930s through 1950s), chronic alcoholics were the population of persons with alcohol problems to whom treatments were first directed. This is understandable, since Alcoholics Anonymous did not start until the mid-1930s and few treatment programs existed prior to that time. Severely dependent individuals were not only those most in need of services, but also the most visible. The concern was with persons who were at risk of dying from drinking-related problems or from severe withdrawals. With an absence of services, and the aura of life-threatening illness, the first priority for health care was to save lives.

While there is not much of a research basis for the use of very intensive treatments with these serious cases, given the low level of functioning of chronic alcoholics, it is clear that many circumstances may need to be addressed for any treatment to be effective. Thus, if the person has no place to live, it is reasonable to think that treatment involving alternative living arrangements would be conducive to recovery. It also may be necessary to help the individual develop a different social environment—one that supports recovery by removing the alcoholic from drinking situations. Other services such as vocational rehabilitation might also be necessary. In terms of treatment aimed at behavior change including cessation of drinking, it might be appropriate to use a fairly directive approach, where the individual is advised and instructed how to act, rather than using an approach that depends on complex thought processes. Even though it has not yet been empirically demonstrated, persons with alcohol-related brain dysfunction would seem poor candidates for approaches that involve considerable abstract reasoning and self-direction. Consequently, the treatment procedures described in this book, which rely on intact cognitive capacities, are not intended for persons who may have brain damage.

What about people who do not fit the definitional criteria of the chronic alcoholic but whose drinking causes them difficulties? Such individuals are often referred to as "problem drinkers." As described in more depth in Chapter 3, problem drinkers typically have either experienced negative consequences of their drinking or drink in ways that place them at risk of such consequences; however, they usually do not drink steadily, do not show major withdrawal symptoms when they stop drinking, and sometimes drink with control, and their lives do not revolve around drinking.

As the result of epidemiological investigations, problem drinkers began to receive attention in the late 1960s and early 1970s. However, despite this recognition, in the ensuing years the treatment system has neither changed nor expanded to accommodate problem drinkers.

In Chapters 2 and 3 we consider problem drinkers as a group in need of different services from those currently available, and we address how the notion of "progressivity" has impeded responding to this need. The issue is not simply that the alcohol field has failed to recognize the need to provide alternative services for problem drinkers, but that clinical practice in the field is discordant with research findings. Even with respect to more serious cases of alcohol problems for which conventional treatments were developed, the procedures demonstrated in the research literature as cost effective have been ignored in clinical practice (Miller & Hester, 1986a). This is probably due to a lack of accountability for treatment effectiveness that has existed until recently (Gordis, 1987; Holden, 1987) and to the fact that the majority of today's treatments are based on a set of strong beliefs about alcohol problems.

In most health care fields practitioners are eager to learn about and to apply research advances in their practice. In the alcohol field, this is different; many practitioners are not interested in research unless it is consistent with their own beliefs.

The Role of Outpatient Services

Since alcohol problems come in many types and severities, a logical premise is that different individuals will respond best to different types of treatment.

Here it is helpful to visualize a continuum of services that vary in the intensity of interventions. Often there will be considerable correspondence between the problem severity and the intensity of the intervention. A main consideration in recommending treatments will be the extent to which the interventions will consume resources, will intrude upon a person's life, and will require lifestyle changes. Obviously more demanding and costly treatments should be reserved for those who have serious problems or impairment. Against this background, and with the understanding that we are not arguing that there is no role for intensive treatments, there are difficulties with prescribing intensive interventions for all types of alcohol problems.

In order to understand and appreciate why outpatient treatment is important, it is helpful to consider addictions services in the context of other health and mental health services. Over the past several years, serious concern has developed about the cost of health care services. From the standpoint of government, there are real economic limits to the amount of public funding that can be dedicated to health care. This is especially true in countries like Canada and Great Britain where health services are wholly publicly funded. Since in such countries nearly all health care costs are paid out of tax revenue, the costs are tied directly to the economy. Very serious attention is given to cost containment because higher costs ultimately mean higher taxes. In the United States some health services are publicly funded but most are provided by private health insurance. Since the costs usually are not directly paid by the government, pressure for cost containment has in the past come from insurance carriers. More recently, however, the need to contain health care costs has become part of the national political agenda and runaway health care costs have been viewed as a major impediment to economic growth. From a government perspective, concern for those with health and mental health problems must be balanced with the need to support other important priorities, such as education and care for the elderly. Consequently, those responsible for formulating public policy must ensure that the funding is spent in ways that are equitable and efficient. In medicine, for example, it is expected that the use of hospital beds will be restricted to cases where inpatient stays can be justified. The concern is not to save money but rather to assure that limited resources are used wisely in order to benefit as many persons as possible. This is one of the natural forces that has contributed to the rise of outpatient treatments.

An important factor encouraging the growth of outpatient services for alcohol abusers has been repeated studies showing that for many individuals in this population, outpatient treatment produces as good an outcome as inpatient treatment. This issue has been investigated for alcohol problems at varying severities, but it is particularly supported for problem drinkers.

We want to stress that when evaluating comparative treatment research, the key question is not whether one treatment is as effective as another, but whether a more expensive or demanding (from the client's view) treatment produces a sufficiently superior outcome to warrant the additional cost or personal investment. Several studies have now examined the relationship between length of inpatient treatment and treatment outcome for alcohol problems (reviewed by Annis, 1986a, and Miller & Hester, 1986a). The findings are straightforward. Controlled studies, without exception, have found no advantage for longer over shorter inpatient treatment, whether treatment occurs over several days or weeks. Taking the issue a step further, one can ask whether residential care is even necessary. Two controlled studies have compared day treatment with inpatient treatment for alcohol problems (McCrady et al., 1986; McLachlan & Stein, 1982) and both found no differences between the two treatments.

Several controlled studies have compared the effectiveness of inpatient versus outpatient treatment for alcohol problems. Edwards and Guthrie (1967) randomly assigned 40 male alcohol abusers either to inpatient treatment averaging 9 weeks in length or to outpatient treatment averaging 7.5 sessions. Not only were no differences found between the groups over a 1-year follow-up but trends for differences favored the outpatients.

A study by Kissin, Platz, and Su (1970) is also informative despite a serious design problem and a low (49%) follow-up rate that makes the findings inconclusive. Alcoholics ($n = 458$) were assigned to either outpatient alcohol treatment, outpatient psychotherapy, inpatient rehabilitation, or no treatment. Unfortunately, random assignment was violated as clients assigned to inpatient treatment were allowed to substitute one of the two outpatient treatments if they wished. Two thirds of those assigned to inpatient treatment chose outpatient treatment instead. While this violation of random assignment destroys the value of the study as a comparative effectiveness evaluation, it demonstrates very clearly that a high percentage of individuals prefer outpatient to inpatient treatment, which bears on the issues of acceptability of treatments to clients and matching of clients to treatments.

Pittman and Tate (1969) randomly assigned 255 alcoholics to either 6 weeks of inpatient treatment plus aftercare or to detoxification lasting 7 to 10 days. At 1-year follow-up, no differences were found between groups. Another study (Stein, Newton, & Bowman, 1975) compared alcoholics who after inpatient detoxification were randomly assigned to outpatient aftercare or to a 25-day inpatient treatment. A 13-month follow-up found no significant differences between groups. Finally, Wilson, White, and Lange (1978) randomly assigned 90 alcoholics to either inpatient or outpatient treatment. At 5-month follow-up, fewer alcoholism symptoms were found for the outpatient group, but by a 10-month follow-up these differences had disappeared.

A controlled study that did not explicitly evaluate inpatient against outpatient treatment but that has direct relevance for the development of self-management treatment is the classic trial of "treatment" and "advice" by

Edwards and his colleagues (Edwards, Orford, et al., 1977; Orford, Oppenheimer, & Edwards, 1976). In that study, 100 married male alcoholics were randomly assigned to receive either a standard package of care that could include outpatient and/or inpatient treatment or to receive a single outpatient session of advice. Although a 2-year follow-up found no difference in outcome between the groups, a trend was noted. More severely debilitated clients had better outcomes when provided the full package of care, and those with less-severe problems did better with a single session of advice. These findings, however, were based on a small number of cases.

In summary, the study by Edwards and his fellow researchers and the other controlled studies reviewed have consistently failed to find evidence that inpatient treatment for alcohol problems produces superior outcomes over outpatient treatment, except for the more impaired clients in the study by Edwards and his colleagues. On this basis alone, outpatient treatment is a more cost-effective alternative to inpatient treatment for the less-impaired alcohol abuser.

Nonintensive Outpatient Treatments

Another type of intervention that has begun to receive widespread attention as a broad public health response to alcohol and drug problems has been called "brief advice," "early intervention," or "brief intervention." This strategy got its initial impetus from a study of smokers by Russell, Wilson, Taylor, and Baker (1979) in Great Britain. These researchers demonstrated that if cigarette smokers were simply advised by their physicians to stop smoking, particularly if they were also provided with a short pamphlet on tips for stopping smoking, about 5% stopped smoking at a 1-year follow-up compared to only 1% to 2% of patients who were not advised to stop smoking. While this finding may not seem dramatic, the results are important when one considers that the vast majority of adults visit their physician at least once every 5 years. Russell estimated that if all general practice physicians in Great Britain advised their smoking patients to stop smoking, this would yield about half a million ex-smokers per year. In contrast, he estimated that it would take at least a 200-fold increase in smoking-cessation clinics to yield an equivalent number of ex-smokers. In terms of the overall health care system, this study revealed a highly cost-effective countermeasure for helping people stop smoking.

A similar strategy has been used to encourage heavy or problem drinkers to reduce or cease their drinking. Interestingly, most of these interventions have not been in response to an individual's request for treatment. Instead, they often involve individuals identified as excessive drinkers by primary care clinicians (typically physicians). An example of such a study with drinkers was reported by Persson and Magnusson (1989). Of 2,114 patients attending somatic outpatient clinics in Sweden, 78 were identified as either reporting excessive alcohol consumption on a questionnaire or as having abnormal liver serum enzyme levels on a blood test. These patients were randomly assigned either to a control group or to a limited intervention that involved an interview with a physician followed by monthly checkups to gather information on the patients' drinking and enzyme levels and to provide patients with feedback. Those patients given the intervention showed positive effects for all of the main variables examined (e.g., drinking levels, serum enzyme levels) over the course of the intervention.

Other studies with less patient contact have yielded similar findings (Chick, Lloyd, & Crombie, 1985; Kristenson, Öhlin, Hultén-Nosslin, Trell, & Hood, 1983; Kristenson, Trell, & Hood, 1981). Such studies are usually hospital or clinic based, and the intervention seldom consists of more than advice to reduce drinking and education about the health risks associated with heavy drinking. Typically, little evidence is provided that the targets of the advice have experienced serious life problems related to their drinking. A similar strategy, but in a nonmedical setting, has been reported by Miller and his colleagues (Miller & Sovereign, 1989; Miller, Sovereign, & Krege, 1988). A "Drinker's Check-up" was offered to the public through media advertisements. Thus far, short-term significant decreases in alcohol consumption have been reported.

With regard to helping persons who self-identify as having alcohol problems, brief interventions have also been positively evaluated. One of the best known studies, conducted by Edwards and his colleagues (1977), has already been discussed. In contrast to Edwards and his fellow researchers, most minimal interventions have been specifically directed at problem drinkers. These treatments usually allow goals of reduced drinking or abstinence or allow clients to choose their own goal (reviewed in Institute of Medicine, 1990), and they often use self-help manuals and/or one or more sessions of counseling. (See Babor, Ritson, & Hodgson, 1986, Heather, 1989, Institute of Medicine, 1990, and Saunders & Aasland, 1987, for reviews of these studies.)

Very often studies of self-identified problem drinkers have found very brief treatments, and sometimes even bibliotherapy (self-help manuals used by clients), to be as effective as more intensive outpatient treatments. For example, Chick and his colleagues (Chick, Ritson, Connaughton, Stewart, & Chick, 1988) randomly assigned 152 clients at an alcohol clinic either to one session of simple advice (5-minute discussion where the client was told that he or she had an alcohol problem and should stop drinking), one session of amplified advice (30- to 60-minute discussion intended to increase the client's motivation to change), or extended treatment that included amplified advice plus individualized further help that could have involved inpatient or day treatment. At a 2-year follow-up, the extended treatment group had suffered less harm from their drinking, but abstinence and problem-free drinking rates did not differ significantly between the treatments.

The study by Chick et al. (1988) was exceptional in the use of an inpatient condition and a 5-minute advice condition. More typical of studies comparing the intensity of outpatient treatment is a study reported by Zweben, Pearlman, and Li (1988). Married couples in which at least one of the partners had an alcohol problem were randomly assigned to eight sessions of conjoint therapy or to one session of conjoint advice and counseling. At the 18-month follow-up there were no differences between the treatments on any outcome measures. Another similar study was reported by Skutle and Berg (1987). Problem drinkers received either 4 hours of instruction in the use of a self-help manual or were assigned to one of three other treatments involving 12 to 16 therapist-directed outpatient sessions (e.g., coping-skills training). At 1-year follow-up, there were no differences between the treatments.

Other studies comparing different amounts of outpatient treatment for alcohol abusers are described in the reviews mentioned earlier. Many of these studies involved relatively small sample sizes, and thus differences between treatments would have to be large to be evaluated as statistically significant (Kazdin & Bass, 1989). However, even when the issue of sample size has been taken into account, no superiority has been demonstrated for more intensive over less intensive treatments (Hall & Heather, 1991).

The above conclusions about the generally equivalent effectiveness of intensive and nonintensive treatments derive from studies where nonselected populations were assigned to treatments. That is, all of the eligible subjects for a given study were assigned nonsystematically among the treatments. While it is possible that some individuals respond particularly well to intensive treatment and others to nonintensive treatment, these interactions cannot be discerned from studies conducted to date. A matching strategy, where clients are purposely assigned or misassigned to treatments thought to "match" their needs would shed some light on this question (Miller & Hester, 1986b). The conduct of high quality prospective matching research, however, is a complicated and resource consuming enterprise (Finney & Moos, 1986).

Several of the following chapters are devoted to a consideration of the literature on issues related to the development and application of self-management treatment of alcohol problems. Although we have written about many of these issues and procedures previously (e.g., L. C. Sobell & M. B. Sobell, 1973, 1983, 1992b; Sobell, Sobell, & Nirenberg, 1988; M. B. Sobell & L. C. Sobell, 1978, 1986/1987; Sobell, Sobell, & Sheahan, 1976), we have never before tied these topics together. That intergration is the primary goal of this book.

2

The Recognition
of Problem Drinkers

Services tailored to problem drinkers have been neglected for several reasons. First, workers in the alcohol field have not made services for problem drinkers a priority. Second, many therapists may be uncomfortable with suitable alternative treatments for problem drinkers as they often involve brief treatment and a reduced-drinking rather than abstinence goal (Sanchez-Craig, 1990; Sanchez-Craig & Wilkinson, 1986/1987; M. B. Sobell & L. C. Sobell, 1986/1987). In our view, however, the major reason why appropriate treatments for problem drinkers have not been offered is conceptual, relating to the traditional notion that alcohol problems are a progressive disorder.

Are Alcohol Problems Progressive?

To suggest that alcohol problems are progressive means that once the problems develop, they will inevitably worsen and follow a predictable course of symptoms if drinking continues. Several decades ago this concept was applied to alcohol problems by Jellinek (1946, 1952, 1960a, 1960b). The main problem with the notion of progressivity is that it lacks empirical support.

The basic approach used by Jellinek and others-who have attempted to replicate his work (reviewed by Pattison, Sobell, & Sobell, 1977) involved retrospectively interviewing severe alcoholics and having them reconstruct the temporal ordering of symptoms they had experienced. Interestingly, Jellinek's first study was not planned. The then-fledgling self-help organization, Alcoholics Anonymous (AA), had prepared a questionnaire that was distributed in their newsletter, the Grapevine. The questionnaire provided respondents with a list of symptoms and asked them to indicate in what year they had experienced each symptom. Of approximately 1,600 questionnaires distributed through the Grapevine, 98 were returned and usable. Jellinek was then asked by AA to analyze the returns, and he agreed, despite knowing the research problems that plagued that survey. Paramount among these were: (1) the sample was highly selective (the typical subject was a long-time member of AA and well versed in AA writings); (2) the subjects were only asked to indicate when a particular event first happened; and (3) the list of potential events was generated by the staff of the Grapevine. Nevertheless, Jellinek analyzed and reported the data, and the notion that alcohol problems follow an inexorable course was born.

Later studies of progressivity, while not as biased in design or in the demands placed on subjects, still obtained retrospective data from severely dependent alcoholics. Although these studies do not agree on the exact ordering of symptoms (see Mandell, 1983), typically severe alcoholics do report that they experienced less serious symptoms earlier in their problem drinking career. Such reports tell us that persons with severe problems will report that they experienced less severe problems in the past, but they do not address the central issue of progressivity. That is, they fail to assess whether people who have an alcohol problem at one time and continue to drink will have a worse problem at a later time.

The appropriate way to determine whether alcohol problems are progressive is by prospective studies, that is, by tracking people who have been identified as having alcohol problems over time. A sizable number of longitudinal studies that have used this methodology have overwhelmingly demonstrated that a minority of cases (about 25–30%) do show a progressive development of alcohol problems (i.e., they worsen over time with continued drinking) (Fillmore, 1988; Mandell, 1983). The more common pattern, however, is one of people moving into and out of periods of alcohol problems of varying severity, with problem episodes separated by periods of either abstinence or of drinking without problems (Cahalan, 1970; Cahalan & Room, 1974; Pattison et al., 1977). Except in a few cases where persons have fairly advanced problems (Fillmore & Midanik, 1984), it is not possible to predict with any confidence that an individual who has an alcohol problem and does not get treatment will still have problems at a later time. It is also impossible to predict how severe the problems will be if they continue. One recent study, for example, found that some persons' problems are less serious at a later point in time (Hasin, Grant, & Endicott, 1990). Findings such as these have led some (e.g., Hill, 1985; Kissin, 1983) to hypothesize that problem drinkers may be qualitatively different from individuals who become chronic alcoholics, and that problem drinkers may never progress to being severely dependent on alcohol. This thesis awaits empirical test.

Despite the lack of evidence for progressivity, the notion is deeply ingrained in the field's thinking about alcohol problems. For example, the *Seventh Special Report to the U.S. Congress on Alcohol and Health* (1990) by the National Institute on Alcohol Abuse and Alcoholism states that "7.2 million abuse alcohol, but do not *yet* show symptoms of dependence" (p. ix, italics added). The word "yet" conveys a clear expectation that these individuals will become dependent unless they are steered from that course.

The progressivity notion is the pivotal justification for the position that anyone with identifiable alcohol problems, regardless of severity, should receive the same treatment. The assumption is that alcohol problems form a uniform disorder, and unless an individual who has developed alcohol problems ceases drinking the disorder will intensify to chronic alcoholism. Many existing treatment approaches are predicated on the notion that anyone who is identified as having an alcohol problem is in the midst of a progressive deterioration into full-blown alcoholism unless they stop drinking. If this approach is taken, then all cases are viewed as suitable for the same treatment because the primary difference between individuals is that some have deteriorated less than others when they enter treatment.

To date, the primary benefit of recognizing problem drinkers has been an increased emphasis on early case identification (Weisner & Room, 1984/1985). This, unfortunately, has led to routing such individuals to conventional treatments. A major element of "early interventions" based on the progressivity notion is an emphasis on convincing such individuals of the futility of their attempting to control their drinking. As illustrated in the next chapter, most problem drinkers do not drink excessively every time they drink. Often they limit their alcohol consumption to nonhazardous levels. Thus, the subjective experience of most problem drinkers contradicts the edict that they lack control over their drinking.

A major field demonstration of how service providers fail to distinguish problem drinkers from chronic alcoholics was reported several years ago by Hansen and Emrick (1983). The authors studied the fates of trained actors sent to five inpatient treatment centers and one outpatient treatment center to be evaluated for treatment of a possible alcohol problem. The five actors were trained to represent varying levels of drinking-problem severity: one was trained to present as someone who was an alcoholic in the past but who had achieved a stable non-problem-drinking recovery and actually needed no treatment; the other four were trained to present as problem drinkers, none of whom would qualify for a diagnosis of alcohol dependence and none of whom would require inpatient treatment. The authors concluded that "there was no apparent consistency as to who was considered 'alcoholic' nor was any relationship observed between the severity of the symptoms presented and the treatment recommended" (p. 164).

Prevalence of Problem Drinkers

In Chapter 1, we briefly mentioned that problem drinkers constitute a much larger group than severely dependent drinkers. In fact, considerable epidemiological and longitudinal research supports this conclusion. In the early 1970s, when the alcohol field started to gain visibility as an area of research, epidemi-ological studies began reporting compelling evidence that the very chronic alcoholics who had the public's eye were only the tip of the iceberg of individuals with alcohol problems. In a national survey of alcohol use in the United States, Cahalan (1970) found that 15% of men and 4% of women had experienced multiple alcohol problems at some time during the 3 years preceding the interview. If a more liberal criterion of alcohol problems is employed, these rates increase to 43% for men and 21% for women. Yet, only a small percentage of respondents reported experiencing alcohol withdrawal symptoms. Although it is impossible to calculate the actual prevalence of severe dependence in Cahalan's sample, the important point is that many people had alcohol problems without accompanying physical dependence.

In another study that conducted a random survey of U.S. Air Force personnel, Polich (1981) found that 4.6% of respondents could be classified as alcohol dependent (symptoms of withdrawal and impaired control over drinking), whereas 9.5% could be classified as nondependent alcohol abusers (based on serious adverse effects of drinking or consumption of >150 ml of ethanol daily). Noting that these findings were based on a selected subgroup within the general population, Polich compared his results with those of major epidemiological studies. He concluded that "the comparative analysis of problem drinking among civilians and military personnel reveals no striking differences between them, after demographic differences are taken into ac-count" (p. 1131). In a Scandinavian study of middle-aged males in the general population, Kristenson (1987) found that 5.4% were alcohol dependent, whereas 9.4% had alcohol-related problems but were not dependent. Similar studies have been reported by Cahalan and Room (1974) and by Hilton (1987, 1991).

Besides the survey findings, several longitudinal studies have examined the prevalence of alcohol problems at a given time as well as interviewed individuals on two or more occasions. These studies have not only failed to support the notion of progressivity but they have also provided evidence for the prevalence of problem drinking. For interested readers, the literature on longitudinal studies has been impressively summarized by Fillmore (1988).

In addition to the general population studies, problem drinkers can also be found in treatment programs. Skinner and Allen (1982) found that alcohol abusers who had voluntarily entered treatment and scored below the median on the Alcohol Dependence Scale were likely to report no history or signs of physical dependence on alcohol, to not self-identify as alcoholic, and to not perceive a need for abstinence as the goal of treatment. Further evidence of problem drinkers in treatment is discussed in Chapter 3, where characteristics of problem drinkers are considered in greater detail.

A recent report by the Institute of Medicine to the NIAAA suggests that the ratio of problem drinkers to those seriously dependent on alcohol is about

4:1 (Institute of Medicine, 1990). As discussed in Chapter 1, the exact ratio of problem drinkers to more severely dependent individuals will depend on the definitions used (Hilton, 1991). Whatever the definition, the important point is that by any reasonable definition, the population of problem drinkers is quite large, and it is considerably larger than the population of persons who are severely dependent on alcohol (Room, 1977, 1980; Skinner, 1990). Clearly, problem drinkers form a sizable population that manifests alcohol problems, but they do not fit the conventional stereotype of individuals physically and chronically dependent on alcohol. The distribution of alcohol use in the adult population is graphically displayed in Figure 2.1, which reflects the estimates by the Institute of Medicine, as well as a gray area of a range of estimates derived from other classifications in which different criteria were used for making the distinction between severely dependent and problem drinkers.

To this point, we have considered how the alcohol field has gradually come to recognize the existence of problem drinkers, a sizable population of

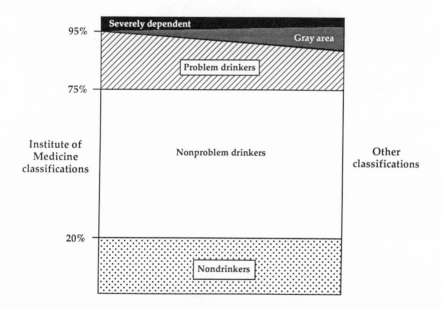

FIGURE 2.1. Distribution of alcohol use in the adult population. From "Treatment for Problem Drinkers: A Public Health Priority" by M. B. Sobell and L. C. Sobell, 1993, in J. S. Baer, G. A. Marlatt, and R. J. McMahon, eds., *Addictive Behaviors across the Lifespan: Prevention, Treatment, and Policy Issues*, Beverly Hills, CA: Sage. Copyright 1993 by Mark B. Sobell and Linda C. Sobell. Adapted by permission.

individuals with alcohol problems. In Chapter 3, we will consider how problem drinkers differ from more severely dependent persons with alcohol problems, and in Chapter 4, we will cover why problem drinkers require different interventions from the intensive treatments that currently dominate the alcohol treatment system.

3

A Closer Look at Problem Drinkers

Studies of Problem Drinkers

Although there is a tendency to consider alcohol problems as a unitary phenomenon, in reality alcohol problems are quite heterogeneous. About the only thing such problems do have in common is that they represent adverse consequences related to alcohol consumption.

Several years ago, Thorley (1980) suggested that three major types of alcohol problems could be distinguished. The first category involves problems related to acute intoxication (e.g., accidental injuries, arrests for drunk driving, fights). The second category includes problems related to regular heavy drinking. Although such problems often involve health consequences (e.g., cirrhosis), other consequences can occur (e.g., financial, marital). These consequences occur in individuals who are seldom "drunk" and who are not physically dependent on alcohol. Jellinek (1960b) noted such consequences among some Europeans who regularly consumed large amounts of wine but seldom in a pattern that would produce a high blood alcohol level. The World Health Organization (WHO) considers these two categories of problems to constitute "alcohol-related disabilities" (Edwards, Gross, Keller, Moser, & Room, 1977).

The final category of alcohol problems consists of problems related to dependence, including the manifestation of alcohol withdrawal symptoms upon the cessation of drinking and consequences related to long periods of intoxication (e.g., job loss). This category combines the WHO categories of alcohol-related disabilities and alcohol dependence (i.e., vocational problems are considered an alcohol-related disability by the WHO).

While the three domains of problems will often overlap (i.e., evidence of all three types of consequences may be apparent), problem drinkers suffer largely from problems related to intoxication. Their drinking is typically not characterized by features such as compulsive alcohol seeking, daily drinking, or by high blood alcohol levels sustained over lengthy periods of time. Yet, it is these features of severe dependence that many existing treatment programs are designed to address. The problem drinker's troubles are more related to drinking episodes that get out of hand, to consequences of drunkenness, and to recognizing that they sometimes consume more alcohol than they planned.

The costs incurred to individuals and society by problem drinkers are formidable, especially when we recall that problem drinkers are more numerous than severely dependent persons. Moore and Gerstein (1981) have reported that the majority of costs attributed to alcohol misuse relate to instances of acute intoxication among persons who are not severely dependent on alcohol. Interestingly, while these costs are eagerly used to lobby for more funding for alcohol services, when funding is received, it is devoted largely to additional services for severely dependent individuals (Cahalan, 1987; Institute of Medicine, 1990; Miller & Hester, 1986a). To some extent, this might be related to the notion of progressivity discussed in Chapter 2. From the standpoint that the same type of service is appropriate for everyone with alcohol problems, it might be argued that the additional funding was being spent for appropriate services. From a public health perspective, however, there is a serious imbalance in the provision of services compared to needs (M. B. Sobell & L. C. Sobell, 1986/1987, 1993). While the next chapter will argue for the need for different services for problem drinkers, the present chapter is devoted to better understanding the nature of problem drinkers.

First the research literature will be examined to identify some general attributes of problem drinkers and compare some of their characteristics to those of more severely dependent individuals. Then assessment data from a group of problem drinkers involved in our own research will be examined in detail.

Problem Drinkers in the Research Literature

The research literature describes problem drinkers in several ways. Since some characteristics are definitional, it would be tautological to cite them as evidence for group differences. For example, one characteristic often used to define problem drinkers is no history of physical dependence, especially major withdrawal symptoms (e.g., M. B. Sobell & L. C. Sobell, 1986/1987). The reason for using major withdrawal symptoms (i.e., hallucinations, seizures, delirium tremens) as a defining characteristic is because they can be objectively measured, whereas the presence or absence of variables such as "impaired control" or "preoccupation with drinking" requires subjective judgments.

Also, just knowing that someone has been severely dependent implies several things about the role of drinking in the person's life. For instance, to manifest serious withdrawal symptoms upon the cessation of drinking, it is necessary to engage in very heavy drinking over an extended period of time (see Pattison, Sobell, & Sobell, 1977). Usually, consumption of the equivalent of at least 30 to 40 oz of spirits (40–50% ethanol) daily for at least a few days is required. For an individual to consume such amounts indicates: (1) considerable tolerance for ethanol, probably relating to an extensive heavy-drinking history; (2) a need to have alcoholic beverages constantly accessible since the cessation of drinking would initiate a withdrawal syndrome; (3) a work or life situation that allows such consumption either without detection or without consequences of detection; (4) the pervasion of most activities with drinking opportunities (i.e., never being very far away from a drink); and (5) in all likelihood, a constellation of consequences that accompanies a long-term heavy-drinking pattern (e.g., disrupted interpersonal relationships, vocational problems, health problems related to long-term alcohol consumption, low self-esteem, a history of failed attempts to reduce or stop drinking). Thus, while a history of severe withdrawal symptoms is only one indication of the problem, it often justifies an educated guess that the individual's lifestyle is centered around drinking and that there is a long-standing history of experiencing alcohol-related consequences.

Problem drinkers will typically score low in the distribution of scores on scales measuring alcohol dependence (Heather, Kissoon-Singh, & Fenton, 1990). They also tend to report problem drinking histories shorter than 10 years, to have fewer health and social consequences related to their drinking, and, often, to have not received prior alcohol treatment (Sanchez-Craig & Wilkinson, 1986/1987). Problem drinkers tend to have greater personal, social, and economic resources and stability than severely dependent drinkers. They tend not to view themselves as "alcoholics" or as basically different from persons who do not have alcohol problems (Skinner & Allen, 1982). There also may be a higher representation of females among problem drinkers compared to more dependent individuals, and overall alcohol consumption of problem drinkers typically is less than that of more severely dependent individuals.

An appreciation of the differences between problem drinkers and more severely dependent individuals can be achieved by comparing pretreatment characteristics of both populations as reported in the literature. Table 3.1 presents such a comparison displaying variables from eight studies involving severely dependent persons and six studies involving problem drinkers, including a study of guided self-management treatment. The severely dependent alcohol abusers were all recruited from inpatient treatment programs except for one study (Kuchipudi, Hobein, Flickinger, & Iber, 1990), which involved persons hospitalized for recurrent alcohol-related pancreatitis, ulcers, or liver disease (62% had diagnosed cirrhosis). All of the problem drinkers received brief outpatient treatment, and in all of the problem drinker studies except

TABLE 3.1. Pretreatment Variables Describing the Client Cohorts from Several Studies of Severely Dependent Alcohol Abusers and Several Studies of Problem Drinkers

Study	n	Females (%)	Married (%)	Employed (%)	MAST score[a]	ADS score[b]	Education (mean years)	Age (mean years)	Drinking problem (mean years)
				Severely dependent samples					
Carver & Dunham (1991)	211	0	11	44	—	—	—	36	—
Chaney et al. (1978)	40	0[c]	43	—	—	—	12	46	17
Chapman & Huygens (1988)	113	20	39	42	8[d]	—	—	42	14
Foy et al. (1984)	62	0[c]	49	40	—	—	12	46	10
Ito et al. (1988)	39	0[c]	38	36	—	20	13	36	15
Kanas et al. (1976)	137	0[c]	45	30	—	—	11	45	16
Kuchipudi et al. (1990)	114	0[c]	—	22	—	—	—	52	—
Vaillant et al. (1983)	100	13	35	27	—	—	—	45	10+[e]
				Problem drinker samples					
Connors et al. (1992)	63	32	33	94	16	—	16	37	6
Harris & Miller (1990)	34	50	—	—	17	—	15	38	8
Sanchez-Craig et al. (1984)	70	26	47	75	19	14	14	35	5
Sanchez-Craig et al. (1991)	96	36	56	98	—	12	15	40	5
Skutle & Berg (1987)	43	21	63	88	—	—	13	43	—
Guided self-management study	100	36	49	88	—	13	15	37	6

[a] Michigan Alcoholism Screening Test (possible scores: 0–53).
[b] Alcohol Dependence Scale (possible scores: 0–47).
[c] Veterans Administration Program.
[d] Short version.
[e] 87% had a drinking problem for more than 10 years.

the one involving guided self-management, the subjects were solicited by newspaper advertisements.

Inspection of Table 3.1 reveals that among the few descriptors for which study comparisons are possible, the problem drinkers were generally younger, had a shorter problem drinking history, and were better educated (however, any difference in education might be attributable to most problem drinkers having been solicited through media advertisement, whereas most of the severely dependent persons were self-admissions to treatment programs). The problem drinkers also showed much greater stability in terms of employment, although they did not differ substantially from the severely dependent in marital status. While most of the studies of severely dependent samples occurred at Veterans Administration hospitals and, therefore, were limited to males, the proportion of females in the problem drinker samples was greater than is typical for alcohol treatment programs (Collins, 1993).

Motivationally, two factors are important clinical considerations when working with problem drinkers. First, while problem drinkers typically have not suffered multiple serious consequences from their drinking, they usually are aware that they could suffer serious consequences if their drinking problem continues. This can provide an incentive for change. However, if treatment demands are too great, then noncompliance can be expected (Miller, 1986/1987; Pomerleau, Pertschuk, Adkins, & Brady, 1978). This occurs because problem drinkers' lives usually have not been so damaged by their drinking problems that they are ready to make large sacrifices to comply with treatment. The demands of treatment compete with their work, family, and personal needs. Since traditional treatments, and especially Minnesota Model treatments, are very demanding, this is another reason why alternative treatments are needed for problem drinkers.

In summary, the research literature tells us several things about problem drinkers as compared to more severely dependent alcohol abusers:

1. Problem drinkers do not have a history of severe alcohol withdrawal symptoms.
2. Problem drinkers tend to have a shorter problem drinking history, typically around 5 years, and seldom over 10 years.
3. Problem drinkers tend to have greater social and economic stability.
4. Problem drinkers tend to have greater personal, social, and economic resources to call upon in treatment (i.e., they have more opportunity to help themselves).
5. Problem drinkers are not likely to view themselves as different from persons who do not have drinking problems (i.e., they do not self-identify as alcoholic, and their self-esteem is usually higher than persons with more severe histories).

6. Problem drinkers can become caught in a motivational dilemma, knowing that they still have a great deal to lose but also feeling that conditions in their life are not so bad as to justify extensive life changes or sacrifices to deal with their drinking.

The above are some of the conclusions that can be drawn from the literature on problem drinkers. A detailed look at a group of problem drinkers will be helpful in conveying a more complete picture and understanding of such individuals.

A Close Look at a Group of Problem Drinkers

A brief look at some of the problem drinkers we recently treated in a study at the Addiction Research Foundation will support many of the features discussed above. These individuals were voluntary admissions to a treatment agency. They did not respond to advertisements as has been common in research studies of treatments for problem drinkers (e.g., Miller, Taylor, & West, 1980; Sanchez-Craig, Annis, Bornet, & MacDonald, 1984; Sanchez-Craig, Leigh, Spivak, & Lei, 1989). That these clients presented themselves for treatment is important because another study conducted at the same agency that used walk-in and solicited clients found that the two groups differed in an interesting way (Zweben, Pearlman, & Li, 1988). Clients solicited by advertisement described themselves as heavier drinkers and perceived themselves as more dependent than those who had sought out treatment. Ad respondents also reported having suffered fewer consequences from their drinking. Two other studies of problem drinkers have reported similar results (Sobell, 1993; L. C. Sobell & M. B. Sobell, 1992a; Hingson, Mangione, Meyers, & Scotch, 1982). These results suggest that it might be the impact of drinking-related consequences rather than the excessiveness of the drinking that motivates problem drinkers to seek treatment.

The 100 problem drinkers we will consider volunteered to participate in a treatment research study with a self-management orientation. Although the literature suggests, as will be discussed in Chapter 4, that many problem drinkers have the capacity to assume the major responsibility for planning and implementing their own behavior-change strategies, the clients discussed here explicitly entered a treatment having that expectation.

Clients' mean age was 37.3 years (range = 21–59 years), and they reported having had alcohol problems for an average of slightly more than 6 years. Although there is a tendency to expect that problem drinkers will be young (perhaps a derivative of the progressivity notion), many clients could be described as having a "middle-age onset" of their problems, a phenomenon reported several times in the literature (Atkinson, Tolson, & Turner, 1990; Fillmore, 1974; M. B. Sobell & L. C. Sobell, 1993).

Some clients in their fifties, for example, had only experienced drinking problems for a few years prior to entering treatment. Thus, at this time, orienting treatment programs for problem drinkers toward specific age groups does not appear warranted.

This group of problem drinkers also showed good evidence of social stability: 88% were employed, and 49% were married. The average education level was nearly 15 years, and 87% had at least a high school education. In another study at the same agency with a different group of outpatients (Sobell, Sobell, Bogardis, Leo, & Skinner, 1992), it was found that those who had at least some university education were significantly more likely to prefer to select their own treatment goal than were those with less education. It may be that education level is a characteristic of the problem drinker population that is attracted to self-management treatments. In areas other than alcohol problems, it has been found that better educated, older adults were most likely to complete self-administered treatment programs (Scogin, Bynum, Stephens, & Calhoon, 1990).

In summary, a typical problem drinker client could be described as a mature, socially stable adult. A final important demographic characteristic is that 36% were female compared to about 21% of the total outpatient admissions to the treatment agency from which the sample was drawn. Sanchez-Craig has suggested that females may find a self-management approach to be particularly appealing (Sanchez-Craig, 1990).

In terms of drinking behavior, an important qualifying condition for the study of self-management treatment was that persons who reported heavy drinking (i.e., ≥ 12 drinks on ≥ 5 days per week for the 6 months prior to admission) were not eligible for the evaluation. Consequently, the sample reported here may be biased toward lighter-drinking problem drinkers. What is important, however, is that these clients definitely had alcohol problems when they sought treatment, although they were not severely dependent on alcohol.

Several features of these clients' drinking for the year prior to entering treatment are of interest and have implications for treatment planning. Pretreatment drinking was assessed using the Timeline Follow-Back method (see Chapter 6; L. C. Sobell & M. B. Sobell, 1992b; Sobell, Sobell, Leo, & Cancilla, 1988). First, daily drinking was uncommon among this population. As a group, they drank on only 68.2% of all days during the year, meaning they were abstinent on about 1 out of every 3 days. Second, when they did drink, on 38.7% of those days they drank ≤ 4 standard drinks (1 standard drink = 0.6 oz of pure ethanol, or 13.6 gm of absolute alcohol). Thus, on nearly 4 out of every 10 drinking days their drinking involved very low amounts. Third, the mean number of drinks they consumed per drinking day was 6.4. This level amounts to an average of a little over 30 drinks per week.

In a study of medical-ward patients with and without alcohol problems, Lloyd, Chick, Crombie, and Anderson (1986) found that a criterion equal to approximately 26 drinks per week was the best cutting point for separating problem and nonproblem drinkers. Sanchez-Craig (1986) found that 12 standard drinks per week (no more than 4 drinks per day on no more than 3 days per week) best distinguished problem-free from problem drinkers. Finally, Hester and Miller (1990) and Harris and Miller (1990) have recommended a weekly limit of 17.5 standard drinks as a success criterion for reduced drinking. While the cohort reported here may have been relatively light drinkers among persons with alcohol problems, prior to treatment they were drinking at or above hazardous levels.

Finally, the mean percent of pretreatment drinking days that involved very heavy drinking, defined as ten or more standard drinks, was 16.8%. Although comparison data are not available, such drinking is probably well below the level of heavy drinking exhibited by severely dependent drinkers. Persons who drink without any problems, however, probably do not consume at least ten drinks on nearly 1 out of every 5 drinking days. In summary, the drinking of our problem drinkers, while not extremely heavy, exceeded hazardous levels and was at a level found to be associated with problem drinking in other studies.

The final major domain of subject characteristics to be discussed is consequences of drinking. In contrast to their pretreatment drinking, the clients reported an abundance of pretreatment drinking-related consequences, perhaps supporting the suggestion from Zweben, Pearlman, and Li (1988) that persons who voluntarily seek out treatment are more likely to have suffered consequences of their drinking. For example, 81% of the clients in our study reported interpersonal problems related to their drinking, 48% reported vocational problems, 78% reported cognitive impairment, 27% reported health problems, 47% reported financial problems, 26% reported an alcohol-related arrest, and 8% reported an alcohol-related hospitalization. Also, 93% reported that they had felt a need for alcohol, 47% stated they had perceived an increase in their tolerance to alcohol, and 42% reported they had at some time felt tremulous as a result of stopping drinking. Moreover, the clients had an average Alcohol Dependence Scale (ADS) score of 12.9 (about the 25th percentile on the norms for that instrument), and due to screening criteria none of them exceeded an ADS score of 21 (the median). Validation studies of the ADS have found withdrawal phenomena to be rare in individuals who score in this range (Skinner & Allen, 1982).

We also asked the clients to subjectively evaluate the severity of their drinking problem during the year prior to treatment using an operationally defined 5-point scale. This was done because for some of the clients, especially those who chose a reduced-drinking goal, it would have been difficult to demonstrate a statistically significant reduction in their drinking in our relatively small sample. Thus, had objective drinking behavior been the only measure, a clinically important change might not have been detected by statistical analysis. The scale we used is shown as Table 3.2.

Overall, 78% of the clients in our study reported that they had suffered at least one serious alcohol-related consequence during the pretreatment year: 56% rated their pretreatment problem as Major, and 22% rated their pretreatment problem as Very Major. No clients reported that their pretreatment drinking was Not a Problem. However, 15% reported that their pretreatment drinking was a Minor Problem, and 7% evaluated it as a Very Minor Problem, the latter meaning that they worried about their drinking but had suffered no identifiable consequences.

In this chapter we focused on describing the problem drinker. In Chapter 4 we provide a review of the research on the treatment of the problem drinker. After summarizing that research, in Chapter 5 we then consider what features of a treatment might appeal to problem drinkers and how treatment for problem drinkers could be easily accomplished by service providers in the community. Attention to the ease of delivery of a treatment in regular clinical settings (as opposed to research settings) is extremely important if there is any hope that a research-based treatment will be adopted by community programs. In the main study in which the guided self-management procedures were evaluated (the focus of this book), 85% of the clients were seen by outpatient therapists rather than by researchers.

TABLE 3.2. Rating Categories for Clients' Subjective Evaluation of the Severity of Their Drinking Problem (Used Pretreatment and Posttreatment)

Not a Problem	—
Very Minor Problem	Worried about it but not experiencing *any* negative consequences from it
Minor Problem	Experiencing some negative consequences from it, but *none* that I consider serious
Major Problem	Experiencing some negative consequences from it, *one* of which I consider serious
Very Major Problem	Experiencing some negative consequences from it, *at least two* of which I consider serious

4

Treatment of Problem Drinkers: The Missing Part of a Comprehensive Approach to Alcohol Problems

Concordance of Advances in the Alcohol Field and in Behavior Therapy

While epidemiological and longitudinal studies were calling attention to problem drinkers, the field of behavior therapy was evolving to embrace cognitive-behavioral treatments. This juxtapositioning of advances in separate areas was fortuitous because the cognitive-behavioral interventions incorporated features that were consistent with the emerging approaches to the treatment of problem drinkers.

Earlier we described the emerging awareness in the alcohol field of problem drinkers as a population in need of services. Here we briefly review how behavioral treatment approaches have evolved, and how recent behavioral treatment approaches have been targeted at problem drinkers.

Learning-theory based approaches to the treatment of alcohol problems predate the development of behavior therapy as a field and the development of Alcoholics Anonymous. An aversive-conditioning treatment for alcohol problems based on the principles of Pavlovian conditioning was reported by Kantorovich (1929). Such an approach involves pairing an aversive event (e.g., painful electric shock, vomiting) with alcohol cues (i.e., sight, smell, taste of alcohol). Aversive-conditioning approaches were used in a few private treatment programs in the 1940s (e.g., Voegtlin & Lemere, 1942) and later resurfaced in a very limited fashion (e.g., Cannon, Baker, Gino, & Nathan, 1986).

In the 1960s behavioral treatments based on operant-conditioning principles became popular. A basic feature of this approach is the supposition that drinking behavior occurs in particular circumstances (i.e., high-risk situations)

26

maintained by reward contingencies. It was at this time that the functional analysis of stimulus and reinforcement contingencies related to drinking became established as a clinical procedure (e.g., Bandura, 1969; Lazarus, 1965). The value of functional analysis was supported by laboratory studies demonstrating that alcohol consumption could be treated as an operant behavior (e.g., Mendelson, LaDou, & Solomon, 1964; reviewed in L. C. Sobell & M. B. Sobell, 1983). This led to tests of treatments based on operant conditioning such as contingency-management treatments (Hunt & Azrin, 1973) and treatments featuring the learning of alternative responses to replace the functions served by alcohol consumption (M. B. Sobell & L. C. Sobell, 1973).

Studies based on operant conditioning were often "broad-spectrum" approaches, incorporating several interventions directed at the multiple dimensions of alcohol problems (Lovibond & Caddy, 1970; M. B. Sobell & L. C. Sobell, 1973). These studies often involved skills training based on the assumption that persons needed to replace functions served by drinking with alternative less-problematic behaviors. In the early years, little research was directed at testing the assumption that skills deficits existed, and what little work existed suggested that any skills deficits were specific to refusing drinks (Foy, Miller, Eisler, & O'Toole, 1976; Twentyman et al., 1982). Broad-spectrum treatments also often involved anxiety-reduction techniques such as relaxation training or systematic desensitization.

The 1970s were marked by the rise of the "cognitive sciences" (see Mahoney & Lyddon, 1988). This had a profound effect on behavior therapy, resulting in the emergence of cognitive-behavioral treatments as a dominant treatment approach. The hallmark of this shift in approach was that thoughts and thought processes were accepted as part of the explanation of abnormal behaviors and as a focus of treatment. Examples of cognitive-behavioral approaches are Bandura's self-efficacy theory (1977, 1986) and Beck's cognitive therapy for emotional disorders (1976, 1991). A cognitive-behavioral emphasis is also apparent in the relapse prevention treatment approach (Marlatt & Gordon, 1985) that receives considerable discussion later in this book.

More recently, Pavlovian conditioning models of addiction have been reintroduced, but in a more sophisticated form. These more sophisticated models are supported by considerable basic research (Niaura et al., 1988). Treatment implications of these models, however, are most relevant to cases of serious dependence, where there is a strong conditioning history. In contrast, cognitive-behavioral approaches are more relevant to the formulation of treatments for problem drinkers.

Treatments for Problem Drinkers: Issues

The rationale for cost-effective treatments for alcohol problems was discussed earlier. If alcohol treatment services were like services in other areas of health care, a tiered system of treatment services would be in place, such as is shown in Figure 4.1. Irrespective of the health problem, the use of highly intensive, costly, and intrusive treatments must be justified as necessary for a particular individual, and it must be shown to be superior to less-intensive approaches. When one considers the range of alcohol problems in our society, the need for a variety of treatment services is obvious. Services should range from advice and assisted self-help through a variety of treatments differing in their intensity and focus. Self-management treatment fits into this spectrum as an outpatient approach suitable for problem drinkers who want to take major responsibility for changing their behavior.

It will be recalled from Chapter 3 that problem drinkers often function satisfactorily in many areas of their lives and that some or even much of the time when they drink, they drink relatively small amounts (four or fewer standard drinks). They also tend to have substantial personal, social, and economic resources available, and they do not view themselves as alcoholics.

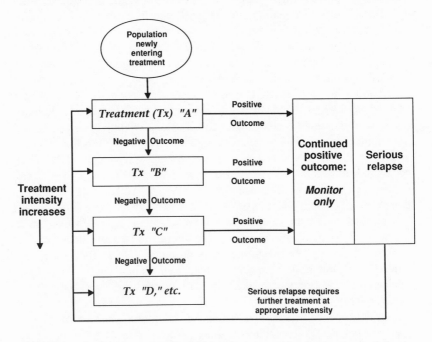

FIGURE 4.1. Tiered system of alcohol-treatment services. As treatment intensity increases, the cost of providing treatment increases, but the number of cases requiring treatment decreases. From "Treatment for Problem Drinkers: A Public Health Priority" by M. B. Sobell and L. C. Sobell, 1993, in J. S. Baer, G. A. Marlatt, and R. J. McMahon, eds., *Addictive Behaviors across the Lifespan: Prevention, Treatment, and Policy Issues*, Beverly Hills, CA: Sage. Copyright 1993 by Mark B. Sobell and Linda C. Sobell. Adapted by permission.

In other words, problem drinkers tend to be resourceful individuals who can assume considerable responsibility for themselves. Self-management treatment, as described in this book, can be viewed as guided self-help, where people are aided in understanding their problem and in formulating their own treatment plan from which they can take credit for their success.

In this chapter, several treatment studies involving problem drinkers are reviewed. This review sets the stage for a description of the treatment approach described in this book. It is important to recognize that guided self-management is a treatment for persons who self-identify as having alcohol problems. Other interventions have been developed for use in case identification and early intervention where the targets of the intervention are people who have not self-identified their drinking as a problem, and for whom the identification is made by primary care clinicians (often physicians). In such cases, brief interventions have sometimes been used with promising results by the primary care clinicians (e.g., Chick, Lloyd, & Crombie, 1985; Kristenson, Öhlin, Hultén-Nosslin, Trell, & Hood, 1983; Kristenson, Trell, & Hood, 1981; Persson & Magnusson, 1989). Although case identification and early intervention are important, they are not the focus of this book. This book centers on ways of helping people who recognize that they have an alcohol problem, and who want to change.

There is now considerable evidence that many problem drinkers who seek treatment respond well to nonintensive, outpatient interventions. There is even some suggestion that more traditional interventions might be counterproductive with this population. One of the best known seminal studies was discussed earlier. The important finding by Edwards et al. (1977) was that persons whose problems were less severe did better in the single session than in the more intensive treatment, while severely dependent persons showed the opposite pattern (Orford, Oppenheimer, & Edwards, 1976).

Several studies have since investigated so-called brief interventions, often aimed at problem drinkers and found that problem drinkers respond well to nonintensive outpatient treatments, and even to bibliotherapy. (See Babor, Ritson, & Hodgson, 1986, Heather, 1989, 1990, Hester & Miller, 1990, Institute of Medicine, 1990, and Saunders & Aasland, 1987, for reviews of these studies.) As will be seen, the majority of studies have compared variants of the same treatment approach. Consequently, while such comparisons can identify the relative contribution of various treatment components, they preclude conclusions about the absolute efficacy of the treatment or about its relative efficacy as compared to widely used alternatives.

The issue of the absolute efficacy of any treatment for alcohol problems, whether for problem drinkers or chronic alcoholics, is a difficult question to answer. First, the assignment to a "no treatment" control group of persons who request treatment would be considered unethical. Second, even if assignment to a no treatment condition was attempted, it is doubtful that the condition could be enforced since multiple treatment programs and profes-sionals, as well as self-help groups (e.g., Alcoholics Anonymous), are readily available. Third, the comparison of treatment recovery rates to natural recov-ery rates (i.e., rates of recovery among persons who have drinking problems but do not seek treatment) may not be a valid comparison because attempts at self-recovery may be the initial approach taken by most people once they decide they have an alcohol problem. If this is so, then the group that seeks treatment will contain many individuals who have attempted and failed at self-recovery. Finally, while the use of waiting list control groups is a promising alternative to a no treatment control procedure, it is possible that the waiting list groups will be confounded for several reasons (e.g., they deliberately postpone changing their behavior until treatment commences; they become angry at the treatment program for imposing a waiting period; they seek alternative treatment during the waiting period). Nevertheless, waiting list control groups can provide useful information not otherwise available.

Two studies have been reported that used waiting list control groups with problem drinkers. Using media-recruited problem drinkers Alden (1988) compared a 12-session behavioral self-management program ($n = 40$) with a 12-session developmental counseling alternative ($n = 33$), an established approach in counseling psychology. An additional 54 subjects were randomly assigned to a waiting list control group and after a 12-week waiting period were randomly assigned to one or the other of the two treatments. A 2-year follow-up found that both treatments were associated with a significant reduction in drinking, but the treatments did not differ in effectiveness. During the 12-week waiting period, the waiting list control group's drinking did not change. This suggests that improvement in drinking was related to treatment, but the use and apparent relative effectiveness of developmental counseling suggests that the specific treatment approach may not be very important. Alden interpreted her study as supporting the use of moderation-drinking goals in treatment for problem drinkers, a feature shared by both treatments. Also, both treatments included the following procedures: establishing goals, self-monitoring of drinking, and discussing problems with empathic counsel-ors. Thus, the treatments did not seem to differ greatly in their major compo-nents, and both involved a substantial self-management emphasis.

The Alden study highlights a problem that complicates evaluating treat-ments for problem drinkers against alternative treatments: Alternative treat-ments are not readily available. To establish an alternative modality to a behavioral self-management approach, Alden had to create an alternative treatment by borrowing from an established approach used for other problems in developmental counseling. In so doing, and in gearing the treatment to a problem drinker population, the result was that the treatments ended up not differing in important ways.

The Alden study points up two current problems with attempting to validate the relative effectiveness of treatments for problem drinkers. First, there is no widely used alternative treatment to brief behavioral self-management interventions. Thus, while brief behavioral interventions could serve as a comparison treatment against which to evaluate a newly crafted alternative approach, there is really no standard against which they can be compared (i.e., they are the standard). Second, while a valuable comparison would be against treatments designed for severely dependent individuals, this raises ethical considerations about purposefully assigning individuals to a treatment hypothesized to be inappropriate and possibly harmful for them (i.e., they might drop out of treatment because they felt the treatment was inappropriate for them).

The second study that used a waiting list control group was reported by Harris and Miller (1990). These researchers evaluated a brief intervention designed for media-solicited persons who had concerns that they were drinking too much. Subjects were assigned to either a self-directed or therapist-directed behavioral self-control treatment or to one of two waiting list control groups. Subjects assigned to one waiting list group were told that their treatment involved an initial baseline phase during which they would record (self-monitor) their drinking. Subjects assigned to the other waiting list group were told they would begin treatment in 10 weeks. After the waiting period, subjects in both waiting list groups participated in either the self-directed or therapist-directed treatment. Even though the self-monitoring procedure could have had a therapeutic effect in and of itself (L. C. Sobell & M. B. Sobell, 1973), improvement for this group occurred only after treatment had commenced. Like Alden's study, this study suggests that treatment does benefit problem drinkers.

A promising alternative comparison procedure was recently introduced by Connors, Tarbox, and Faillace (1992) in a study of the effects of aftercare on problem drinkers. Media-solicited problem drinkers participated in an eight-session outpatient treatment and were then randomized to either group aftercare, telephone aftercare, or no aftercare conditions. A no treatment comparison group was recruited through media solicitations for problem drinkers who were concerned about their drinking but were neither in nor seeking treatment. While not a true "no treatment" control group because of the absence of random assignment and because the subjects had not sought treatment, this procedure provides a group that can be followed indefinitely over time, whereas persons assigned to a waiting list control group can at best have their entry into treatment delayed by several weeks. Moreover, any purposeful delay that is not due to an inability to provide timely treatment raises ethical questions.

Connors and his colleagues found no evidence that treated problem drinkers who got aftercare did better than those who did not get aftercare, and they found that the nontreated problem drinkers (i.e., comparison group) improved as much over time as those who were treated. In terms of the latter finding, these authors suggest that the comparison subjects may have been ready to make changes in their drinking and that the experience of being interviewed and followed over time may have been sufficient to help them change their behavior.

Treatments for Problem Drinkers: Evaluations

Of the several treatment research studies that have evaluated treatments for problem drinkers, many have used self-management procedures. Miller and his colleagues conducted several studies using procedures they refer to as behavioral self-control training (Miller, 1977; Miller & Baca, 1983; Miller, Gribskov, & Mortell, 1981; Miller & Taylor, 1980; Miller, Taylor, & West, 1980). These studies largely involved media-solicited problem drinkers, and they have tested variations of a basic treatment paradigm involving the use of a self-control training manual. The variations have consisted of testing the manual alone (i.e., bibliotherapy, but usually accompanied by at least one session of instruction in use of the manual) or assisted by a therapist either in individual or group treatment sessions (typically eight to ten sessions). In most of these studies a relatively small number of subjects (i.e., about 8 to 12) have been assigned to a specific group. Hester and Miller (1990) described behavioral self-control training as involving "goal setting, self-monitoring, specific changes in drinking behavior, rewards for goal attainment, functional analysis of drinking situations, and the learning of alternative coping skills" (p. 141). A key feature is that the client is responsible for making significant treatment decisions. This series of studies has found no differences in outcomes between group and individual therapist-assisted treatments. Also, the self-directed treatment did not differ significantly in outcome from therapist-directed treatment.

Sanchez-Craig, Annis, Bornet, and MacDonald (1984) evaluated a cognitive-behavioral treatment for problem drinkers in a study that compared abstinence and moderation (i.e., controlled-drinking) treatment goals. The 70 socially stable problem drinkers treated in the study were largely media solicited. The only procedural difference between treatments was that problem drinkers in the moderation-goal condition received counseling about how to regulate their drinking. Also, those assigned to the abstinence-goal condition were not aware that they could have been assigned to a moderation-goal treatment. Both groups significantly reduced their drinking over 2 years of follow-up, but they did not differ from one another in outcome. Irrespective of the assigned goal, most of the subjects who had a successful outcome had reduced rather than ceased their drinking. It is also notable that individuals advised to be abstinent drank significantly more during treatment and that moderation was the vastly preferred goal for these problem drinkers (i.e., even most of those assigned to abstinence ended up reducing rather than stopping their drinking). This theme of moderation as a preferred treatment goal and as the most likely successful outcome (even if it is not a goal) pervades treatment studies of problem drinkers, although some problem drinkers do favor and achieve abstinence.

Graber and Miller (1988) also randomly assigned problem drinkers ($n = 24$) to treatment goals, although their subjects had more severe alcohol problems than those in the 1984 study by Sanchez-Craig and her colleagues. At the start of Graber and Miller's study, the subjects had no clearly stated preference for either abstinence or moderation goals. The subjects assigned to a moderation goal were taught goal setting and given a self-help manual that included a section about controlling their drinking. The abstinence-goal subjects were given the same manual but without the controlled drinking section. They were also introduced to the disease model of alcoholism as a rationale for their abstinence, and they were informed about denial as a defense mechanism used by persons with alcohol problems.

Despite the rather clear differences between procedures and the use of a slightly more severe sample of problem drinkers, outcomes for the two groups did not differ significantly at a 42-month follow-up or at shorter follow-ups. At the 42-month follow-up, using very stringent classification criteria, four subjects had been abstinent for at least 1 year and three had been moderate and asymptomatic drinkers. The relatively low (30%) success rate in this study may relate to the use of very strict criteria for asymptomatic moderate drinking or to the use of a more severe sample than in the 1984 study by Sanchez-Craig and her fellow researchers.

In Norway, Skutle and Berg (1987) used a treatment similar to that used in Miller's earlier behavioral self-control training research. Media-recruited problem drinkers were randomly assigned to (1) bibliotherapy (involving 4 hours of instruction in use of a self-help manual); (2) therapist-directed self-control treatment; (3) training in coping skills; or (4) a combination of the two therapist-directed treatments. At 1-year follow-up, although all groups showed significant reductions in drinking, there were no differences between groups. The majority of clients had reduced their alcohol consumption before treatment started. This suggests that the treatment was not responsible for the initiation of behavior change, although it may have helped maintain the change.

In Scotland, Heather and his colleagues (Heather, Robertson, MacPherson, Allsop, & Fulton, 1987; Heather, Whitton, & Robertson, 1986) evaluated a controlled-drinking self-help manual for media-recruited problem drinkers. Subjects were randomly assigned to receive by mail either the manual or a booklet of general advice and information. At 1-year follow-up, both groups of subjects had reduced their consumption by about one third. In an interesting subanalysis, subjects who had received other help for their problem were excluded from the sample. It was then found that subjects who had received the self-help manual had significantly lower alcohol consumption than the control group. In this and the Sanchez-Craig and Lei (1986) study, high consumers at assessment showed greater reductions in consumption than low consumers at assessment. Heather and his colleagues cautioned that differential attrition from follow-up between the groups may have accounted for the observed group difference.

Robertson, Heather, Dzialdowski, Crawford, and Winton (1986) randomly assigned 37 problem drinkers to either three or four sessions of advice or to about nine sessions of cognitive-behavioral therapy. The brief treatment had many features of a self-management treatment including functional analysis of drinking, the formulation of drinking guidelines, and provision of a controlled-drinking advice sheet. The intensive treatment involved problem-solving skills training, marital contracting, relaxation training, cognitive restructuring, self-management training, controlled drinking counseling, and sexual counseling as needed. At follow-up, an average of 15 months after treatment, the intensive treatment subjects showed a significantly greater reduction in their average monthly consumption compared to those in the advice group. However, since females were overrepresented in the intensive treatment group, gender differences are an alternative explanation for the difference between groups.

Moderation as a goal and outcome of treatment has been a central issue in the development of treatments for problem drinkers (M. B. Sobell & L. C. Sobell, 1986/1987). Such goals are now viewed as a reasonable treatment alternative for problem drinkers (Institute of Medicine, 1990; Sanchez-Craig & Wilkinson, 1986/1987; Wallace, Cutler, & Haines, 1988). It has been suggested that allowing clients to make decisions about treatment goals increases their commitment to achieving their goals (Bandura, 1986; Miller, 1986/1987). This proposition has been tested in some studies.

Using a population that included problem drinkers and more severely dependent clients, Orford and Keddie (1986a, 1986b) assigned alcohol abusers who strongly preferred either abstinence or moderation to their preferred goal, and randomly assigned goals to alcohol abusers who did not express a strong goal preference. They concluded that treatment was most effective when it was compatible with the client's preferred goal. This study failed to find any relationship between type of successful recovery (abstinence or moderation) and the severity of alcohol dependence. A study by Elal-Lawrence, Slade, and Dewey (1986) also allowed a broad range of alcohol abusers to select their own goals and reached conclusions similar to those of Orford and Keddie (1986a, 1986b). However, they reported that goal choice at assessment was not predictive of outcome. Finally, Booth, Dale, and Ansari (1984) used procedures similar to those of Elal-Lawrence, Slade, and Dewey (1986) and found that alcohol abusers were most likely to achieve the goals they had chosen for themselves.

In the studies discussed in the previous paragraph, all of the alcohol abusers were assigned to goals that were preferred or at least acceptable to them. It is interesting that in the Sanchez-Craig, Annis, Bornet, and MacDonald (1984) study, the majority of problem drinkers assigned to an abstinence goal ended up reducing rather than stopping their drinking, meaning that the overwhelming majority of successful outcomes for clients in the abstinence-goal group were moderation outcomes. In conjunction with problem drinkers' preference for goal self-selection, this strongly suggests that the availability of moderation goals is imperative for providing treatments likely to be perceived as attractive by problem drinkers.

It is not just mandatory-abstinence approaches that have been thought to be counterproductive for problem drinkers. There is also some evidence that other aspects of conventional approaches are associated with higher rates of attrition or noncompliance with the treatment regimen compared to short-term behavioral treatments.

A study by Pomerleau and his colleagues (Pomerleau & Adkins, 1980; Pomerleau, Pertschuk, Adkins, & Brady, 1978) compared problem drinkers randomly assigned to a multicomponent behavioral treatment emphasizing moderation or to a traditional group-encounter therapy emphasizing abstinence. At 1-year follow-up, 14% of the traditionally treated subjects had maintained abstinence compared to 6% in the behaviorally treated group. However, 72% of the behaviorally treated subjects and 50% of the traditionally treated subjects had improved outcomes (the difference was not statistically significant). Most of the improvement involved a reduction in drinking rather than abstinence. Thus, consistent with other studies, the requirement of abstinence had little effect on treatment outcome for problem drinkers.

A key finding in the study by Pomerleau and his fellow researchers was that attrition during treatment differed markedly between groups; 43% (6 out of 14) of the traditionally treated subjects dropped out compared to only 11% (2 out of 18) of the behaviorally treated subjects. Unfortunately, since the treatments differed in many ways, it is difficult to draw conclusions about how the treatments and goals affected attrition. The authors noted, however, that the majority of dropouts from the traditional treatment condition occurred shortly after a confrontational group session.

In summary, several studies have investigated treatments for problem drinkers. Overall, these studies have shown considerable reductions in drinking. The two studies that used waiting list control groups showed positive gains from treatment, although another study that used a control group of problem drinkers not seeking treatment found that these subjects reduced their drinking as much as those who had been treated. A central feature of this literature is the use of moderation treatment goals and the attainment of moderation outcomes. In fact, a perplexing aspect of these studies is that it does not seem to matter whether one advises problem drinkers to abstain from or to moderate their drinking: The majority of successful outcomes occur through moderation. Since some studies have also found very brief (i.e., one-session) interventions to produce similar changes in problem drinkers, it is unclear that even the relatively modest treatment intensity found in short-term treatments is necessary in most cases. Finally, there is some suggestion that conventional treatment approaches may be inappropriate for problem drinkers. In the next chapter, these and other issues are examined in light of a recent trend to conceptualize motivational interventions. Following that discussion, the framework of the guided self-management approach to treatment of problem drinkers is presented.

5

A Self-Management Approach to Treating Problem Drinkers

Earlier chapters reviewed how problem drinkers have become recognized as a population in need of services and the types of approaches that have been shown to be effective for such individuals. This chapter describes the development of a self-management treatment based on the research literature. Our objective was to develop a treatment approach that would appeal to and be suitable for problem drinkers. Problem drinkers were selected as the target population because (1) few treatments exist for this group; (2) it represents a sizable population; and (3) the limited research conducted to date suggests that self-management approaches might work well with such individuals. The resulting approach called "guided self-management," or "guided self-change," has been evaluated in different settings with positive results (Romach et al., 1991; Sellers et al., 1991; Sobell, Sellers, & Sobell, 1990; M. B. Sobell & L. C. Sobell, 1990; Sobell, Sobell, & Leo, 1990).

While detailed statistical analyses of the findings will be presented in peer-review journal articles, this book provides the findings from a clinical perspective, allowing for the discussion of certain topics (e.g., therapists' and clients' views of the treatment) that are clinically important but do not receive detailed attention in journal articles.

This chapter presents the basic principles of and rationale for the guided self-management treatment. Subsequent chapters present the procedures and related assessment tools, treatment outcome information, and a discussion of therapist and client perceptions of the treatment. Based on these findings, recommendations are offered for how the treatment might be modified and used by clinicians. We want to emphasize that treatment can always be improved, and those who use this approach should not feel constrained by the guidelines presented here. In applying the method, readers should make changes that are consistent with current knowledge.

Development of a Treatment Tailored to Problem Drinkers

Based on the preceding chapters, one can draw several conclusions about the nature of an intervention that would be expected to appeal to and be effective with problem drinkers. Such conclusions were used to develop the guided self-management approach. In particular, the starting point in developing a treatment tailored to problem drinkers included the following premises:

• Treatment should be outpatient and nonintensive.
• Treatment should be largely a motivational intervention.
• Treatment should offer flexibility of treatment goals.

Nonintensive Treatment

Treatment of problem drinkers can be highly cost effective compared to services typically provided for alcohol problems. For problem drinkers, intensive treatments are usually no more effective than nonintensive outpatient treatments. An important qualification is that the treatment outcome findings that form the basis for this conclusion, as with most research-based conclusions, come from studies that compared groups of clients. Although the averaged group outcomes did not differ, it is possible that some individuals benefited more from one treatment than the other. Thus, from the perspective of an efficient health care system, most treatments for problem drinkers should be nonintensive, although for some clients intensive treatment may be warranted. However, intensive treatment should be the exception rather than the rule.

The evidence that very brief interventions can have positive outcomes for problem drinkers (see Chapters 1 and 4) suggests that the major function of treatment with problem drinkers is motivational—to help these individuals use their own resources to bring about behavior change. A behavioral orientation, as exemplified in cognitive-reappraisal therapy (Sanchez-Craig, 1980), individualized behavior therapy (M. B. Sobell & L. C. Sobell, 1978), behavioral self-control (Miller, 1977; Miller & Taylor, 1980), and other behavioral treatments (e.g., Alden, 1988; Chaney, O'Leary, & Marlatt, 1978; Heather, Robertson, MacPherson, Allsop, & Fulton, 1987), is consistent with a motivational focus. All of these treatments emphasize the functional analysis of drinking and the replacement of excessive drinking by alternative behaviors. Most of these approaches also include skills-training procedures, procedures that appear unnecessary for most problem drinkers. For such individuals, all that may be needed is to learn a general strategy for identifying and responding to risk situations. In this regard, Edwards (1980) has incisively observed that *"the intensity of treatment* should be kept to a sensible minimum with emphasis on facilitating the patient's own exploitation of his natural resources, on clarification of his own working methods, with treatment an aid to monitoring rather than its being a massive or escalating intervention" (p. 318, italics in original). This conclusion has also been echoed by Miller and Hester (1980), who asserted that "current research suggests that perhaps minimal interventions, rather than 'total push' efforts, would be the prudent norm for treatment in this area" (p. 98).

Based on the above, the therapeutic value of a short-term treatment might be enhanced by: (1) helping individuals learn how to identify generic situations that pose a risk of problem drinking and to use alternative ways of dealing with those situations; (2) helping individuals recognize their own strengths for dealing with risk situations (i.e., a person might possess the necessary skills but not realize how those skills can be used to avoid drinking excessively); (3) increasing the individual's motivation to avoid problem drinking by identifying and emphasizing the adverse consequences of such drinking; and (4) helping the individual recognize the benefits derived from avoiding problem drinking.

Not all agree, however, that nonintensive interventions should be the treatment of choice for problem drinkers. Heather (1989) examined several complex issues relating to such a conclusion and asserted that if one ignores cost-effectiveness considerations, the evidence is insufficient to dislodge intensive outpatient treatment as a treatment of choice for problem drinkers. Part of Heather's argument, however, was based on the contention that many of the brief-intervention studies used sample sizes too small to show a statistically significant difference between brief and more intensive interventions. A later study by Hall and Heather (1991) tested this notion and found that sample size did not account for the failure to find differences between approaches.

Another problem in evaluating the brief-intervention literature has been the combining studies of highly limited interventions (e.g., Chick, Ritson, Connaughtton, Stewart, & Chick, 1988, used a 5-minute advice session) with interventions that involve a few sessions. In a later paper, Heather (1990) teased apart some of these factors and concluded that brief interventions have a reasonable place in the front lines of a system of care for alcohol problems, provided that additional services are available when necessary. This is a well-justified position since the health care system has limited resources, and a consideration of what strategies are most advantageous for the total population in need of services must be a guiding principle in service planning. The important point is that brief treatments should be conceptualized as part of a treatment system where alternative strategies are available for persons for whom brief treatments are not effective.

No treatment is effective for everyone. With brief treatment there is a special obligation to identify those clients who are not benefiting and to offer other services to them. Also, building a relapse-prevention and management orientation into the treatment might help clients minimize the effects of problems that recur after treatment. A test of the benefits of doing this was the main objective of the seminal study that tested the effectiveness of the guided self-management treatment.

Motivational Interventions

What accounts for the effectiveness of nonintensive interventions? Consider the extreme case where one session of advice/counseling was as effective as much more intensive treatment. Assuming that both treatments were more effective than no treatment, what accounts for the improvement shown by the single-session group? Since the changes cannot be attributed to any intensive or involved procedure (e.g., skills training), it is obvious that the clients already had the skills required to change their behavior and that the advice/counseling session probably served to catalyze the clients to bring their skills to bear on the problem.

Miller (1983, 1985, 1986/1987, 1991; Miller, Sovereign, & Krege, 1988), who has written extensively on motivational interventions with alcohol abusers, feels that such interventions are particularly suited for problem drinkers. He has emphasized that motivation is a state (and therefore changeable over time) of commitment directed toward some course of action rather than a personal characteristic of an individual.

In a recent book on motivational interventions, Miller and Rollnick (1991) identified several ways that motivation can be enhanced: giving advice; removing barriers to change; allowing clients as much perceived choice as possible in the treatment process; decreasing the attractiveness of drinking; arranging external contingencies to encourage and support change; providing personalized feedback (e.g., blood serum enzyme levels) about the effects of alcohol and using feedback to reinforce progress in treatment when appropriate; setting clear and feasible goals; and expressing an active helping attitude. From a therapist's perspective, this latter characteristic is defined as "a therapist being actively and affirmatively interested in your client's change process" (Miller & Rollnick, 1991, p. 27).

An important factor related to enhancing motivation is the therapist's interviewing style or what Miller calls "motivational interviewing" (1983; Miller & Rollnick, 1991). The intent is to minimize resistance by the client and to have the client take responsibility for evaluating his or her own problem and for making a commitment to change. The specific features of motivational interviewing include (1) avoiding labeling; (2) using an inquisitive rather than confrontational style to raise clients' awareness of risks and consequences related to drinking; (3) providing objective feedback to clients in a low key style so as not to elicit resistance; (4) reassuring clients that change is possible;

and (5) allowing clients choices in treatment planning and goal setting. This type of interviewing style may describe the way many clinicians interact with their clients. The importance of Miller and his colleague pulling these features together is that they relate them to a large body of psychological literature (such as attribution theory and theories of attitude change) that may suggest other ways to enhance motivation (Miller, 1985; Miller & Rollnick, 1991). Many aspects of the guided self-management treatment approach are motivational.

Selection of Treatment Goals

An interesting aspect of successful interventions with problem drinkers is that they often involve a moderation rather than an abstinence outcome (Heather, 1990; Heather & Robertson, 1983; Hester & Miller, 1990; Hill, 1985; M. B. Sobell & L. C. Sobell, 1986/1987). Curiously, this occurs whether or not moderation is a treatment goal (Polich, Armor, & Braiker, 1981; Sanchez-Craig, Annis, Bornet, & MacDonald, 1984). That problem drinkers gravitate toward moderation outcomes when successful, regardless of the advice received in treatment, suggests that offering an alternative to abstinence may be an essential characteristic of services that hope to attract problem drinkers. In fact, the lack of a relationship between treatment goal recommendations and type of treatment outcome is not restricted to problem drinkers. (For a report of a study involving seriously dependent individuals, see Foy, Nunn, & Rychtarik, 1984.)

Since type of successful outcome (abstinence or moderation) has not been found to be significantly related to therapist assigned goals, this raises the question of whether it might be advantageous to have clients select their own goals. Recently, some studies have offered problem drinkers the opportunity to select their own treatment goals (usually with advice from the therapist) (see M. B. Sobell & L. C. Sobell, 1986/1987). Not only has self-selection of treatment goals been hypothesized to increase a person's commitment (i.e., motivation) to goal achievement, but many problem drinkers would prefer to select their own goals (Sobell, Sobell, Bogardis, Leo, & Skinner, 1992).

From the perspective of motivation for change, the major concern is not with the type of goal a client will pursue, but rather with how that decision is made. In guided self-management treatment, clients are asked to specify their own goal. This is done for two reasons. First, the literature suggests that there is no basis for expecting that assigning goals to clients will effect their behavior. Second, self-selection of goals appears to increase commitment to change (i.e., motivation).

According to Bandura's (1986) cognitive social-learning theory of behavior change, goals represent internal standards used by people to evaluate their own performance. He suggests that when goals are explicit, proximal, and perceived to be attainable, people strive to make their performance match their goals (i.e., having goals increases motivation). Bandura cites psychological research indicating that people perform better when they have been actively involved in the goal selection process than when their goals have been designated by others. He hypothesizes that making commitments "under conditions of perceived choice" (p. 478) serves to encourage people to strive to fulfill their goals. Likewise when goals are imposed by others, people do not necessarily feel obliged to fulfill those goals.

Miller (1986/1987) also considers perceived goal choice as important. Part of his exposition on motivational interventions suggests that clients will be more likely to comply with a treatment procedure when they view themselves as having made the decision to pursue that strategy. He hypothesized that allowing alcohol abusers to self-select their own goal would attract more persons to treatment, reduce attrition from treatment, and enhance the likelihood of successful outcomes.

In another study we conducted, alcohol abusers in outpatient treatment were asked to indicate how they would prefer their treatment goals to be determined. Nearly two thirds stated they would prefer to select their own goal, while slightly more than a quarter preferred the therapist to assign their goal. Clients who preferred goal assignment by the therapist had significantly more severe problems than clients who preferred to self-select their goal. Nearly two thirds of all clients reported they would be more likely to achieve a goal they had set for themselves, even if they had expressed no opinion about whether they or a therapist should select their goal (M. B. Sobell et al., 1992). This study lends support to the notion that problem drinkers would find goal self-selection to be a reasonable treatment approach, and that such a procedure might increase motivation (i.e., that they would be more likely to strive toward a goal they had set for themselves).

There are several other reasons why a goal self-selection procedure is consistent with a self-management approach to treatment. From a long-term perspective, when people achieve goals they have set for themselves, this should strengthen their self-efficacy and consequently help maintain their behavior change. While a person who achieves a goal specified by the therapist might give credit to the therapist for having set the goal, from the standpoint of self-efficacy theory (Bandura, 1986), it would be preferable for the individual to attribute the accomplishment to himself/herself.

Another important benefit of goal self-selection relates to instances when the goal is not achieved. When the goal has been set by the therapist, there are multiple ways that a client can rationalize failure to achieve the goal (e.g., the goal was too demanding; I didn't want to change just to satisfy my therapist; I didn't have the same goal as my therapist). When the pursuit of a self-established goal fails, the issue of goal appropriateness must be confronted directly because the failure cannot be attributed to someone else. Failure to achieve the goal not only sets the stage for discussion about whether the goal should be changed but also for a discussion of the client's commitment or motivation to change.

Although guided self-management treatment allows clients to select their own goals, if there are medical contraindications to drinking, this should be discussed with clients, and they should be advised to choose a goal of abstinence. Likewise, when there are nonmedical reasons why drinking would constitute too great a risk (e.g., if it would provoke serious marital conflict or job loss), clients should be advised against pursuing a goal of reduced drinking. Goal self-selection and specification, integral features of guided self-management treatment, are taken very seriously and conducted in the context of safeguards to prevent the procedure from being misused (e.g., to prevent clients from using goal self-selection as a justification for continued heavy drinking).

Finally, it is advisable to review the selected goal with the client on more than one occasion. Since most clients will not know what goal is the most appropriate for them at the start of treatment, they should be allowed to change their goal if justified. Treatment is a dynamic process, so some treatment decisions will depend on whether particular strategies have been successful. Over the course of treatment a learning process occurs; what is learned can suggest changes in the treatment plan, including a change in goals.

Cognitive Relapse Prevention in Guided Self-Management Treatment

Several decades ago, Wikler (1948) pointed out that there was an extremely high frequency of relapse among substance abusers after treatment. He suggested that environmental factors associated with drug use that were not present during treatment triggered relapse. At the time he proposed his hypothesis, it did not stimulate much research interest. However, in the ensuing years research has accrued yielding a picture of treatment outcomes marked by the recurrence of drug problems, including alcohol problems. The majority of outcomes include relapses, particularly within the first 6 months following treatment (Allsop & Saunders, 1989b; Gordis, Dorph, Sepe, & Smith, 1981; Hunt, Barnett, & Branch, 1971; Miller & Hester, 1986a; Polich et al., 1981).

Marlatt and his colleagues (Cummings, Gordon, & Marlatt, 1980; Marlatt, 1980; Marlatt & Gordon, 1985) gathered alcohol and other drug abusers' retrospective reports of the occurrence and precipitants of relapse. They found a high frequency of relapse, and they identified three general types of precipitants, which accounted for 74% of relapse episodes among alcohol abusers: negative emotional states, interpersonal conflict, and social pressure. These same factors have demonstrated remarkable consistency across different types of substance abuse, accounting for 72% of relapses among smokers, heroin addicts, gamblers, and uncontrolled eaters (Cummings et al., 1980).

Research on situations associated with relapse underlies the cognitive-behavioral model of relapse formulated by Marlatt and his associates (Marlatt & Gordon, 1985). That model, advanced as applicable to all addictive behaviors "attempts to describe the individual's reaction to a relapse and to examine the relationship between the first relapse episode and subsequent use" (Cummings et al., 1980, p. 297). Although the model applies most directly to persons seeking abstinence (in such cases the first instance of substance use can be defined as a relapse), it can be extended to individuals who seek to moderate their drinking. In such cases, a relapse can be defined as any instance when a person's drinking transgresses self-imposed rules (Larimer & Marlatt, 1990). Marlatt's approach to understanding relapse involves a social learning perspective (Bandura, 1977, 1986) that includes operant-conditioning and cognitively mediated learning explanations of behavior in addition to classical conditioning. A distinction is made between changing behavior (the acquisition of change) and the maintenance of behavior change, with relapse conceptualized as a failure to maintain change after treatment.

A social learning model of abusive drinking understands relapse as a response to specific stimuli. Therefore, treatment should focus on the client's learning to identify and cope effectively with such stimuli. The relapse prevention model enlarged the social learning approach to specifically include procedures for dealing with relapse, including procedures for maintaining a commitment to behavior change in spite of a relapse, with an emphasis on cognitive aspects of relapse.

Marlatt's model of the relapse process assumes that certain types of situational antecedents, designated as high-risk situations, set the stage for a relapse to occur. The critical determinant of whether or not a relapse occurs is whether the person recognizes the situation for its inherent risk and exercises an appropriate coping alternative. If an appropriate alternative is exercised, the individual not only avoids relapse but also experiences an increased sense of personal control (i.e., confidence in one's ability to avoid relapse) that makes it less likely that relapse will occur in the future. If the individual does not exercise a coping alternative, three factors combine to greatly increase the likelihood that a relapse will occur: (1) failure to cope; (2) diminished sense of personal control resulting from knowing that one has not attempted to cope with a high-risk situation; and (3) short-term positive outcome expectancies for substance use.

If a relapse (or violation) does occur, a "rule violation effect" is presumed to follow. As first proposed, this was referred to as an "abstinence violation effect" because the relapse prevention model was based on an analysis of relapses by chronic alcoholics who were trying to maintain abstinence. The effect refers to an individual attributing a lapse (i.e., initial violation) to a constitutional failing ("I'm just the type of person who has no control over their behavior"). Such thinking leads the individual to become self-deprecating and feel helpless. This sets the stage for the lapse to develop into a full-blown relapse. Such an experience is hypothesized to increase the likelihood of future relapses. Thus, in relapse prevention there is an emphasis on avoiding the initial violation and then on preventing relapse once a lapse has occurred.

In practice, the relapse prevention approach has focused on two major areas. The first has been on the *prevention of relapse*, which involves the functional analysis of drinking to identify high-risk situations and the use of coping-skills training to prepare individuals to deal with high-risk situations by means other than drinking. It has also been suggested that clients should be educated to estimate their own blood alcohol levels and that they should be encouraged to use a minimum 20-minute waiting interval between an initial rule violation and continued drinking (Cummings et al., 1980). This delay provides a person with an opportunity to reevaluate the situation and take actions to preclude further drinking. It also separates the triggering events from continued drinking and allows for the possibility that during the delay interval the strength of the triggering events may decrease, better enabling the client to exercise alternatives to continued drinking. Although an emphasis on functional analysis and coping-skills training is integral to relapse-prevention treatments, these are basic behavioral counseling techniques that were used several years before the term relapse prevention was introduced (e.g., Lovibond & Caddy, 1970; M. B. Sobell & L. C. Sobell, 1973; Sobell, Sobell, & Sheahan, 1976). The major contribution of this part of the relapse prevention model has been to highlight general types of situations associated with relapse, which allowed for the development of treatments that could have applicability across individual cases (e.g., Chaney et al., 1978). For example, the identification of interpersonal conflict situations as high risk for relapse suggests that social skills training could be a useful treatment strategy.

The second major area of focus of the relapse prevention model has been the development of approaches for dealing with relapses once they occur. We will refer to this contribution from the model as approaches to *relapse management*. It is this aspect of the relapse prevention model that we believe has made a unique contribution to the alcohol treatment field. The model has provided a context for discussing with clients the likelihood that relapses will occur. Previously, many therapists would avoid discussing the possibility of relapse lest clients misinterpret such discussion as reflecting a lack of confidence in them. Since the introduction of the relapse prevention model, discussion with clients of the possibility of relapse has become commonplace. In fact, the term "relapse prevention" is so well known it has been applied to many other forms of treatment, possibly because it can be asserted the virtually all treatments are intended to prevent relapse. For example, the trade magazine *Alcoholism and Addictions* features a center section titled "Relapse Prevention" that has nothing in common with Marlatt's model except the name.

Relapse management stresses the importance of dealing with relapses that occur by (1) minimizing the negative impact of the relapses and (2) construing relapses as learning experiences rather than as disastrous personal failures. This can help to lessen the significance of relapses that do occur as well as to maintain the subject's motivation for a successful long-term outcome. Considered from this perspective, recovery is viewed as a learning process rather than an all-or-none phenomenon. The occurrence of initial problems and how they are managed are seen as important determinants of long-term outcome. Continued success experiences are expected to lead to long-term maintenance of behavior change. Similarly, continued failure experiences are expected to rapidly dissipate treatment gains.

Relapse management has two key components. The first concerns *how clients react to the onset of a relapse*. The important point for clients to grasp is that the quicker the relapse is interrupted, the fewer risks they will take, and the fewer consequences they will suffer. Clients are told that just because they have crossed the line does not mean that they must stay there. They can minimize the harm by cutting the episode short.

The second relapse management component deals with *the effects of a relapse on future motivation for change* in terms of the way a person deals with a relapse that has occurred. Here clients are encouraged to view the relapse as a learning experience, to see what lessons can be gained from the experience to help prevent future relapses, and then to put the relapse in perspective and get it behind them (i.e., to view it as a setback along the trail to recovery, not as a reason to abandon attempts to change). The dual emphases on a taking a long-term perspective on recovery and on dealing with adverse episodes constructively complement self-management treatments and are consistent with self-help strategies. Thus, relapse prevention can be viewed from a motivational perspective as fostering clients' perseverance in their attempts to change their behavior.

The relapse prevention approach, which had its origin in research conducted primarily with chronic alcoholics (Marlatt, 1978), requires some modifications to be consistent with the research findings relating to problem drinkers. In terms of alternative responses to drinking in high-risk situations, the guided self-management approach focuses on helping clients identify and use existing coping skills rather than providing clients with skills training. Encouraging clients to identify and capitalize on their own strengths and coping styles is less value laden than a coping-skills training approach, and thus it might be more appealing to problem drinkers. For example, if confronted with social pressures to drink, a person could do several things:

(1) resist those pressures by being appropriately assertive; (2) resist those pressures by less assertive means (e.g., "My doctor told me that I shouldn't drink"); (3) leave the situation; (4) enlist the help of others (e.g., spouse, friend) in resisting the pressures; or (5) ignore the pressures. While any of these methods might be effective, coping-skills training requires designation of what skills would be good to acquire. The self-management approach, however, allows clients to determine the type of response they believe will be most effective and feasible for them. Thus, one important way that the guided self-management treatment approach differs from traditional relapse prevention is that it does not involve explicit skills training.

The traditional relapse prevention approach also needs to be modified to include moderation goals. For clients with a reduced-drinking goal, instead of any drinking constituting a violation of intention (i.e., the abstinence violation effect), it is drinking that violates limits specified by the client's goal that constitutes the rules violation effect (Larimer & Marlatt, 1990).

Evaluations of Relapse Prevention

In several recent reviews of the relapse process, Saunders and Allsop (Allsop & Saunders, 1989a; Allsop & Saunders, 1989b; Saunders & Allsop, 1987; Saunders & Allsop, 1992) have discussed the advantages and disadvantages associated with the relapse prevention model. One major problem is that although the model has intuitive appeal, it has not been adequately tested (Saunders & Allsop, 1987). Another is that "there is a very real difference between being skill deficient and having skills but deciding not to use them" (Allsop & Saunders, 1989b, p. 18). A skills deficiency would suggest the use of a skills training intervention, whereas a failure to use skills would suggest the need for a motivational intervention. There have been relatively few evaluations of the efficacy of relapse prevention, and little work has attempted to evaluate the unique contribution of the cognitive aspects of relapse prevention procedures. Almost all of the investigations have involved social skills training as the primary relapse prevention procedure. Those few studies that have evaluated the relapse prevention model will be reviewed here.

Although that report did not use the term "relapse prevention" when it was published the best known relapse prevention study is Chaney, O'Leary, and Marlatt (1978). In addition to their regular treatment, chronic alcoholics in inpatient treatment were randomly assigned to participate in social skills training (relapse prevention), to participate in a discussion group where high-risk drinking situations were discussed but skills training was not provided, or to receive no additional treatment. Although the skills-training group did not differ from the other two groups in outcome 3 months after treatment, it had a significantly better outcome (i.e., decreased duration and severity of relapse episodes) at 1 year posttreatment. This finding is consistent with viewing recovery as a learning process (Marlatt, 1983).

In Norway, Eriksen, Björnstad, and Götestam (1986) randomly assigned groups of 12 alcohol-dependent clients to receive either eight sessions of social skills training in addition to a standard alcoholism group counseling treatment or only the standard treatment. Subjects who received skills training had their first drink a mean of 51.6 days following treatment compared to 8.3 days for control subjects. They drank about one-third less alcohol per week than the control subjects. Also, their consumption was comparable to Norwegian norms and was judged by their significant others as socially acceptable.

Ito, Donovan, and Hall (1988) compared the effects of two aftercare conditions (a cognitive-behavioral skills-training relapse prevention or an interpersonal-process orientation) for hospitalized male alcoholic veterans. At the 6-month follow-up both groups showed comparable outcomes on several variables, although there were trends favoring the relapse-prevention treatment. Sjoberg and Samsonowitz (1985) similarly compared an outpatient drinking-related coping-skills program with a counseling program focusing on strategies for abstinence and found no difference between groups.

Another randomized controlled study of the relapse prevention method utilizing skills training has been reported by Annis (Annis, 1986b; Annis & Davis, 1988a, 1988b). In this study, 41 clients who participated in a program for employer-referred problem drinkers received eight outpatient counseling sessions of relapse prevention treatment over 3 months. Although the clients improved significantly over 6 months of follow-up, there was no comparison group. Thus, it is not possible to evaluate the relative effectiveness of the relapse prevention approach.

A positive finding for relapse prevention has been reported by Saunders and Allsop (1992), who compared 60 problem drinkers randomly assigned to a cognitive-behavioral relapse prevention treatment group and a routine treatment group, a relapse-discussion group and a routine treatment group, or a routine treatment group only. At 6-month follow-up, subjects who had been in the relapse prevention group had longer periods of abstinence, fewer symptoms of dependence, and fewer and less severe alcohol problems. At 1-year follow-up, the time to first drink and time to first heavy-drinking day were significantly longer for the subjects who had received relapse prevention than for the other subjects in the study.

The relapse prevention model has been extensively evaluated in the area of smoking research. Consistent with the model, Condiotte and Lichtenstein (1981) found in a prospective study that a large proportion (about 80%) of subjects who relapsed "appeared to demonstrate aspects of the abstinence violation effect" (p. 656). Consistent with findings by Cummings and his colleagues (1980), a microanalysis of relapse situations found a significant relationship between subjects' posttreatment perceived self-efficacy (i.e., confidence in their ability to cope) and the types of situations in which relapse occurred: Relapses occurred in situations for which subjects had reported low self-efficacy. Shiffman (1982), in a study of relapse of ex-smokers, found data supportive of Marlatt's model. However, while situational antecedents were important, they were not sufficient determinants of relapse. Within risk situations, the most important determinant of relapse appeared to be whether subjects performed any coping responses; those who performed any coping response were less likely to relapse. This finding provides indirect support for a motivational component for relapse prevention rather than for specific skills training.

Killen and his colleagues (Killen, Fortmann, Newman, & Varady, 1990) evaluated a relapse prevention component among behavioral treatments and nicotine gum interventions for smokers and found no effect for the relapse prevention component. They reported that "although participants in the trial said they liked the relapse prevention strategies presented to them and that they 'made sense,' subjects failed to put such strategies into practice" (p. 90).

Roffman and his colleagues (Roffman, Stephens, Simpson, & Whitaker, 1988) reported preliminary findings for a relapse prevention treatment of marijuana dependence. The subjects were generally well-educated, employed, and in their 30s. The relapse prevention treatment ($n = 54$) was compared with a social-support treatment ($n = 56$) that emphasized developing and using a support network. Treatments involved ten group sessions and booster sessions at 3- and 6-month follow-ups. At 1-month follow-up, abstinence rates did not differ significantly between the groups. At a 3-month follow-up, for subjects run later in the study, the social-support subjects had a better abstinence rate than the relapse prevention subjects. However, at the 6-month follow-up the difference was no longer significant, despite the fact that slightly more subjects were abstinent in the social-support group (31.3%) than in the relapse prevention group (24.7%). At a long-term follow-up (30 months), there was no significant difference in outcome between groups (Roffman, Stephens, & Simpson, 1990), leading the authors to conclude that they had found no advantage for the relapse prevention group.

Finally, Hawkins, Catalano, and Wells (1986) randomly assigned 70 drug abusers in a therapeutic community to a skills-training intervention, and another 60 to the regular therapeutic community program as a control condition. Experimental effects were noted for the skills-training group on within-treatment measures of social skills, but no between-treatment outcome data were presented.

Other studies have examined the relapse prevention model but not the relapse prevention treatment. Hall, Havassy, and Wasserman (1990), for example, studied 221 alcoholics, opiate users, and cigarette smokers who were followed after treatment for either 12 weeks or until they had relapsed with their problem drug for 7 consecutive days. The authors found that relapse precipitated by negative moods could only be assessed after the fact (most studies of relapse precipitants have used retrospective assessments). When the relationship between negative moods and substance use was examined in a prospective manner, no association was apparent. This suggests that rather than precipitating relapse, negative moods may simply be a convenient attribution made by clients when they are attempting to explain why a relapse occurred. Also, clients with the most restrictive goal (i.e., abstinence) were less likely to lapse, and less likely to progress from a lapse to a relapse, than were clients with less-demanding goals. This finding is contrary to the relapse prevention model, which predicts that a stringent goal would increase the probability of a relapse after a slip.

In another study testing the relapse prevention model, Birke, Edelmann, and Davis (1990) examined whether illicit drug users would show an abstinence violation effect. They concluded that factors such as health and criminal involvement were more important variables in predicting drug use and relapse than were cognitive attributions about an initial use.

In evaluating the various tests of the relapse prevention approach, it is clear that in most cases relapse prevention treatment, as it has been tested to date, has been inextricably confounded with other treatment procedures, most notably skills training. To some extent, a certain amount of confounding is unavoidable. For example, it is not clear how one could enact a relapse prevention treatment that did not include a functional analysis of drinking behavior. However, it is possible to conduct relapse prevention in the absence of skills training. Also, while there is support for using a skills-training version of relapse prevention treatment with severely dependent alcohol abusers (i.e., such individuals may be deficient in certain skills) (Twentyman et al., 1982), to date no studies suggest that less severely dependent alcohol abusers have similar deficits. Indeed, the finding that short-term treatments can be efficacious for such persons suggests that most of these individuals have adequate coping skills, which, with some guidance, they can use successfully to deal with potential or actual relapse situations.

In conclusion, while the studies published to date provide limited support for the effectiveness of social skills training for alcohol abusers, the findings are inconsistent. Also, the unique contributions of the key cognitive features of the relapse prevention approach have not been evaluated, except in our own research, which will be discussed later in this book. The lack of tests for the cognitive aspects of relapse prevention is unfortunate because it is the emphasis on cognitive aspects of relapse (i.e., how relapses are construed) that primarily differentiates the model from previous behavioral treatments. There is also a need to evaluate whether relapse prevention has general applicability or should be restricted to clients who tend to catastrophize about a lapse.

Summary and Integration

Based on the positive track record of brief interventions, and realizing that the effectiveness of such approaches cannot be attributed to intensive skills training, it is clear that many people have sufficient resources to modify their behavior patterns if they wish. The guided self-management orientation is intended to facilitate self-change by encouraging people to identify reasons for changing, by providing general strategies for achieving and maintaining change, and by providing advice. The emphasis is on helping people to identify their own strengths and resources and to capitalize upon those assets as they seek a life free from alcohol problems. The intervention is intended to be minimally intrusive on a person's life-style. A strong emphasis is placed on practicality, that is, developing treatments that can be readily applied by clinicians and other health care providers in community-based treatment programs. The majority of the treatment in guided self-management studies was conducted by clinicians rather than researchers.

In the following chapters, the major components of the guided self-management treatment program are described. While the treatment involves a small number of sessions, it is most appropriately described as a "program" of treatment. This is because it gets off to a running start with the first treatment components being set in place at the assessment, and it continues past the formal sessions if a need for further treatment is indicated. There is no "magic number" of treatment sessions for any given individual. Different people will have problems of differing complexity, will have different life circumstances, and will be capable of different rates of change. Flexibility and adapting to the needs of each client should be the major consideration when applying the procedures described here. Although the treatment is discussed as a set of procedures, we wish to stress that it is an approach rather than a regimen. The guiding themes of the approach are its emphasis on increasing clients' motivation (commitment to change) and on finding ways to help people help themselves.

6

Assessment: A Running Start

The subtitle of this chapter—a running start—conveys a very important aspect of guided self-management treatment. Since not much time is spent with a client, the treatment is designed to cover a great deal of material quickly and efficiently. Thus, the assessment not only gathers data but also provides the start of an accelerated treatment process.

Entering Self-Management Treatment

First, and foremost, it is important to determine that the client will accept a self-management treatment approach. In our case, since the treatment provided was one of many services offered, clients were screened at a central intake. When a new client was identified as eligible for the self-management program, the intake worker explained that the treatment was being evaluated and that if the client participated in the treatment, he or she would be part of a research study. The client was then provided with a written description of the treatment, which follows in an abbreviated form:

About Guided Self-Management Treatment

Guided self-management is a treatment program developed specifically for certain types of persons with alcohol problems; namely, persons who do not have severe alcohol problems. The treatment program emphasizes helping persons recognize and use their own strengths to resolve their drinking problems. It involves a comprehensive assessment, which gathers information about the person's drinking problem and factors that might be important to take into account in order to understand the problem. After the assessment, clients read two short booklets describing the treatment approach, complete two homework assignments relevant to their treatment, and attend two 90-minute outpatient treatment sessions. Following this, clients can receive additional treatment at their request.

A brief written description was used so clients would understand from the start that the treatment would involve their taking major responsibility for formulating and enacting their own treatment plan. The role of the therapist and of the program materials is to provide guidance to help clients accomplish these tasks, but the focus is on helping people help themselves. These points can be communicated by a therapist just as easily as by written description. What is important is that clients understand what they are getting into before they make the commitment.

Describing self-management as an approach designed for people who want to take responsibility for helping themselves and whose problems are not very severe is a motivational strategy intended to reinforce clients' self-confidence that they can succeed in conquering their drinking problem. It is considered important in brief treatments to provide clients with a sense of optimism (Zweben, Pearlman, & Li, 1988).

Finally, we recommend that all clients be alcohol free when clinically assessed. This recommendation derives from a large body of research conducted by ourselves and others on the validity of alcohol abusers' self-reports of drinking and drinking-related information. In general, it has been found that alcohol abusers' self-reports are reasonably accurate if clients are interviewed when alcohol free, are seen in a clinical or research setting, and are given assurances that the information they provide will be confidential (Babor, Stephens, & Marlatt, 1987; O'Farrell & Maisto, 1987; L. C. Sobell & M. B. Sobell, 1986, 1990; Sobell, Sobell, & Nirenberg, 1988). The latter condition is part and parcel of all clinical treatment (Rankin, 1990).

In addition, there is evidence that if clients are not alcohol free when interviewed, their self-reports of drinking are not reliable. In a study of new admissions to an outpatient treatment program, we found that in 50% of the cases in which a client had a positive blood alcohol level, the client's self-report of drinking was discrepant with the breath-test reading (Sobell, Sobell, & VanderSpek, 1979). In nearly all cases with a positive blood alcohol level (92 out of 93), the client substantially underreported how much he or she had drunk prior to the interview.

To determine that clients are alcohol free, we recommend breath testing. Numerous inexpensive breath testers are available for use in offices (e.g., M. B. Sobell & L. C. Sobell, 1975). While such devices are screening rather than evidential testers (i.e., they are not legally binding), they are sufficiently accurate for clinical use, are quick and easy to administer, and require no special training. Breath testing is a relatively unobtrusive way of determining whether clients have alcohol in their system. In our experience, it has been extremely rare for a client to object to the test. If the test indicates more than a negligible blood alcohol concentration, we recommend that the client be instructed that it is necessary to be alcohol free for the assessment and that the assessment be rescheduled.

In our opinion, breath testing communicates to the client a professional approach to the treatment of alcohol problems. People are familiar with the use of tests when health problems are being assessed (e.g., urine tests for glucose levels), or treated (e.g., hypertension), and alcohol problems are no different. It is good clinical practice, especially at the assessment, to test whether the client is alcohol free rather than taking the client's word for it.

One might expect that the clinical opinion of experienced staff is all that is needed to identify clients who have been drinking, and thus that breath tests for blood alcohol level are unnecessary. The above study (Sobell et al., 1979) also addressed this point. Experienced clinicians first recorded their own judgment about whether the client had been drinking, then recorded the client's self-report of recent drinking, and finally breath tested the client. These experienced clinicians failed to identify 50% of the clients who gave self-reports that were discrepant with their breath test.

The above results illustrate the phenomenon of tolerance. Tolerance is an adaptation in the individual that occurs as a result of drinking, especially frequent drinking. This adaptation can be thought of in two ways. First, with repeated drinking experiences, it takes an increasing amount of alcohol to achieve the same response in an individual that previously was produced by a smaller dose. The alternative way to conceptualize tolerance, and a way that may have relevance for explaining why some people come to increase their consumption over time, is that it takes a greater amount of alcohol than in the past to achieve the same degree of effect. Thus, a person who previously felt "intoxicated" after consuming three or four drinks might with repeated drinking experiences find that he or she needs to consume six or seven drinks to feel the same way. Acquired tolerance to alcohol helps explain why even trained clinicians are not good judges of a person's blood alcohol level, especially if they have not had much prior experience with the client in a sober state. A person with high acquired tolerance may have a substantial blood alcohol level yet not display obvious drunken behavior.

Assessment as a Therapeutic Process

The assessment information that clients provide their therapists yields a picture of the client's drinking and related problems. Clinicians with little experience with problem drinkers may be surprised that the assessment process sometimes constitutes the first time that clients have given any intensive thought to their drinking and related problems. When considered in context this becomes understandable. While problem drinkers sometimes drink to excess, on many other occasions they drink without problems or the risk of problems. Often when they seek treatment their alcohol problems do not dominate their lives, and sometimes the problems are even perceived as a nuisance rather than as a major threat to their well-being (Thom, 1986, 1987). For problem drinkers who have not spent much time thinking about their drinking patterns, and whose drinking has not seriously disrupted their lives, just completing an assessment interview can be an illuminating and, it is hoped, motivating experience.

At the end of the assessment clients in guided self-management treatment are given Reading 1, which provides a framework they can use to organize their thoughts and the assessment information that they have reported. They are also given Homework Assignment 1, which asks them to perform a functional analysis of their drinking. These two features of the treatment constitute the main components of getting a running start. A few points are pertinent at this time.

First, Reading 1 provides an overview of the cognitive-behavioral self-management approach that forms the basis for treatment. While most clients who have gotten this far accept the approach and find it consistent with their view of their problems and of what they need to do, there will be some clients who cannot accept the approach or who on reflection feel that it does not really fit their case. In such cases, clients should be reassessed and offered appropriate alternatives. Thus, the first reading can also serve a screening function.

Second, Reading 1 and Homework Assignment 1 prepare the client to perform a functional analysis of their own drinking. The reading describes the basic components of a functional analysis of drinking, and Homework Assignment 1 requires that clients perform such an analysis on their own drinking. Thus, the reading and assignment enable the client to integrate the information covered during the assessment and to organize it in a meaningful manner. This helps to give them an early start on their treatment. Prior to starting the first treatment session, they have a basic knowledge and understanding of the treatment approach that will be taken, and they have formulated major portions of a functional analysis of their own drinking. As a result, clients enter formal treatment prepared to go ahead at full speed.

The assessment also serves to prepare the therapist for dealing with the client. If the assessment is conducted by someone other than the therapist, we recommend that the therapist be provided with a clinical summary of the assessment, known as a "Clinical Assessment Summary," and be given the assessment materials in advance of the first treatment session. A sample of a completed Clinical Assessment Summary appears as Figure 6.1. Even when the therapist performs the assessment, a Clinical Assessment Summary can be useful because it provides a concise, readily available reference about important aspects of the case. Furthermore, since most therapists have a large caseload, the Clinical Assessment Summary facilitates recall of important

Name: _____   Date Completed: _____

CLINICAL ASSESSMENT SUMMARY

ADS Score: _9_   ADS Components: _Hangovers; acute effects; tried unsuccessfully to cut down._

Age: _41_   Sex: (M)   F   Yrs. Education: _18_   Marital Status: (M/CL)   NM   S   D   W

Employment Status: _Full-time_   Occupation: _Truck dispatcher_

No. of Alcohol- or Drug-related Arrests: _0_   No. of Jobs lost due to Alcohol or Drug use in past year.: _0_

Ever purposely abstinent: (Y)   N   Longest no. mos. purposely abstinent : _2_   Family History of Alc. Problems: (Y)⁻²   N

Prior A/D treatment: Y   (N)   Describe: _____

Problem Self–Appraisal: _Major problem. Spouse threatens to leave if he doesn't bring his drinking under control._

Alcohol Consequences: _Blackouts; interpersonal conflict; late for work._

Other Drug Use: _Nil_

No. of Yrs. problem drinking: _4_   No. of Yrs. heavy drinking: _7_   No. days morning drinking in past yr.: _1_

Timeline	_172_ No.. of days Abstinent	_72_ No. of days 5 – 9 SDs
Past 360 days	_81_ No. of days 1 – 4 SDs	_35_ No. of days ≥ 10 SDs

Drinking (Patterns, features, or use characteristics): _Weekdays drinks lightly or not at all. Many weekends (Fri., Sat., Sun.) drinks about 8–12 drinks on a day, sometimes 15. With friends at a bar, whiskey. Cut down recently to 1 day/week._

☐ **IDS** (heavy use situations in past yr.): _Elevations on positive affect scale suggest a good times drinker. A bit of control testing._

☐ **SCQ** (vulnerability): _Perceives major vulnerability when control testing. Somewhat vulnerable when feeling good._

Goal: _3 drinks on 5 times per week; 1 time a month as many as 5 drinks. Always in the presence of spouse and with her approval._

Additional Observations: _Spouse has already been helping him to cut down._

FIGURE 6.1. Example of Clinical Assessment Summary.

aspects of a given case, and it avoids having to review all the assessment material. The time needed to prepare a Clinical Assessment Summary of the type shown here is minimal.

In summary, assessment as conducted in guided self-management treatment is more than a data-collection procedure: Assessment is the start of treatment. Clients are informed about the basic principles of the treatment and are given the task, following the assessment session, of beginning to functionally analyze their drinking. They come to the first treatment session familiar with the orientation of the treatment and with materials to talk about. Likewise, the therapist entering the first session is familiar with the case and ready to begin the treatment. This "running start" for the client is an integral part of guided self-management treatment as a motivational intervention, and it is a procedure that is not typical of other brief treatments.

Selected Assessment Tools and Procedures

The assessment recommended here has the central features of any good clinical assessment of an alcohol problem (e.g., gather information on sociodemographic factors, drinking-problem history and drinking patterns, consequences of drinking, other substance use) as well as some added features. Various ways of gathering basic sociodemographic information are not discussed here, nor are assessment instruments that only serve research purposes. Instead, the focus is on instruments and procedures that we have found to have exceptional clinical utility.

Screening Procedures

Since the self-management approach discussed in this book is intended for and has only been evaluated with persons who are not severely dependent on alcohol, one needs some way of identifying such clients. A combination of procedures can be used for this purpose: (1) clients' scores on a self-report measure of dependence; (2) their report of never having experienced severe withdrawal symptoms; and (3) a medical assessment to verify those reports. The medical assessment that we have used primarily for research studies is usually unnecessary in clinical practice.

For assessing dependence, we recommend using the Alcohol Dependence Scale (ADS) (Skinner & Allen, 1982; Skinner & Horn, 1984). The ADS is a well-validated instrument for which a user's manual and normative data are available. While the ADS is one of several scales (Davidson, 1987; Sobell, Sobell, & Nirenberg, 1988) developed to measure the alcohol dependence syndrome (Edwards & Gross, 1976), some of the available instruments have been criticized for not actually measuring that construct (Davidson, 1987; Edwards, 1986). For the present purposes, the issue of whether such scales truly tap all dimensions of the hypothesized dependence syndrome is secondary to how well they identify problem drinkers.

While most of the available dependence scales are relatively sensitive for differentiating among levels of severe dependence (e.g., Severity of Dependence Questionnaire) (Stockwell, Murphy, & Hodgson, 1983), very few are sensitive at lower levels of dependence (Davidson, 1987). The ADS, however, is able to differentiate among persons with lower levels of dependence (Skinner & Allen, 1982). An alternative instrument sensitive to lower levels of dependence is the Short Alcohol Dependence Data (SADD) questionnaire (Davidson & Raistrick, 1986). The ADS and the SADD are relatively comparable; the major difference is that since the SADD is not copyrighted it can be reproduced at no charge. Both scales are quick to administer (ADS = 25 items; SADD = 15 items), and both have satisfactory psychometric characteristics.

A conservative cut-off criterion on the ADS is a score of 21 or less (the 50th percentile on norms constructed at the Addiction Research Foundation, Toronto). Persons scoring below the 50th percentile on the ADS rarely have experienced severe withdrawal symptoms (i.e., seizures, hallucinations, delirium tremens) (Skinner & Horn, 1984). The ADS also has individual items about severe withdrawal symptoms that can be double checked to insure that none of the items were answered positively by the client.

In our studies, we have also briefly screened for evidence of probable organic brain syndrome using two standardized tests: (1) the Trail Making Test, using age adjusted scores (Davies, 1968) and (2) the Digit Symbol and Vocabulary subscales on the Wechsler Adult Intelligence Scale (Wilkinson & Carlen, 1981). Since certain parts of the intervention involve reading materials, we have also screened clients for their reading ability using the Wide Range Achievement Test (Jastak & Jastak, 1965). However, unless there is a question about brain damage or reading ability, clinicians can assess their clients without such tests. The major concern is to exclude clients who have low levels of literacy or for whom there is evidence of impaired cognitive function, especially impaired abstracting abilities. These kinds of exclusion factors are applicable to conducting any type of cognitive treatment with alcohol abusers.

Finally, for research purposes we have often excluded clients who are frequent heavy drinkers. In one study, for example, clients were excluded who reported that over the past 6 months they had consumed an average of at least 12 standard drinks on at least 5 days per week. This criterion was based on a pilot study in which other screening criteria had failed to identify some extremely heavy drinkers, and for whom a low-intensity, self-managed treatment did not seem a good treatment choice. Based on clinical experience, it is our recommendation that very heavy drinkers should not participate in self-management treatment, unless the number of sessions and length of time in treatment are increased. While some of the principles of self-management treatment might have applicability for more serious cases, such applications should be prudent.

Measuring Drinking: The Timeline Follow-Back Method

The assessment of drinking is a critical feature of any treatment for alcohol problems. Clinically, it is helpful to have a complete picture of the drinking. However, the assessment procedure should not be unduly burdensome. To gather drinking data, we have used the Timeline Follow-Back method.

The Timeline Follow-Back technique was developed a little over 20 years ago as a research follow-up data procedure to provide information on posttreatment drinking (L. C. Sobell & M. B. Sobell, 1973, 1992b; Sobell, Sobell, Leo, & Cancilla, 1988). It was an alternative to procedures popular at that time, such as classifying individuals as either drinking or abstinent, with no further information on the amount or pattern of drinking.

Another popular procedure at the time was the quantity–frequency (QF) method, whereby people estimate on average how many days per week they drink, and how much they typically drink on a drinking day. QF procedures have limited utility for assessment or follow-up in clinical populations (Room, 1990; L. C. Sobell & M. B. Sobell, 1992b) because they force people to impose a pattern on their report of their drinking, when their drinking might actually be quite unpatterned. Also, days of heavy drinking, if in the minority, tend to go unreported in QF estimates (i.e., they are not part of the "average" or "typical" pattern). The Timeline Follow-Back procedure avoids these problems by asking people to recall as well as possible all of their drinking that occurred during a specified interval.

The Timeline method asks people to reconstruct their drinking on a day-by-day basis over a particular interval using a blank calendar. Readers unfamiliar with this technique might think that clients are not able to reconstruct their drinking over an extended period of time. However, a sizable body of research shows this can be done with reasonable reliability (i.e., reports of the same interval tend to be stable over time) and validity (i.e., reports of significant others agree well with those of the clients; official records verify instances of alcohol-related consequences. (See Babor et al., 1987, L. C. Sobell & M. B. Sobell, 1992b, and Sobell, Sobell, Riley, 1988, for reviews of this research.)

The Timeline method is a retrospective procedure and as such requires people to provide best-recall estimates of their past drinking. If a client reports having consumed 14 standard drinks on January 17th, when it may have been 16 or 12 drinks, and it may have been on the 15th or the 18th, this degree of reporting error is no greater and probably less than that incurred by other methods. The important point is that the Timeline will provide a reasonably accurate summary of the major features of the drinking: amount, frequency, pattern, and degree of variability.

In order to understand the richness of Timeline data for clinical purposes, it is important to know something about the instructions people are given regarding how to reconstruct their drinking. Clients completing a Timeline calendar are told that what is most important is that they reconstruct their drinking as well as they can. They are told that it is not expected that their report for long intervals will be absolutely accurate, but that it should be as close to what really occurred as possible. Clients understand that the purpose of the procedure is to provide the therapist with a visual summary of their drinking over the reporting period.

In research studies, the pretreatment Timeline typically covers the 12 months prior to the interview. In clinical practice, however, the interval can be shortened to 90 days prior to treatment, particularly if the client reports that that interval is representative of the pretreatment pattern. Clients are asked to record their drinking on the calendar, thereby providing a picture of what their drinking was like, including patterns of drinking (e.g., heavy weekend drinking) and any changes in the pattern over time (e.g., switched from mostly heavy weekend drinking to drinking almost daily for the month prior to entering treatment). Clients are also asked to record the amount of alcohol they consumed in standard drink units (a standard drink contains a specified amount of ethanol irrespective of the type of alcoholic beverage, see Chapter 7). If the client reports that the 90 days prior to entering treatment are not representative of a longer pretreatment interval (e.g., 1 year), then the client can complete a second calendar reflecting a "typical" 90-day period or can be asked to indicate in what ways the 90-days period just preceding treatment was atypical.

Since providing Timeline data is often perceived by clients as a formidable task, they are also apprised of several aids that may help ease the task of reconstructing their drinking. One important memory aid is to have clients identify the dates of significant events during the reporting period. These may be generic events (e.g., New Year's Day, major sporting event, major news event) or idiosyncratic events (e.g., their own or others' birthdays, dates of important personal events such as changing jobs, dates of vacations or personal holidays). It is helpful to write these events on the Timeline calendar. Clients will often remember what they were doing around these "anchor" dates and can use them to reconstruct their drinking for substantial periods. Calendar aids have also been used to help clients recall alcohol-relapse episodes (McKay, O'Farrell, Maisto, Connors, &

Funder, 1989), drug use (Adams & Henley, 1977), and other events (Gorman & Peters, 1990).

Another aid to constructing a Timeline is to have clients recall lengthy periods of time when they completely abstained, drank in a very patterned manner (e.g., 6 drinks every day; 2 to 4 drinks per day on Monday through Thursday and 10 to 12 drinks Friday through Sunday), or drank heavily for an extended time period. Other techniques can be used to target in on approximate levels of consumption in difficult cases. For example, if a client reports having drank "a lot" of beers on a day but claims an inability to specify what "a lot" means, "bracketing" can be helpful. The client can be asked "does 'a lot' mean 24 beers or 6 beers?" A typical response to this question by the client might be "certainly not 24 beers, more like 12 or so." If desired, one can target in further by asking "was it 12 beers or could it have been more like 9 or 15 beers?" For research studies, the probing continues until the specification is as precise as possible. For clinical purposes, however, the important questions usually involve how frequently clients drink, the pattern of drinking, and how often they consume large amounts and small amounts when they drink. Thus, it makes little practical difference if a large amount is 12 drinks or 15 drinks or if a small amount is 2 drinks or 3 drinks, as long as the major features of the drinking are captured.

The clinical value of the timeline goes beyond simply providing drinking data, however. Studying the completed Timeline, the therapist and the client can readily gain a picture of the main features of the drinking during the period in question. For example, did drinking increase over the pretreatment period? Was there a distinct pattern to the drinking? Did the drinking bear obvious relationships to possible antecedents (e.g., holidays, recreational activities, paydays, weekends)? Figures 6.2 through 6.4 provide examples of Timelines taken from actual cases, illustrating how a completed Timeline can provide a clinically useful summary of clients' drinking.

A computer-administered software program of the Timeline Follow-Back method is currently being developed, and a preliminary version of the program has been field-tested. The computer program contains instructions for completing the calendar; it provides users with a country-specific standard drink conversion menu (e.g., for the United States, Canada, Great Britain, Australia); it facilitates recall by listing major events and holidays on the calendar; and it also allows users to list personal holidays and events. The computer version has some advantages over a paper-and-pencil method. Most notably, the drinking data can be automatically analyzed and graphed, and immediate feedback can be provided to the user. A recent publication describing the Timeline method in considerable detail provides some samples of the types of data that can be generated by the computerized version of the Timeline (L. C. Sobell & M. B. Sobell, 1992b).

360-day Timeline

Subject No.: ______

Today's Date: June 10 Start Date: June 15 End Date: June 9

	SUN	MON	TUES	WED	THURS	FRI	SAT
J	1	2	3	4	5	6	7
U	8	9	10	11	12	13	14
N	15 Father's Day 2	16 2	17 0	18 3	19 0	20 10	21 7
	22 0	23 3	24 10	25 0	26 3	27 7	28 7
	29 2	30 8	1 Canada Day 4	2 3	3 3	4 10	5 7
J	6 0	7 3	8 10	9 0	10 3	11 7	12 7
U	13 2	14 0	15 3	16 0	17 3	18 10	19 7
L	20 HOLIDAY 6	21 6	22 10	23 2	24 10	25 10	26 10
	27 2	28 0	29 0	30 2	31 0	1 10	2 7
A	3 8	4 Civic Holiday 4	5 10	6 0	7 3	8 7	9 7
U	10 2	11 0	12 3	13 0	14 3	15 10	16 7
G	17 0	18 3	19 10	20 0	21 3	22 7	23 7
	24 2	25 0	26 3	27 0	28 3	29 10	30 7
	31 8	1 Labour Day 2	2 10	3 0	4 3	5 7	6 7
S	7 0	8 3	9 10	10 0	11 3	12 10	13 7
E	14 0	15 3	16 10	17 0	18 3	19 7	20 7
P	21 2	22 0	23 3	24 0	25 3	26 10	27 7
	28 0	29 3	30 10	1 0	2 3	3 7	4 7
O	5 2	6 2	7 0	8 0	9 3	10 10	11 Birthday 10
C	12 7	13 Thanksgiving 3	14 10	15 0	16 3	17 7	18 7
T	19 2	20 0	21 3	22 0	23 3	24 10	25 7
	26 0	27 3	28 10	29 0	30 3	31 Halloween 7	1 7
N	2 2	3 10	4 3	5 10	6 3	7 12	8 10
O	9 0	10 10	11 Remembrance 3	12 10	13 3	14 10	15 10
V	16 2	17 0	18 3	19 0	20 3	21 10	22 7
	23 0	24 3	25 10	26 0	27 3	28 7	29 7
	30 2						

	SUN	MON	TUES	WED	THURS	FRI	SAT
		1 0	2 3	3 10	4 0	5 10	6 7
D	7 0	8 3	9 10	10 0	11 3	12 7	13 7
E	14 2	15 0	16 3	17 0	18 3	19 10	20 7
C	21 0	22 3	23 10	24 5	25 Christmas 6	26 7	27 7
	28 2	29 0	30 3	31 12			
					1 New Year's Day 2	2 10	3 7
J	4 0	5 3	6 10	7 0	8 3	9 7	10 7
A	11 Florida 2	12 0	13 3	14 0	15 3	16 10	17 7
N	18 2	19 1	20 10	21 5	22 9	23 12	24 3
	25 10	26 1	27 2	28 2	29 2	30 10	31 7
F	1 0	2 3	3 10	4 0	5 3	6 7	7 7
E	8 2	9 0	10 3	11 0	12 3	13 10	14 Valentine's Day 7
B	15 0	16 3	17 10	18 0	19 3	20 7	21 7
	22 2	23 0	24 3	25 0	26 3	27 10	28 7
M	1 0	2 3	3 10	4 0	5 3	6 7	7 7
A	8 2	9 8	10 3	11 5	12 5	13 10	14 7
R	15 0	16 6	17 12	18 3	19 0	20 10	21 10
	22 2	23 10	24 3	25 10	26 14	27 10	28 12
	29 8	30 3	31 15	1 0	2 0	3 0	4 6
A	5 0	6 3	7 0	8 3	9 0	10 5	11 6
P	12 0	13 3	14 0	15 3	16 0	17 Good Friday 7	18 8
R	19 Easter Sunday 2	20 Easter Monday 3	21 3	22 0	23 3	24 8	25 6
	26 0	27 2	28 3	29 0	30 3	1 7	2 7
M	3 2	4 0	5 3	6 0	7 3	8 10	9 7
A	10 Mother's Day 2	11 3	12 10	13 0	14 3	15 10	16 8
Y	17 8	18 Victoria Day 2	19 0	20 3	21 3	22 10	23 7
	24 2	25 2	26 10	27 0	28 3	29 7	30 7
	31 0	1 9	2 7	3 0	4 3	5 11	6 7
J	7 0	8 9	9 0	10	11	12	13
U	14	15	16	17	18	19	20
N	21 Father's Day	22	23	24	25	26	27
	28	29	30				

FIGURE 6.2. Example of Timeline for pretreatment drinking.

360-day Timeline					Subject No.: ____		

Today's Date: Nov. 26 Start Date: Dec. 1 End Date: Nov. 25

	SUN	MON	TUES	WED	THURS	FRI	SAT
		1 0	2 0	3 5	4 5	5 3	6 20
D	7 0	8 0	9 0	10 5	11 3	12 20	13 2
E	14 2	15 0	16 0	17 5	18 2	19 4	20 20
C	21 5	22 0	23 0	24 5	25 Christmas 3	26 20	27 0
	28 0	29 0	30 0	31 20			
					1 New Year's Day 3	2 3	3 20
J	4 0	5 0	6 0	7 5	8 3	9 20	10 2
A	11 2	12 0	13 0	14 5	15 2	16 0	17 20
N	18 5	19 0	20 0	21 5	22 0	23 20	24 0
	25 0	26 0	27 0	28 5	29 5	30 4	31 20
F	1 2	2 0	3 0	4 5	5 3	6 20	7 2
E	8 5	9 0	10 0	11 5	12 2	13 3	14 Valentine's Day 20
B	15 0	16 0	17 0	18 5	19 0	20 20	21 0
	22 2	23 0	24 0	25 5	26 5	27 0	28 20
M	1 5	2 0	3 0	4 5	5 3	6 20	7 2
A	8 0	9 0	10 0	11 5	12 2	13 20	14 0
R	15 2	16 0	17 0	18 5	19 0	20 4	21 20
	22 5	23 0	24 0	25 5	26 5	27 20	28 0
	29 0	30 0	31 0	1 5	2 2	3 3	4 20
A	5 0	6 0	7 0	8 5	9 0	10 20	11 0
P	12 2	13 0	14 0	15 5	16 3	17 Good Friday 4	18 20
R	19 Easter Sunday 0	20 Easter Monday 0	21 0	22 5	23 0	24 20	25 2
	26 2	27 0	28 0	29 5	30 2	1 3	2 20
M	3 0	4 0	5 0	6 5	7 0	8 20	9 0
A	10 Mother's Day 2	11 0	12 0	13 5	14 3	15 4	16 20
Y	17 0	18 Victoria Day 0	19 0	20 5	21 0	22 20	23 2
	24 2	25 0	26 0	27 5	28 5	29 3	30 20
	31 5						

	SUN	MON	TUES	WED	THURS	FRI	SAT
		1 0	2 0	3 5	4 2	5 20	6 0
J	7 5	8 0	9 0	10 5	11 0	12 4	13 20
U	14 5	15 0	16 0	17 5	18 3	19 20	20 2
N	21 Father's Day 5	22 0	23 0	24 5	25 0	26 3	27 20
	28 5	29 0	30 0	1 Canada Day 5	2 5	3 20	4 0
J	5 5	6 0	7 0	8 5	9 0	10 4	11 20
U	12 5	13 0	14 0	15 5	16 2	17 20	18 2
L	19 5	20 0	21 0	22 5	23 3	24 3	25 20
	26 5	27 0	28 0	29 5	30 0	31 20	1 0
A	2 5	3 Civic Holiday 0	4 0	5 5	6 5	7 4	8 20
U	9 5	10 0	11 0	12 5	13 0	14 20	15 2
G	16 5	17 0	18 0	19 5	20 2	21 3	22 20
	23 5	24 0	25 0	26 5	27 3	28 20	29 0
	30 2	31 0	1 0	2 5	3 0	4 4	5 20
S	6 0	7 Labour Day 0	8 0	9 5	10 5	11 20	12 2
E	13 2	14 0	15 0	16 5	17 0	18 3	19 20
P	20 0	21 0	22 0	23 5	24 2	25 20	26 0
	27 2	28 0	29 0	30 5	1 3	2 4	3 20
O	4 0	5 0	6 0	7 5	8 0	9 20	10 2
C	11 2	12 Thanksgiving 0	13 0	14 5	15 5	16 3	17 20
T	18 0	19 0	20 0	21 5	22 0	23 20	24 0
	25 2	26 0	27 0	28 5	29 2	30 4	31 Halloween 20
N	1 0	2 0	3 0	4 5	5 0	6 20	7 2
O	8 5	9 0	10 0	11 Remembrance 5	12 3	13 3	14 20
V	15 2	16 0	17 0	18 5	19 2	20 20	21 0
	22 5	23 0	24 0	25 5	26	27	28
	29	30	1	2	3	4	5
D	6	7	8	9	10	11	12
E	13	14	15	16	17	18	19
C	20	21	22	23	24	25 Christmas	26
	27	28	29	30	31		

FIGURE 6.3. Example of Timeline for pretreatment drinking.

360-day Timeline

Subject No.: ______

Today's Date: April 24 Start Date: April 29 End Date: April 23

	SUN	MON	TUES	WED	THURS	FRI	SAT
		1	2	3	4	5 Good Friday	6
A	7 Easter Sunday	8 Easter Monday	9	10	11	12	13
P	14	15	16	17	18	19	20
R	21	22	23	24	25	26	27
	28	29 0	30 0	1 0	2 0	3 0	4 7
M	5 8	6 0	7 0	8 0	9 0	10 0	11 9
A	12 Mother's Day 7	13 0	14 0	15 0	16 0	17 0	18 8
Y	19 9	20 Victoria Day 7	21 0	22 0	23 0	24 0	25 8
	26 9	27 0	28 0	29 0	30 0	31 0	1 7
J	2 8	3 0	4 0	5 5	6 0	7 5	8 9
U	9 7	10 0	11 0	12 0	13 0	14 0	15 7
N	16 Father's Day 8	17 0	18 0	19 0	20 0	21 0	22 9
	23 7	24 0	25 0	26 5	27 0	28 5	29 8
	30 9	1 Canada Day 8	2 0	3 0	4 0	5 0	6 7
J	7 7	8 0	9 0	10 0	11 6	12 6	13 7
U	14 6	15 7	16 6	17 0	18 0	19 6	20 7
L	21 8	22 0	23 0	24 5	25 0	26 5	27 9
	28 7	29 0	30 0	31 0	1 0	2 0	3 8
A	4 9	5 Civic Holiday 7	6 0	7 0	8 0	9 0	10 9
U	11 7	12 0	13 0	14 5	15 0	16 5	17 8
G	18 9	19 0	20 0	21 0	22 0	23 0	24 7
	25 8	26 0	27 0	28 0	29 0	30 0	31 9
S	1 7	2 Labour Day 8	3 0	4 0	5 4	6 0	7 9
E	8 7	9 0	10 0	11 0	12 0	13 0	14 9
P	15 8	16 0	17 0	18 0	19 0	20 0	21 7
	22 9	23 0	24 0	25 0	26 4	27 0	28 8
	29 7	30 0					

	SUN	MON	TUES	WED	THURS	FRI	SAT
			1 0	2 0	3 0	4 0	5 9
O	6 8	7 0	8 0	9 0	10 0	11 0	12 7
C	13 9	14 Thanksgiving 7	15 0	16 0	17 4	18 0	19 8
T	20 7	21 0	22 0	23 0	24 0	25 0	26 9
	27 8	28 0	29 0	30 0	31 Halloween 0	1 0	2 7
N	3 9	4 0	5 0	6 0	7 4	8 0	9 8
O	10 7	11 Remembrance 0	12 0	13 0	14 0	15 0	16 9
V	17 0	18 0	19 0	20 0	21 0	22 0	23 0
	24 8	25 0	26 0	27 0	28 4	29 0	30 7
D	1 9	2 0	3 0	4 0	5 0	6 0	7 8
E	8 7	9 0	10 0	11 0	12 0	13 0	14 9
C	15 8	16 0	17 0	18 0	19 4	20 0	21 7
	22 9	23 0	24 1	25 Christmas 6	26 4	27 0	28 8
	29 7	30 0	31 7				
				1 New Year's Day 5	2 0	3 0	4 9
J	5 8	6 0	7 0	8 0	9 0	10 0	11 7
A	12 9	13 0	14 0	15 0	16 0	17 0	18 8
N	19 7	20 0	21 0	22 4	23 5	24 0	25 9
	26 8	27 0	28 0	29 4	30 5	31 0	1 7
F	2 7	3 0	4 0	5 0	6 0	7 0	8 8
E	9 8	10 0	11 0	12 4	13 5	14 Valentine's Day 0	15 9
B	16 9	17 0	18 0	19 4	20 5	21 0	22 7
	23 7	24 0	25 0	26 5	27 0	28 0	1 8
M	2 8	3 0	4 0	5 0	6 0	7 0	8 9
A	9 0	10 0	11 0	12 0	13 0	14 0	15 0
R	16 7	17 0	18 0	19 0	20 0	21 0	22 7
	23 8	24 0	25 0	26 0	27 0	28 Good Friday 4	29 4
	30 Easter Sunday 4	31 Easter Monday 4	1 0	2 0	3 0	4 0	5 7
A	6 7	7 0	8 0	9 0	10 0	11 0	12 8
P	13 8	14 0	15 0	16 0	17 5	18 0	19 9
R	20 9	21 0	22 0	23 0	24	25	26
	27	28	29	30			

FIGURE 6.4. Example of Timeline for pretreatment drinking.

Assessing High-Risk Drinking Situation

Another instrument originally developed for research purposes that we have found very useful for treatment planning is the Inventory of Drinking Situations (IDS) (Annis, Graham, & Davis, 1987). Based on self-efficacy theory (Bandura, 1977) and on reports of the importance of situational factors in relapse (Marlatt, 1978; Marlatt & Gordon, 1985), Annis formulated a 100-item questionnaire assessing situations in which a person drank heavily over the year prior to being interviewed. Although a 42-item version of the IDS is now available (Annis et al., 1987), we have used the 100-item instrument in our research, and we feel that this version has the greatest clinical utility. Annis et al. (1987) also have recommend using the 100-item version for clinical purposes.

The items on the IDS represent eight categories of potential high-risk situations for drinking, based on a classification system developed by Marlatt and his colleagues (Marlatt & Gordon, 1985). The eight categories form subscales that combine to form two major classes of situations, Personal States "in which drinking involves a response to an event that is primarily psychological or physical in nature" (Annis et al., 1987, p. 1) and Situations Involving Other People where "a significant influence of another individual is involved" (Annis et al., 1987, p. 1). Clients are asked to respond to each item with regard to how often they "drank heavily " in that situation, using a 4-point scale ranging from 1 = Never to 4 = Almost Always.

One problem with the IDS is that the determination of heavy drinking is left to the client's discretion, and there is no provision on the questionnaire for gathering information about the client's subjective definition of heavy drinking. Since knowing how a client defines heavy drinking can be essential for evaluating the client's responses, it is recommended that an additional question be routinely appended to the form asking: "By 'heavy drinking' I mean drinking at least _____ standard drinks in any particular situation."

The classes and subscales, along with one sample item for each subscale of the IDS follow:

Personal States
Unpleasant Emotions (When I felt that I had let myself down)
Physical Discomfort (When I felt nauseous)
Pleasant Emotions (When I felt satisfied with something I had done)
Testing Personal Control (When I started to think that just one drink could cause no harm)
Urges and Temptations (When I suddenly had an urge to drink)

Situations Involving Other People
Conflict with Others (When other people treated me unfairly)
Social Pressure to Drink (When I was in a restaurant and the people with me ordered drinks)
Pleasant Times with Others (When I wanted to celebrate with a friend)

The psychometric characteristics of the IDS are satisfactory and are described in the User's Guide for the instrument (Annis et al., 1987). Others have also validated the IDS (Cannon, Leeka, Patterson, & Baker, 1990; Isenhart, 1991). The recommended scoring method is to convert answers into Problem Index scores which range from 0 to 100. This can be done by hand or by computer. A personal computer version of the IDS that includes automatic scoring and a computer-generated client report is available (Annis et al., 1987). The Problem Index scores for the subscales can be used to create a profile for clients describing the types of situations most associated with their heavy drinking over the year prior to the interview. Case examples including IDS profiles are presented in Chapter 11.

When interpreting clients' answers to the IDS, it should be noted that the situations covered by the questionnaire derive from Marlatt's (Marlatt & Gordon, 1985) research on alcohol abusers' reports of situations associated with their initial relapse to substance use following treatment. The assessments made for the IDS, however, involve clients' reports of how often they "drank heavily" in particular situations over the past year. Conceptually, it may be that situations that trigger an initial relapse differ from those regularly associated with heavy drinking. For example, for someone attempting to be abstinent, interpersonal conflict might be the situation most likely to result in a return to drinking, although drinking with friends may be the situation where most of the person's heavy drinking has occurred. At the present time, we are not aware of any studies disentangling these two aspects of drinking situations.

For problem drinkers, we find the IDS (which identifies situations associated with heavy drinking) to have more face validity and clinical utility than an approach asking clients about relapse precipitants. This could be because the drinking of problem drinkers is largely inconsistent with a relapse prevention model. The problem drinkers we have studied do not describe their drinking as involving extended periods of abstinence interrupted by "relapses" where initial drinking leads to continued heavy drinking. With regard to the initiation of drinking, when problem drinkers drank they frequently did not drink heavily (they reported drinking four or fewer drinks on nearly 40% of their pretreatment drinking occasions). The majority of our clients reported that on the day following a day of heavy drinking they either did not drink or drank substantially smaller amounts.

Another reason we recommend the IDS is that we found high concordance between the scale scores and the types of situations that clients identified in their homework assignments as most problematic (see Chapter 9). However we do not recommend substituting one for the other: The IDS provides a broad generic picture of the clients' heavy drinking situations, whereas the homework answers provide a detailed evaluation of a few of the client's most serious problem situations.

An important feature of the drinking of the problem drinkers we have studied that was identified both in their IDS and in their homework answers was the frequently reported relationship between positive affect and heavy drinking, a finding that parallels data collected by others using the IDS (Annis, Graham, & Davis, 1987; Cannon, Leeka, Patterson, & Baker, 1990; Isenhart, 1991). This finding has important implications for appetitive motivational theory (Baker, Morse, & Sherman, 1987; Stewart, DeWitt, & Eikelboom, 1984), which postulates that both positive and negative affective states can set the occasion for drug use. It also has implications for the conduct of treatment. This will be discussed further in Chapter 11, when we consider treatment procedures and case examples from the guided self-management approach.

Assessing Self-Efficacy

A parallel instrument to the IDS, which measures self-efficacy, is the Situational Confidence Questionnaire (SCQ) (Annis & Graham, 1988). The SCQ contains the same 100 items as the IDS, but asks persons to indicate on a 6-point scale (ranging from 0 to 100, inclusive, in steps of 20) how confident they feel at the time they complete the scale that they could resist the urge to drink heavily in that situation. The SCQ is intended to measure clients' feelings of self-efficacy in the same situations covered by the IDS. In our experience, most clients' answers to the SCQ parallel their responses to the IDS, and thus the clinical value of the SCQ for treatment planning is questionable. Occasionally, however, clients report high self-efficacy for a high-risk situation and vice versa. Thus, if the SCQ is not used, it is important to at least ask clients how confident they are that they can refrain from heavy drinking in the situations identified on the IDS as previously associated with their heavy drinking.

Treatment Goal Assessment

We asked all clients to complete a Goal Statement on several occasions, including assessment. A copy of the Goal Statement appears in Chapter 7, where its contents and use are discussed. The Goal Statement is first administered at assessment in order to learn what expectations the client has brought to treatment. For example, if at assessment a client indicates an intention to seek to reduce his or her drinking, but the desired drinking levels are clearly hazardous, this gives the therapist forewarning of an important area for discussion.

Guided self-management is a program of treatment that begins at assessment. The first attempt at integration of assessment materials starts when the client, after reading Reading 1, completes Homework Assignment 1 and brings it to the first treatment session. This facilitates a natural flow from assessment into the treatment sessions.

7

Treatment Procedures: Preparation, Goal Setting, Monitoring Drinking

The Need for Flexibility

While guided self-management treatment has several components, there is no hard-and-fast prescription for ordering or combining the procedures. Practitioners are strongly encouraged to adapt the procedures to their own style and to each particular case. Thus, the order in which the component treatment processes occur can be tailored to each client. For this reason, in the following discussion the treatment procedures are not presented in the context of a strict session outline. Although session outlines are provided later in this book, they are only guidelines for how the therapeutic process might be structured. Finally, in a nonintensive program, it is important that the treatment sessions be well focused and efficient.

In clinical settings where standardization is not needed, the criterion that makes the most sense for determining the length of treatment is how the client responds. For some people a positive response might be evident after a few sessions; for others it may take several sessions. There is nothing inherently wrong with extending the number of treatment contacts beyond that for which the approach was developed, as long as it is kept in mind that the approach was designed as a short-term intervention. Once the procedures have been completed and if progress has not occurred, then it is necessary to evaluate barriers to change and to assess whether this type of treatment should be continued. Questions that can be asked include: Is a self-management approach appropriate for this client? Do the client's life circumstances weigh against change occurring, and if so, can those circumstances be modified to support change? From the client's perspective, is there insufficient motivation for change (i.e., the costs of reducing or stopping drinking are seen as higher than the benefits that would result), and if so, is there any chance that this situation will soon change?

Preparing for Treatment Sessions: The Client's Obligations

Prior to the first treatment session, clients should be informed about certain conditions applying to the treatment. Typically, these can be discussed at the end of assessment as a therapeutic contract specifying obligations for the client (therapist obligations are presented in the next section):

• Clients should be instructed to be alcohol free when they arrive for sessions. They should know that a breath test can be conducted to verify their status, and they should know that if they arrive for a session with a positive blood alcohol level the session will be rescheduled. This procedure also sets the tone for honesty in the relationship between client and therapist. As mentioned in Chapter 6 and discussed later in this chapter, the availability of an objective test of blood alcohol level is important because of the phenomenon of tolerance; even experienced therapists are not reliably able to identify whether alcohol abusers have a positive blood alcohol level (Sobell, Sobell, & VanderSpek, 1979).

• Clients need to understand the importance of completing the readings and homework assignments prior to the sessions and of bringing them to the session. They should understand that what makes the treatment a "program" is the continuity of procedures from assessment through aftercare. Reading 1, given to clients at the end of assessment, is intended to help them integrate the information that has been discussed during assessment. The Homework Assignment 1 is intended to capitalize on the assessment experience by helping clients become aware of and define their high-risk drinking situations. These procedures build on the momentum generated by the assessment process. Likewise, Reading 2 and Homework Assignment 2 build on the first session. If clients fail to do the readings and homework excercises, questions about their commitment to change should be raised. Our experience to date suggests that the vast majority of problem drinkers will comply with the procedures.

Preparing for Treatment Sessions:
The Therapist's Obligations

It is not just the client who is expected to get a running start in the guided self-management treatment. For treatment sessions to be focused, it is important for the therapist to review the assessment materials prior the first session, determine where additional information is needed, and consider possible treatment directions. Likewise, prior to further sessions, notes and materials from previous sessions should be reviewed. One way to facilitate the review process is for the therapist to use a Clinical Assessment Summary (see Figure 6.1) and to update it with any important information obtained in treatment sessions.

Starting the First Session: Setting the Tone

To insure a common understanding and mutual expectations between the client and therapist, the following introductory comments, taken from the script used in guided self-management treatment training for therapists, should be communicated to the client using the therapist's own words.

- The guided self-management treatment approach is not suitable for all people. The primary characteristic of persons who benefit from short-term treatment is that they are not severely dependent on alcohol. They have varying degrees of life problems related to their drinking, but they do not drink to the point where they become physically dependent on alcohol. If they stop drinking they do not suffer major withdrawal symptoms (e.g., hallucinations, seizures, delirium tremens). They do not drink extremely large amounts, and they do not drink every day.
- Studies have shown that certain types of persons with alcohol problems often benefit as much from short-term treatment as from more intensive treatment.
- Guided self-management is a treatment approach that was developed specifically for people who have the personal strengths and resources to overcome their drinking problem on their own if given some guidance.
- The treatment provides a framework, based on research, within which clients can gain an understanding of their drinking problems and develop strategies for avoiding future drinking problems.
- It is important to remember that this is a program of treatment that, although it includes a small number of formal treatment sessions, begins at assessment and can continue on an "as needed" basis after the formal sessions have been completed.
- For some people, the formal treatment sessions and the associated reading materials and homework assignments will be sufficient, while others will need more help.

Goal Setting

A key part of the guided self-management treatment program is that clients are asked to choose their own drinking treatment goal. As discussed earlier, goal self-selection is a treatment component intended to increase clients' commitment to change. Clients appear to do better when the treatment orientation is consistent with their own beliefs, and problem drinkers are more likely to seek to reduce their drinking rather than abstain regardless of the advice they receive in treatment.

During guided self-management treatment, clients are provided with recommended guidelines for reduced drinking, and they are strongly advised of any medical contraindications to drinking. In our experience, while few problem drinkers will have medical contraindications to a reduced-drinking goal, an assessment is still recommended. To facilitate obtaining objective assessments of medical contraindications to alcohol consumption, it is helpful for therapists treating problem drinkers with a self-management approach to cultivate a working relationship with physicians who are supportive of such an approach. Physicians who value public health approaches to alcohol problems are likely to find compelling the arguments supporting treatments developed for problem drinkers, including ones that offer a reduced-drinking goal. There are exceptions, however, and these typically involve individuals who hold strong conventional beliefs about alcoholism. Such individuals may adopt the empirically unfounded position that anyone who has any problem with alcohol should never drink again. The likelihood of altering such a belief-based conviction is probably small to nonexistent.

The key question in the medical evaluation is whether there are any existing health problems that would be exacerbated by consumption of limited amounts of alcohol. For example, if the client suffers from certain medical problems (e.g., diabetes, gout), then reduced drinking would not be advisable because even limited drinking could worsen such conditions. The medical evaluation should not consider whether the person can achieve reduced drinking, but rather if any serious health problems would be aggravated if the client engaged in limited drinking.

In research studies, we have assessed goal selection at several different points in the program, including at follow-up. In clinical practice, it is recommended that the client's goal be assessed at assessment, and at the first and last treatment session. Goal specification at assessment helps the therapist form a picture of the client and of reasonable treatment expectations. The goal at assessment reflects the client's immediate (i.e., without advice from the therapist) preference for either a reduced-drinking or abstinence goal, and it provides information about how realistically the client has appraised his or her situation. For example, a client whose goal is to reduce consumption to seven drinks a day on 6 days per week would be deemed to have an unrealistic idea of what constitutes nonhazardous drinking.

The vast majority (about 80%) of clients in the guided self-management treatment studies chose a reduced-drinking goal at assessment. Most set relatively conservative and realistic limits for their desired level of drinking, for example, three drinks on about 3 days per week. Thus, there is no indication that clients would misuse the goal-choice situation to rationalize heavy drinking, although this may occasionally occur. This is one reason that the therapist should provide very explicit information on suggested guidelines if the client chooses a reduced-drinking goal.

There are two reasons why it is very important that a reduced-drinking goal be carefully defined: (1) so the client has specific, well-thought-out rules about drinking limits and the circumstances under which he or she may drink, and (2) so the goal definition does not change over time as a way of rationalizing behavior that does not conform to intentions. For goal specification, it is recommended that a Goal Statement be used, a copy of which appears later in this chapter. After completing this form, clients are given a copy so that they have a record of their commitment.

The first time clients are asked to complete the Goal Statement, the following points should be emphasized:

- It is important for the therapist to know what specific type of change in drinking clients are seeking because this provides a basis for evaluating whether clients' efforts are successful.
- Since people sometimes change their goals, the form is completed on more than one occasion. Clients should notify the therapist whenever there is a goal change.
- Upon administration of subsequent Goal Statements, clients are told that there is no need to change answers from the previous goal. The readministrations are only intended to give clients an opportunity to change their goal if desired and to allow discussion of the change.
- Although goals are discussed in treatment and advice is provided, clients are told that they ultimately must make the decision about whether to drink, and what the limits should be if they choose to drink. For some people, not drinking at all is the best way to deal with their drinking problems. For others, especially if their problems are not very severe, they may be able to reduce their drinking to a level at which it is unlikely to cause problems.

Alcohol Education

It is appropriate to provide some alcohol education at the time the Goal Statement is discussed. Because some clients will enter treatment better informed than others, the extent of information will vary. The main topics for discussion can include absorption, metabolism, and disposition of alcohol by the body; blood alcohol level; standard drink conversions; and tolerance.

Educational pamphlets can also be used to provide some of this information, as long as the pamphlets are scientifically accurate.

Those who can make a personal computer available to clients may be interested in a new computer program that uses several factors (e.g., body water, gender, age, drinking rate) to predict blood alcohol concentrations (Kapur, 1991). The program can be used to educate therapists and clients about factors influencing blood alcohol concentration. Using this program, clients can explore blood alcohol concentration issues in depth.

In discussing various educational topics with clients, it is helpful to use examples that the client will be able to understand. For example, the analogy of the body as a funnel is a useful way of explaining what happens to alcohol when it enters the body. Without discussing technical details about the metabolism of alcohol, the funnel analogy communicates the point that while a lot of alcohol can be consumed quickly, the rate at which it leaves the body is steady and small, which has implications for blood alcohol levels. Such a discussion leads easily into a discussion of standard drinks.

If an assessment procedure such as the Timeline Follow-Back has been used, standard drink conversions may already have been explained. Most clients can readily understand a standard drink nomenclature and have little difficulty reporting their drinking using standard drinks. Familiarizing clients with a standard drink reporting format is also useful in educating clients about the amounts of ethanol in the different types of standard drinks (e.g., beer vs. wine). While therapists can give some general guidelines to clients for calculating blood alcohol levels (Devgun & Dunbar, 1990), it is important to note that there is large individual variability in blood alcohol levels produced in different individuals by a given dose of alcohol.

A discussion of legal definitions of intoxication (e.g., drunk driving) can follow a discussion of blood alcohol levels and lead to a discussion of tolerance. In most states in the United States the legal limit for drunk driving is 10 mg of ethanol per 100 ml of blood (0.10%). In Canada, the legal limit is 0.08%, while in some European countries the limit is as low as 0.04%. It is important for clients to know how much they can drink before they will be legally drunk. This can be simplified by referring to each 0.01% of ethanol as "1 point"; thus, the level of legally defined intoxication in most states in the United States is 10 points. For example, a male client weighing 200 pounds might be advised that each standard drink consumed is likely to increase his blood alcohol level by 2 points within about 20 minutes of drinking. Although factors such as having food in the stomach can slightly delay absorption, the effect of such factors will for most purposes be negligible. The rate at which an individual's body metabolizes alcohol may also be considered as roughly 2 points per hour. Various combinations of consumption associated with a constant rate of metabolism can then be used to show how metabolic rate (funnel example) will determine an individual's blood alcohol level at any given time.

It is also important that clients understand the phenomenon of tolerance. Recall that tolerance means that with repeated drinking experiences the same dose of alcohol affects an individual less. Thus, to achieve the same effect in terms of feeling intoxicated, more alcohol must be consumed. There are two reasons why the notion of tolerance should be discussed with clients. First, tolerance is somewhat independent from blood alcohol level. As tolerance to alcohol is acquired, the person will feel less intoxicated (and be less impaired on several tests) at the same blood alcohol level. The critical issue is that it is unwise for people to gauge their blood alcohol level by their subjective feelings of intoxication. As tolerance is acquired, what changes is the response to a given dose of alcohol, not the resulting blood alcohol level. The legal definition of being "under the influence," however, is tied to a blood alcohol level criterion. In court, what matters is whether the individual's blood alcohol level was above the criterion value.

Making the Point about Tolerance

An example of tolerance is reflected in the story of an intoxicated pilot, who flew a Northwest Airlines passenger jet without incident from South Dakota to Minnesota ("Flying and Alcohol," 1990). The flight crew was reported to have been drinking heavily prior to boarding the plane. Although the authorities were notified of this, they were not able to intercept the airplane before it departed. While the crew flew the plane without consequence, upon landing they were required to take a breath test. The pilot was found to be legally intoxicated with a blood alcohol level of 0.16%. In court, the pilot's lawyer maintained that the pilot was an alcoholic who had acquired considerable tolerance to alcohol, and, therefore, his performance was not impaired despite having a high blood alcohol level. While highly alcohol-tolerant individuals can perform well-practiced tasks with minimal impairment, it is on unfamiliar tasks and on certain cognitively complex tasks (e.g., attending and responding to multiple events such as might occur in a flight emergency) that impairment shows up, even at lower blood alcohol levels. Needless to say, the pilot was convicted. This example demonstrates the phenomenon of tolerance and underscores the importance of linking drunk driving to blood alcohol levels and not to performance.

The second reason why a discussion of tolerance is important relates to goal specification. Clients should understand that if their drinking is strongly motivated by a desire to feel intoxicated, then the phenomenon of tolerance can be expected to place them at high risk if they pursue a reduced-drinking goal. That is, if they are drinking for the effect, then they are likely to find that over time they need to consume more to reach the desire state. A wish to become intoxicated often signals a high-risk situation where drinking should be avoided. It is important for clients to understand that if they choose to have a reduced-drinking goal, their drinking should not be motivated by the purpose of achieving a particular state of intoxication or effect. Drinking for effect is inconsistent with a goal of nonhazardous drinking.

Discussing the Goal Statement with the Client

In discussing the Goal Statement with the client, the emphasis should be on the feasibility and reasonableness of the chosen goal. It is useful to provide clients with a set of general recommendations should they seek to pursue a reduced-drinking goal. The recommendations we have used are as follows:

- Consume no more than three standard drinks on no more than 4 days per week. These limits are based on several studies in the literature (Babor, Kranzler, & Lauerman, 1987; Sanchez-Craig & Israel, 1985). It is important to have abstinent days for two reasons. First, by avoiding daily drinking the habitual components of drinking (i.e., drinking a certain amount every day at a certain time) are minimized. Second, abstinent days help avoid developing excessive tolerance to alcohol (i.e., tolerance reverses somewhat in the absence of drinking).
- Do not drink in high-risk circumstances. It makes no sense to drink if there is substantial risk of a negative outcome.
- Drink at a rate no faster than one standard drink per hour, especially if driving.
- In line with a recommendation by Marlatt and colleagues (Cummings, Gordon, & Marlatt 1980), it is suggested that clients impose a thinking period of 20 minutes between deciding to have a drink and acting on that decision. Such a procedure helps to counteract impulsive drinking, and it gives clients time to reevaluate the reasons for drinking and perhaps to decide not to drink or continue drinking. During this "time-out," clients should consider the risks involved in the particular situation.

About one out of every four or five problem drinkers in treatment will seek to abstain from drinking. The choice of a nondrinking goal, however, should result from a reasoned decision of the likely costs and benefits of that goal, and it should not be based on the client believing that he or she is physically unable to engage in limited drinking. In other words, clients should choose a nondrinking goal because they feel that there is a serious risk that their drinking could result in health and social problems, and this is a risk they are not prepared to take. The motivation for an abstinence goal should be "I have chosen not to drink because that is the best way for me to avoid future problems." It is important that clients be able to provide sound reasons for being abstinent, reasons that relate to what would be risked by drinking. It is the list of reasons for not drinking that will support the long-term commitment to abstinence. Multiple and clearly understood reasons will provide a more stable foundation for abstinence than a belief that control over drinking is not possible.

The purpose of the discussion of the client's Goal Statement is to assess the strength of the clients' commitment to the goal and to reinforce the goal, not to undermine the goal (unless the evidence suggests it is contraindicated). The emphasis should be on evaluating the feasibility and reasonableness of the goal. In many cases, the rationale for the goal will be apparent from the assessment and from the client's description of adverse consequences in Homework Assignment 1 (see Chapter 9).

A good technique for discussing goals with clients is to ask them a series of questions (Miller & Rollnick, 1991). For example, if the goal is abstinence, one can ask clients to discuss their reasons for refraining from drinking. If the goal is to reduce drinking, then the clients should be asked about proposed limits and guidelines, whether the goal is realistic given their history, and whether it is consistent with the avoidance of high-risk drinking (i.e., there should be no substantial likelihood of immediate or long-term consequences of drinking within the limits specified by the goal). Has the client ever been able to drink at low levels and without problems, especially in the past year (see Chapter 9, Homework Assignment 1)? If not, why does he or she believe that it could be achieved now? One question that is sometimes useful in helping clients decide whether a nonabstinence goal is feasible is to ask them whether they feel it would be easier to not drink at all or to limit their drinking to only one or two drinks per day. When clients respond that it would be easier to not drink at all, often it is because having just one or two drinks would serve no purpose for them (i.e., their drinking is for the effect and because of tolerance would place them at risk of drinking too much).

Finally, although it is recommended that clients be given the opportunity to change or revise their goal, two caveats accompany this recommendation. First, goals should not be changed while the client is drinking or when a high-risk situation is present or imminent. Second, clients should be very careful about changing the goal to allow more drinking. In all cases, the goal should only be modified after full consideration of the potential consequences of the change.

Filling Out the Goal Statement

The Goal Statement, shown in Appendix 7.1, asks clients to specify their goal for the next 6 months. There is nothing special about 6 months; it simply reflects the intervals over which follow-up data were collected on clients in our studies. Such restrictions do not apply to clinical practice. For clinical settings, it is suggested that the therapist negotiate with the client the length of time over which the goal statement will be binding and enter that information on the form. Such a procedure has the advantage of establishing a future date when progress will be evaluated and the goal renegotiated if necessary.

The first question on the form asks clients whether they seek to abstain or to drink in a limited manner. The next set of questions about specific drinking limits are irrelevant for clients whose goal is abstinence. Clients who choose a reduced-drinking goal, however, are required to specify the exact limits they wish to place on their drinking. The amount of drinking is described in terms of standard drinks. The required specifications include the planned average quantity of drinking, the frequency of drinking, the planned upper limit of consumption, and the maximum frequency of reaching that limit. The inclusion of upper limits on the Goal Statement recognizes that while drinking that deviates from the general limits may occur, it should still be kept within planned limits.

The specification of limits is followed by two open-ended questions that ask clients to specify the situations and circumstances in which they will and will not drink. This communicates to clients that situational variables (the drinking context and their personal state) influence the risks involved in drinking. The conditions specified by clients can be used in treatment. Examples of the types of conditions specified by clients appear in Chapter 11, where case examples are presented.

Although the last two questions on the form were originally included for research purposes, they also have clinical value. The first question asks clients how important it is for them to achieve their goal. Few of our clients have reported that accomplishing their treatment goal is the "most important" thing in their lives. This suggests that if treatment demands become overwhelming, problem drinkers might drop out of treatment.

The second question is a global self-efficacy rating about curtailing their drinking. While there is controversy in the scientific literature about whether self-efficacy can be a global as well as situational variable (Smith, 1989; Tipton & Worthington, 1984; Wang & RiCharde, 1988), for the present purposes this is not important. This question asks clients how confident they are that they will achieve their goal. Evidence from several self-efficacy studies, many with smokers attempting to quit, suggests that an individual's self-confidence in being successful is an important predictor of outcome. Clinically, both of these questions (importance of achieving goal and confidence in the likelihood of achieving goal) provide a clear picture of the client's motivation.

What happens when clients specify limits or circumstances that are inconsistent with the therapist's advice? First, it is prudent to ask clients to provide information honestly, even if it is not in accord with the therapist's advice. It is better to know that a client does not intend to follow the therapist's advice, than to have them try to please the therapist by listing limits that they have no intention of honoring. Knowing that a client is intending to drink more than recommended is useful information. It indicates that drinking at a particular level or frequency is important enough to the client that he or she is willing to incur the risk of negative consequences in order to engage in that behavior. Although clients should be honest in completing the form, it is also important to call their attention to any inconsistencies between their goal and the therapist's advice and to make clear that they understand that what they are proposing is contrary to advice. It is also important to document such situations in a client's record. Thus, while clients should be informed before acting on their decision, it is their decision to make.

In later treatment sessions, the therapist can compare the clients' drinking with their goal. Failure to meet the goal can serve as the starting point for a discussion of whether the treatment goal should be changed. Adherence to the goal can serve as a basis for reinforcing clients' efforts. Since it is the clients' responsibility to make and enact decisions, when they meet their goals they should view themselves as having constructively changed their own behavior. Conversely, when clients do not meet their goals, they should view themselves as responsible for doing something about that, whether it involves changing the goal or changing the way they go about trying to meet the goal. The therapist is an advisor, but the responsibility is the clients'!

Self-Monitoring

It is helpful for clients to self-monitor their alcohol consumption between contacts, beginning with the assessment, and to bring these records to the sessions. Self-monitoring involves recording one's own behavior. In alcohol treatment this includes alcohol consumption and related behaviors such as urges, settings, moods, and other features of drinking situations.

Self-monitoring of drinking is not a recent innovation. In 1973, we reported using the method for alcohol abusers in outpatient treatment, and we discussed ways in which the procedure assisted the treatment process (L. C. Sobell & M. B. Sobell, 1973). One major benefit of self-monitoring is that it forces clients to be constantly aware of their drinking, thereby providing a safeguard against subjectively distorted perceptions of drinking. Over the years, clients have repeatedly said that despite thinking that they knew how much they drank, keeping a record of their drinking provided them with feedback that they were drinking more than they had thought.

Self-monitoring has much clinical utility: (1) it provides a picture of the client's drinking during treatment; (2) it provides a basis for evaluating whether change in drinking is occurring; and (3) it allows for a discussion of drinking without awkwardness. A client's record of the situations and circumstances in which he or she drank between sessions provides a basis for discussion of those events in treatment. An example of the type of form that can be used for self-monitoring appears in Appendix 7.2.

Unfortunately, while the use of self-monitoring has been reported in several studies (Annis & Davis, 1988a; Hester & Miller, 1990; Toneatto et al., 1991), there has been little evaluation of its therapeutic effectiveness. It is possible that just recording one's own drinking might have a "reactive effect" on the drinker and precipitate behavior change (Nelson & Hayes, 1981). Two studies of reactive effects of self-monitoring have been conducted to date, one with normal drinkers (Sobell, Bogardis, Schuller, Leo, & Sobell, 1989) and one with alcohol abusers (Harris & Miller, 1990). Both studies found that self-monitoring did not have a reactive effect on drinking.

Some clients will refuse to self-monitor even when the logs require little information. When this happens, we recommend that the client reconstruct his or her drinking at the session using the Timeline technique. The Timeline and self-monitoring techniques both provide the same type of data—daily drinking. Since the period between sessions tends to be short, the reconstruction using the Timeline technique does not take very long, and discussion of drinking-related event can usually be conducted at the same time that the data are gathered.

In the next chapter our discussion of treatment procedures continues with consideration of materials clients are asked to read. These readings communicate to clients the conceptual basis of the treatment, and they form the foundation for the client to undertake completing the homework assignments.

APPENDIX 7.1. Blank Goal Statement Form

On this form describe your goal regarding your use of alcohol *over the next 6 months.* Do you intend to not drink at all, or to drink but only in certain ways and under certain conditions?

Do not feel tied to any earlier Goal Statement that you filled out as part of this program.

What is your goal now? If your goal mentions drinking, describe what you mean in terms of amount of drinking and circumstances when you would drink.

1. For the next 6 months, my goal is (Check either Box A or Box B):
   ☐ A. Not to drink at all

   If you checked this goal, go on to question 2, next page.

   ☐ B. Only to drink in certain ways

   If you checked this goal, then answer the following questions, using the following definition of one standard drink:

   <u>One standard drink is equal to:</u>
   - 12 oz of *beer* (5% alcohol)
   - 1½ oz of hard *liquor* or spirits (e.g., whiskey)
   - 5 oz of *table wine* (11–12%)
   - 3 oz of *fortified wine* (20%)

(i) On the average day when I do drink, I will probably drink about _____ standard drinks during the course of that day.

(ii) I plan to drink no more than _____ standard drinks during the course of any single day. That will be my Upper Limit.

(iii) Over the course of an average week (7 days), I plan to drink on no more than _____ days. (If you plan to drink on less than one day per week, check here: _____)

(iv) Over the course of 1 month (30 days), I plan to drink my Upper Limit of drinks on no more than _____ days. (If you plan to drink to your Upper Limit of drinks less than one time per month, check here: _____)

(v) I plan to drink *only* under the following conditions:

_____

_____

_____

_____

(vi) I plan *not to drink at all* under the following conditions:

_____

_____

_____

_____

People usually have several things that they would like to change in their lives. Changing their drinking behavior can be one of those things. You have just described your drinking goal for the next 6 months. With regard to that goal, answer the following two questions.

2. At this moment, how important is it that you achieve your stated goal? (How hard are you willing to work, and how much are you willing to do, to achieve your drinking goal?)

   Answer this question by writing a number from 0 to 100 in the designated space below, using the following scale as a guide:

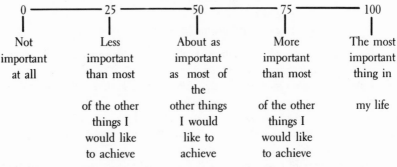

Write your goal importance rating (from 0 to 100) here: _____

3. In the designated space below, indicate how confident you feel at this moment that you will achieve your stated goal. In other words, what is the probability that you will achieve your goal? Use the following scale as a guide:

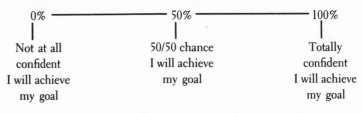

Write your confidence rating (from 0% to 100%) here: _____ %

APPENDIX 7.2. Blank Daily Alcohol Monitoring Form

Name: _____

GOAL: _____

DATE	ABLE TO RESIST PROBLEM DRINKING	NO. OF DRINKS BY BEVERAGE TYPE				TOTAL NO. OF DRINKS	SITUATION (Check all that apply)				THOUGHTS, FEELINGS
Record: Month & day	**1** = Yes **2** = No **3** = No urges	Beer	Hard liquor	Table wine	Fortified wine	If no drinking occurred on this day, write "o" here.	Alone	With others	In a private place	In a public place	Indicate any thoughts or feelings (e.g., stress, anger, happiness) you experienced just prior to and after drinking.

USE OTHER SIDE OF PAGE FOR ADDITIONAL NOTES RELATED TO YOUR DRINKING (e.g., reasons for use)

From *Problem Drinkers: Guided Self-Change Treatment* by Mark B. Sobell and Linda C. Sobell. Copyright 1993 by The Guilford Press. This form may be reprduced by book purchasers for professional use with their clients.

8

Treatment Procedures: Readings and Conceptual Framework

The use of readings in guided self-management treatment serves multiple functions. Some of these functions have been briefly mentioned in previous chapters:

- They communicate the treatment approach in an understandable and consistent way.
- They provide a framework that clients can use to evaluate and change their own behavior.
- They are constantly available to the client.
- Providing clients with the first reading at assessment helps to capitalize upon the self-change momentum that started when the client called for an appointment.
- The readings and the associated homework provide the "running start" for treatment (see Chapter 6).
- The readings provide background information so that the session time can be spent on assessing the client's understanding of the treatment approach rather than explaining the approach.
- Compliance with the readings and homework can indicate the client's commitment to making serious efforts to change.

The readings, which are reproduced in this chapter, are not copyrighted and may be used freely without charge or permission.

Two aspects distinguish these readings from other self-change readings (e.g., Miller & Muñoz, 1982; Sanchez-Craig, 1987; Vogler & Bartz, 1982). First, they are considerably shorter. Some bibliotherapy materials go into extreme detail and include relatively complicated skills-training exercises. As discussed earlier, the evidence suggesting that even a single session of advice can produce benefits calls into question the value of skills training as an exercise for all alcohol abusers, especially problem drinkers.

Second, these readings were written with he help of a professional journalist (a newspaper columnist). The reason this was done was to produce readings that would be comprehensible to persons who had at least some high school education. Thus, the readings were purposely written to be nonscientific and nontechnical. They have been well received by a wide range of clients.

In the formal evaluation of guided self-management treatment, two versions of the treatment were compared, one that incorporated relapse prevention components and one that was limited to behavioral counseling (Sobell, Sobell, & Leo, 1990). The readings for the two conditions differed in that the relapse prevention sections were not included in the behavioral counseling readings. For this book, the only version of the readings provided is the complete version (i.e., the version that includes the relapse prevention sections).

Reading 1

Reading 1 (Appendix 8.1) explains that the purpose of the treatment is to help people help themselves, and it presents a general behavioral analysis of drinking. It also emphasizes that recovery is a long-term goal, an approach intended to help the client persevere in efforts to change if difficulties are encountered. A dieting analogy is used to communicate the main point that a slip need not lead to abandonment of efforts to change. In explaining the importance of setting events, referred to as "triggers," and of short- and long-term consequences of drinking, it is stressed that each analysis must be tailored to the individual—the configuration of each client's drinking problem is different. The notion of "risk" of consequences is also introduced. This is particularly relevant for problem drinkers because such individuals may find it easier to identify risks than actual consequences of their drinking because by definition problem drinkers are individuals whose drinking difficulties are not severe. Reading 1 ends with an introduction to Homework Assignment 1. This homework complements the self-evaluation that will have begun at assessment by instructing clients to systematically summarize and elaborate on factors related to their own drinking.

Since an understanding of Reading 1 is necessary for satisfactory completion of Homework Assignment 1, and since the reading conveys the basic treatment approach, it is important early in treatment (i.e., the first treatment session) to determine that clients understand the material and feel the approach is suitable for them. A technique that often works well is to ask the client to paraphrase or summarize the major points of the handout. For example, the therapist might say: "Please tell me what you think are the main points in the reading and how they apply to you?" The key is to ascertain whether the client understands the important concepts and issues. If not, the therapist should attempt to guide the client to such an understanding. In cases where the approach does not fit the client's perception of his or her problem, alternative approaches should be considered.

The discussion of Reading 1 provides a good opportunity to discuss the rationale for short-term treatment with aftercare. The objective is to create a situation in which clients feel comfortable with the brevity of the formal treatment but also know that they can request additional sessions. The following is an example of content that could be used in a discussion of the treatment. This narrative was prepared as part of therapist training materials for the guided self-management treatment. It was not prepared as a "script" to be used with all clients, but rather as a way of communicating to the therapists how they can facilitate clients' understanding of the main points of the treatment. Thus, it reads as though it were a communication from the therapist to the client.

• First, let's discuss the self-management approach, and how you can prevent slips from occurring. The focus is on learning to recognize situations where you are at risk of problem drinking and to develop other ways of dealing with those situations. You may already use an approach similar to this in dealing with other problems you encounter or in giving advice to others. If this is the case, it will be even easier to extend the approach to dealing with your drinking problem.

• Although we will be discussing specific aspects of your drinking problem to illustrate how to apply this approach, these are just examples. What is important is that you apply this general approach on a regular basis—as a way of thinking about and dealing with potential problem drinking situations.

• An important point is that beyond this general approach, everything about the self-management program is individualized—tailored to your case. The situations in which you drank, the consequences you experienced, and what you can do to avoid future drinking problems are all specific to you. There are no right or wrong answers, except for you. What works for you may not work for others.

• We will also be emphasizing the need for you to identify and use your own strengths and resources in dealing with your drinking problem. People who qualify for this program, although they have a drinking problem, often are quite effective in dealing with many other areas of their lives. Examining how you deal with problems that do not involve drinking can help you identify what works for you. Many of the ways in which you deal effectively with other problems in your life may be applicable to dealing with your drinking.

• Our starting point is to identify the types of situations in which your problem drinking has occurred or is likely to occur. Problem drinkers do not always drink, and even when they drink it is not always to excess. We will call those situations in which you have a high likelihood of problem drinking "risk" situations. As discussed in the reading, various features of risk situations can be thought of as "triggering factors," since they tend to trigger your drinking. The first step in dealing with your drinking problem is to identify those factors that tend to "trigger" your drinking.

• In many cases, it is not difficult to understand why these factors tend to trigger your drinking. Most behaviors serve a purpose, and drinking is no different. So if you give it some thought you can usually identify certain situations in which you find drinking helpful. Drinking may not be the best way to respond to these situations, but it works to an extent at the time. The problem is that excessive drinking also tends to produce negative consequences, although many are delayed.

• In addition to identifying triggering factors, it is important to identify the results of drinking. This is not difficult, but since drinking often produces several results, it can be somewhat complex. Understanding the positive consequences of drinking and what drinking does for you is helpful in understanding why you drink. Understanding the negative consequences of drinking, which often occur at some time later than the drinking, is very important because they are what makes drinking a problem for you. It is the likelihood of suffering these negative consequences that gives you your best reason for not drinking to excess or for not drinking at all. When you are at risk of problem drinking, thinking about the negative consequences that might occur can be a useful way of reinforcing your commitment not to drink.

• As discussed in the reading, overcoming a drinking problem seldom happens overnight. However, research has also found that over time many people resolve their drinking problems. For some, the change is abrupt, and they never have drinking problems again. For many, however, the change is more gradual, but the outcome is the same: They successfully overcome their drinking problem. Although it would be most desirable that you never have any further drinking problems from this day forward, in many cases the road to recovery is a bit more bumpy. In this self-managment program our approach is to hope for the ideal outcome, no further drinking problems, but also to recognize that for many the road to recovery will have some problem periods, commonly called slips or relapses.

• If you should have some bumpy periods, these can be very critical occasions, because how you react to slips can affect whether you continue to strive to change your behavior. Much of what we will be doing in treatment is intended to help you avoid slips by identifying when they are likely to occur and taking actions to prevent them. However, we also must deal with the possibility that a slip might occur.

• The most important thing is that you have a successful outcome over the long run. The dieting example, as presented in the reading, makes this point. You set yourself a long-term goal, and you work toward it. If you encounter problems along the way, don't become discouraged and give up your goal. This does not solve anything. In the case of drinking problems it usually makes things worse since the risks you take by drinking excessively are far more serious than those of overeating. You should think of your recovery as a long-term goal. The sooner you get there the better, but even if delays and setbacks occur, you still want to get there. This kind of outlook is crucial if you encounter some bumps in the road. You can accept them as a temporary setback, or you can let them defeat you. More accurately, you can defeat yourself. This can be a very sharp two-edged sword. If you view a slip as a temporary setback, there are things you can do to minimize the impact it will have on you. If you see a slip as a defeat, such thinking will often feed into the slip to make it worse, such as "everything's already lost so I might as well blow it." If you let a slip become a defeat, recovery may be more difficult. Too much is at stake to let a temporary setback defeat you.

• This is where your Goal Statement can come into play. Your goal represents the rules that you have set for yourself. When you do not follow your rules, that is what we mean by a "slip." (For clients whose goal allows drinking, it should be stressed that this is why the rules must be well specified). Whether or not a slip occurred should not be a matter of judgment.

• If a slip occurs, you should view it as an unfortunate but surmountable and temporary setback. The reason you should view a slip in this way is simple. It lets you do something constructive, to make the best of the situation. It also helps you get back on track as quickly as possible.

• A problem that occurs for many people who are attempting to deal with their drinking problems is that if a slip occurs, they consider it to be a serious personal failure that indicates that they cannot deal with their drinking. This provides the easy explanation that they are not capable of doing what they think is best for themselves over the long run. This kind of thinking is self-defeating. It provides an excuse for giving up. A much healthier way of dealing with a slip is to just consider it what it is: a setback and nothing more. Dwelling on the slip is self-defeating because there is nothing you can do to change it, and the bad feelings will just increase. The important thing is to get back on track and put the slip behind you. This may involve riding out the bad feelings. They are natural, and they will disappear. And over the long run, you will feel better that you did not let them get the better of you.

• If you take the approach of viewing the slip as a temporary setback, but not a catastrophe, there are two things you can do to make it a constructive experience. First, even while in the midst of drinking, you can limit a slip's seriousness. If you slip, you slip, but there is no need to roll all the way down Mount Recovery! One obvious way to lessen the impact of a slip is to stop drinking as soon as possible. Find a way out of the situation. Perhaps you can get others to help you, such as havng someone drive you home or stay with you. If you are at home, you might consider throwing out the remaining alcohol. There are many things you can do to make the slip less serious, and you will feel better in the long run for having intervened early. Needless to say, if you do this, the negative consequences are also likely to be fewer, or perhaps will not occur at all. Later, although you may still regret the setback, you can take pride in having done something constructive about it.

• Another constructive thing you can do if a slip occurs is to turn it into a learning experience. What was different about this time, as compared to other occasions when you did not slip? How could you deal more constructively with the same type of situation if it occurred again? Were there any warning signals that you failed to notice? Sometimes the triggering factors, when taken separately, are not that apparent. Perhaps, a series of small events added up until you finally drank. Sometimes people can inadvertently set themselves up for a slip, structuring their life so that they have the opportunity to drink excessively or find various reasons to excuse their drinking. When this occurs, we refer to drinking that occurs as the result of seemingly irrelevant decisions. Each decision, in itself, contributed only a small increase to the likelihood of drinking to excess, but together the decision to drink excessively was a collective result. If this happens, how could you recognize the warning signs in the future?

• Also, a slip can signal that your motivational balance or commitment to change is shifting dangerously. Thus, a slip suggests it would be valuable to review your commitment to long term change. Is your commitment being challenged? If so, why is it being challenged now? How can you recapture the strength of commitment you had earlier?

• In summary, rather than putting yourself down for having slipped, do whatever you can to minimize the effects of the slip and see what you can learn from it. Turning a slip into a learning experience can have an important effect on your long-term recovery. If you have a piece of chocolate cake while on a diet, you need not give up the goal of losing weight, and you certainly should not let the initial slip be an excuse for having more cake!

Probing for high-risk situations can also be used to examine the client's understanding of relapse management concepts and the importance of how one might handle a relapse. The following are some examples of ways of probing the client's understanding of high-risk situations and whether a relapse prevention approach might be useful:

• Ask the client to describe how he or she has reacted to slips in the past.
• Ask the client to discuss any feelings of guilt that have been associated with prior slips.
• Ask the client to describe what kinds of events could lead to a slip and how he or she would handle a hypothetical future slip.
• If clients are defensive, ask them to discuss how others they know have handled slips.

- Ask clients to describe how others they know have reacted to their slips. How does the reaction of others affect their reaction to their own slip?
- Analogies, such as dieting, may be particularly useful for helping clients understand the basic treatment approach.

Finally, the discussion of Reading 1 provides an opportunity to discuss the client's answers to Homework Assignment 1 and to introduce Reading 2. The therapist could say:

"Let's take a look at your homework answers and see what we can learn about what triggers your problem drinking. Of course, identifying the triggers and being motivated to avoid problem drinking may not be enough. The trick is not so much 'wanting' not to drink as putting that wish into action. That is where your evaluation of your problem drinking all comes together. Action is the topic of the second reading and homework assignment."

Introducing Reading 2

When presenting the client with Reading 2, it can be helpful to provide a very brief summary of the reading's content. We present this, as we did for Reading 1, in the form of a communication from the therapist to the client.

- This second reading concerns how to make and carry out plans to avoid problem drinking. First, you identify those factors that tend to trigger your drinking along with the results or consequences that the triggering factors tend to produce. It is easier to avoid problem drinking if you can anticipate in advance when a triggering situation is likely to occur.
- Knowing the positive consequences of your drinking is also important because finding a satisfying alternative to drinking will be the first big step. This may not always be possible, however, and sometimes you may just have to tough it out and refrain from drinking to avoid problems. On many occasions, though, you will probably find that you can do something other than drinking to deal effectively with the situation.
- The second step is to think of other possible ways you can deal with the risk situation. We call these your options, because there usually is more than one thing you can do.
- The third step is to evaluate your options in terms of the outcomes they are likely to produce and the likelihood that you will be able to carry them out. On this basis, you then decide which options are best for you.
- The final step is to put the best option into practice. This is not always as easy as it may sound, but the effort is worth it when you consider the

alternative of continued problems. Developing alternative ways of dealing with problem drinking situations will be a central topic of our discussion.

Reading 2

Reading 2 (Appendix 8.2) focuses on problem-solving skills and on actions related to relapse prevention. Although the homework assignments focus on particular types of problems, it is important to emphasize to clients that while relevant examples are considered in the sessions, they do not represent all the ways in which clients can deal with high-risk situations. In other words, the purpose of the reading is to impart a general strategy for dealing with a part of the client's life that has gotten out of hand. It is expected that after the formal treatment sessions, clients can continue to expand on and improve the specific methods they use for avoiding problem drinking. Thus, what is important for clients to learn is a strategy for developing effective ways of dealing with high-risk situations. The individual examples in Homework Assignment 2 are relevant to the client's problem, but they are intended as exercises to help the client learn how to apply the rules.

Since Homework Assignment 2 is an exercise in applying problem-solving rules, it usually is most convenient to combine probing of the client's understanding of the problem-solving approach with a discussion of the client's answers to Homework Assignment 2. Since part of Reading 2 stresses that clients can take an active role in preventing relapse, a review of the major points of the relapse prevention approach can be helpful.

A good way to lead into a discussion of the client's answers to Homework Assignment 2 is to briefly review the problem-solving guidelines. As with Reading 1, a good way to assess the client's understanding is to ask the client to paraphrase the main points of the reading. The following examples, used in training therapists to conduct guided self-managment, illustrate some points that can be covered in the review. As before, it is in the form of a communication from the therapist to the client.

• Typically, when you encounter a high-risk situation, many options or ways to deal with the situation are available. What you want to avoid is a harmful outcome. In most cases, you will need to think not only about how you can avoid excessive drinking but also about what else you can do to handle the situation. There are no "right" answers. You need to consider what is best for you. You can do this in the following way:

—List a set of realistic options for yourself.
—Evaluate the options in terms of their feasibility and what you judge to be their likely overall outcomes.

   —Decide upon your best option and have at least one backup plan.
   —Think of the steps needed to put your option into practice. A series
     of small steps will allow you to better monitor your own progress.

  • The problem-solving strategy can be applied in two types of situations.
First, you can use it to deal effectively with high-risk situations. It is best
when you can anticipate the situation well in advance because this gives you
more time and usually greater freedom to develop alternative plans. However,
every time you find yourself ready to take a drink, you are potentially in a
risk situation. Even if you did not anticipate the situation developing, however, you can still apply the strategy when confronted with a drink. The stakes
are too high to make hasty or impulsive decisions. It is always possible to
stop and think—to buy some time before taking the drink.

  • As noted earlier, to avoid making impulsive decisions, some people
have found it helpful to commit themselves to waiting some period of time,
preferably at least 15 to 20 minutes, between when they decide to have a
drink and when they actually begin drinking. This assures that the decision
is not impulsive. During this "time-out" period, a person can evaluate the
potential risks in more detail and can reverse the decision if he or she decides
that the risk is too great.

  • A second use of the problem-solving strategy is if you have a slip. In
such circumstances, you can still apply this strategy for cutting off the slip as
early as possible. Evaluate your options for stopping the slip as quickly as
possible, and do whatever you need to achieve that goal.

    Chapter 9 discusses how to review the homework assignment answers
with clients, and Chapter 10 covers how the various components fit together
to become an integrated treatment. This is followed in Chapter 11 by the
presentation of case examples, which will illustrate how the various procedures
and assignments "hang together" in practice.

APPENDIX 8.1. Reading 1
Understanding Your Drinking Problem

You are now in a self-help treatment program. The "self-help" means that although we're here to help you in every way, the success of the treatment will depend on you.

This is the first of two readings you should study carefully because they outline the program you'll be developing—a program based on **your own** strengths and resources. For although problems with alcohol have affected your life in various ways, there are obviously many aspects of daily life that you cope with quite effectively.

These readings, therefore, will help you realize when you're in danger of problem drinking and help you plan other ways of dealing with these situations. But only **you** can make sure these plans are put to use. It is **your** life that will benefit most by overcoming your problems with alcohol or drugs.

* * *

Generally, a person's alcohol problem does not develop overnight. And seldom does it disappear overnight. While a few people may never have further problems with alcohol from the day they decide to do something about it, for most people the solution takes some time. Resolving an alcohol problem can often be compared to a hike up a bumpy hill. Your goal is to get to the top. Most of the time you make steady progress. But sometimes you may hit dips in the path—sudden slumps in your recovery. This type of pattern is shown in the drawing on the next page. If you follow this pattern, then the way in which you react to these dips is vital to your future improvement.

It is much the same as dieting. If you break your diet during one meal, it could affect you in one of two ways:

1. You could consider your entire dieting attempt a failure and decide you don't have the determination to continue. So you simply give up and return to your old ways of eating. If you follow this pattern, then obviously your goal will not be reached.

OR

2. You could consider it a momentary slip that sets you back only slightly in reaching your goal. But then you press on, determined to lose weight. If this is your attitude, you'll be better able to achieve your goal.

Mount Recovery — Hill of Decisions, Decisions, Decisions!!!

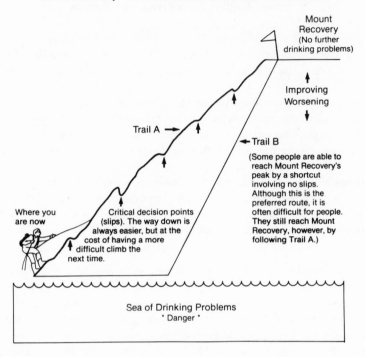

Exactly the same kind of thinking can be applied to your drinking problem. Ideally, you will never use alcohol to excess again. But there's always the possibility of a slip. And if you do slip, the way you react to it is important. You can look at how far you've come and what lies below, take a deep breath, and continue your climb uphill. If you're prepared to accept the slip as only a temporary setback, and then press on to your goal, you are far more likely to achieve your goal. Or you can get discouraged, forget how far you've come, give up on your goal, and turn back. If you let the slips get the better of you, and simply give up, you won't get to Mount Recovery. And the next time the climb may be even more difficult.

Treat your recovery as a long-term goal, and accept a slip for what it is. One slip, and nothing else. What counts is getting to the top of Mount Recovery. Dips along the way may slow you down. But they **never** have to stop you.

*   *   *

The purpose of this first reading is to **IDENTIFY YOUR PROBLEM**. Presumably, none of us acts without a purpose. And, although we don't always act in our best interests, or the way we think we should, there are usually reasons or our behavior.

Generally these causes fall into two major categories. We will call the first **TRIG-GERING FACTORS** because they consist of things which "trigger off" your desire to drink. They are events that set the scene for drinking, events that lead to the final decision to drink—although they sometimes continue triggering while you're using alcohol.

The second category is the **CONSEQUENCES**, or results, of your drinking. Some consequences occur while you're using alcohol (immediate results). Others occur later on (delayed, or long-term, results). Yet drinking usually results in several consequences. Some are admittedly helpful. Most of us, in fact, would probably say we use alcohol to get happy or carefree, ease tension, forget our problems, socialize more easily. But many other consequences are obviously harmful, and it is these harmful consequences that make drinking a problem. In other words, when your drinking is having harmful consequences, then it's a problem.

With most drinking, however, there's a direct relation between the **Triggering Factors** and the **Consequences**. For instance, some people drink at a party (a triggering factor) when they feel ill at ease (another triggering factor) in order to become more relaxed (an immediate result). Yet such drinking, of course, can also lead to hangovers and remorse about our behavior (delayed results).

But it's important to realize that the events that trigger your own drinking problems are not necessarily the same as someone else's. Some of you may have serious family problems, others do not. Some may have problems at work, others are pleasantly employed. There are no right or wrong answers to fit us all.

You must think only in terms of **yourself**, and your own problems. And don't be embarrassed to face or discuss **anything** you feel is relevant to your use of alcohol. Don't judge it—simply confront it. If it's causing you problems, then you need to deal with it.

At this point, just so we know we'll be talking about the same things, the following are some basic terms and definitions that we'll be using in the program.

Triggering Factors

This expression refers to those situations which are usually associated with your heavy drinking. Yet many circumstances may qualify as **Triggering Factors**. For instance, they could include:

1. **Unexpected Situations:** You're on a plane, and the flight attendant offers you a drink. Or, after a meeting, your boss suggests you join him in a bar.

2. **Situations You Seek:** Dropping into your local pub. Going to a party where there's heavy drinking.

3. **Emotional Situations:** The aftermath of an argument or a heavy business negotiation. Bumping into an old friend.

4. **Personal Problems:** Frustrations over debt. Anxiety about a job interview or court appearance.

Situations, as you see, can vary enormously. Sometimes a single **Triggering Factor** may set off your heavy drinking. To use an extreme example: Learning you need auto repairs doesn't usually result in drinking to excess. But, if you learned your brakes were shot at the same time that you had to renegotiate your mortgage, and you sprained your back and heard you may be laid off work, that cluster of situations may form a Collective Triggering Factor that sets off your drinking.

It's rare, of course, that such misfortunes would strike all at once. But problem drinking is often preceded by more than one triggering factor.

Consequences

As stated earlier, some **Consequences** occur during or shortly after drinking or using drugs (immediate results), while others occur later on (long-term results). But the difference between them is important.

We often overlook the immediate results of our drinking, which are often viewed as helpful. These can range from a desired change in your mood (from tense to relaxed) to breaking down one's inhibitions (feeling more comfortable in company) to simply having a good time. If the immediate results of your drinking tend to be beneficial, this is important. Research shows that immediate results usually have a stronger effect on a person's behavior than long-term results. Unfortunately, sometimes the long-term result can be quite serious.

But long-term results are often hard to identify. We often fail to link them with the drinking that actually caused them. For instance, liver disease can be a long-term result of heavy alcohol use that goes unnoticed for years because it develops over time. Loss of a job could be another long-term effect of drinking; although it may not be directly related to any single drinking episode, the quality of your work may have gradually declined. Also, because of drinking your relationship with family or friends could slowly deteriorate.

Thus, when analyzing the consequences or results of your drinking, it is vital to include those things that **could** have occurred or **may** occur in the future. We call these **"RISKS."** As an example: You drove home from a bar intoxicated, yet the police didn't stop you. But although you made it, the risk of arrest, or having an accident, was substantial. You risked serious consequences.

Finally, a bad consequence to you may not be considered bad by someone else. Or you might consider a consequence bad at one time and good at another time. For example, a hangover on New Year's morning can be considered the result of a once-a-year celebration, and you can sleep it off. Yet the same hangover on a Monday morning, which makes you miss work, could have a far more harmful result.

So when we speak of the **"OUTCOME"** of a drinking episode, we mean **all the combined consequences** that occur. In short, we must look at the overall picture. When the consequences are generally more harmful than helpful, that's a drinking problem.

* * *

Identifying Consequences and Triggering Factors

By now you're no doubt aware that identifying Triggering Factors and their Consequences might be more difficult than it first appeared. The key to this program is being extremely **careful and specific in your definitions**. For example, the expression "feeling depressed" is often used by people as a reason for excessive drinking. But the definition is not specific enough. You need to know what kinds of events and circumstances make you feel depressed. And again, they vary widely. You might feel depressed "after losing an argument" or "realizing you said something stupid" or "losing your temper." But it's easier to avoid a feeling of depression if the reasons that cause it can be identified. Analyze yourself and get to know the specific factors that most affect you.

The same is true for identifying Consequences. "Feeling better" is not specific enough. What happened to make you feel better? Was your change of mood (feeling better) associated with your drinking? Again, make a careful analysis.

* * *

Put Your Understanding into Action

By now you should be ready to identify the major Triggering Factors and Consequences of your drinking. Set aside a few hours in the next 2 or 3 days to carefully analyze the causes and effects of your problem. Then write them down seriously and honestly. Make lists of your Triggering Factors and of your Consequences—both good and bad, short-term and long-term. Often, you'll find that a particular group of Triggering Factors is closely associated with a particular group of Consequences.

If at this point you feel eager to get on with the task of developing alternatives to problem drinking, that's natural. But for your alternatives to have any meaning, it is essential to **first identify** your Triggering Factors and Consequences. Do not rush through this exercise. Take your time. Your drinking problems are complex. Give them the thought and consideration they deserve.

After you're satisfied with your analysis, complete Homework Assignment 1 and bring it to your next session.

APPENDIX 8.2. Reading 2
Dealing with Your Drinking Problem

Now that you've identified the **Triggering Factors** and **Consequences** related to your drinking, the next step is to learn to **use this information** to avoid drinking problems in the future. This section is intended to help you develop **Options**, or **Alternatives**, to excessive drinking. Again, the issues are probably more complicated than they first appear; otherwise, far fewer people would have drinking problems.

*   *   *

Types of Options

The following diagram shows four ways in which you might react to various Triggering Events (situations):

OPTIONS	EXPECTED OUTCOME
1. Drinking to Excess	⇒ HARMFUL
2. Drinking, **BUT** Not to Excess	⇒ BENEFICIAL
3. **NOT** Drinking, **AND** Acting Constructively	⇒ BENEFICIAL
4. **NOT** Drinking, **BUT** Still Acting Unconstructively	⇒ HARMFUL

Option 1 is the most familiar, and its outcome is obvious.

Option 2 may, or may not be, a reasonable alternative for you. It involves drinking in limited amounts—in order to avoid harmful results. But it usually means **not drinking** when in the midst of those Triggering Factors or situations associated with your drinking problem. Some people drink at certain times and experience problems, while at other times they are able to drink without problems (for instance, a glass or two of wine with dinner). But whether or not **any** drinking is a reasonable option for you depends on your evaluation of **three** things.

A. How seriously the Triggering Factors will affect your drinking. For example, you may feel at ease when with friends but anxious when asking for a raise—a situation causing stress.

B. An honest appraisal of the Triggering Factors, and your ability to handle them. Can you drink in certain situations without it resulting in problems?

C. What are the possible Consequences you will risk by drinking? The more serious the risks, the less likely it is that any drinking is a reasonable option.

Option 3 is, naturally, a harder course to follow, but it is by far the most beneficial. We'll discuss this in more detail in a moment.

Option 4 means that although you refuse to drink in the midst of strong Triggering Factors, you may behave in other ways that result in equally harmful consequences. For instance, instead of drinking, you may lose your temper and abuse someone—for which you later feel remorse.

As seen in the preceding diagram, just because a person responds to certain **Triggering Factors** by not drinking, it doesn't mean the results are always positive. Since we've seen that nondrinking options can be both "beneficial" and "harmful," it's important to understand these terms. The **"appropriateness" of any alternative** to drinking is **determined by the outcome** it is likely to produce.

Again, there are no absolute answers for everyone. Any single option may be appropriate only to you, but not to someone else. For example, if your boss is constantly critical of your work, you may drink as a frustrated, angry reaction. If your boss will listen to reason, however, one option may be to discuss the problem with him or her. Ask your boss what's wrong and how you might correct it. It could be something very simple. Or your boss's criticism may be totally undeserved, in which case you can explain it to him or her.

On the other hand, if your boss is simply stubborn or arrogant, such a discussion might cause him or her to fire you. In such circumstances, it might be wiser to start looking for another job, complain to a higher authority, or simply quit. These are extremes, of course. But the point is: Consider not only the alternatives but their **likely outcomes**.

*   *   *

Comparing Options

At this point, having identified the **Triggering Factors** and **Consequences** related to your drinking, the next step is to decide on the **best options** for you. Some of them might involve things you do; others may involve ways of **coping**, such as learning to relax, or to accept things you can't change. The main thing, though, is to **forget about making value judgments** at this time. Simply consider all the feasible options that you have.

By "feasible," we don't mean they won't take work to accomplish. We simply mean options that are **realistically possible**. For instance, you may have marital problems. But instead of constant bickering or fighting (which drives you to drinking), how about considering alternatives such as seeking therapy, talking to your clergyman or clergywoman, discussing the problems with your spouse—or even considering separation or divorce. The options may be simple, or harsh. But the main thing is to consider **all realistic options**. It helps to list them. **Then evaluate the options in terms of their overall outcomes.** This is where value judgments come in.

When you've done that, you're in a position to make the best decision. How effective, in the long run, are the options likely to be? What will it take to reach them? Will it be worth it? and why?

The final step in choosing your best options is **planning how to use them**. For instance, you must consider:

1. Are you ready to see them through?

2. Are some easier to accomplish than others?

3. What personal costs will they involve? (Example: Will avoiding **every** drinking situation cause greater problems than simply learning to say "no thanks" with polite, but firm authority?)

These questions require serious thought, and it's little wonder we only tend to consider them when we have to.

Putting Options into Effect

Now that you've picked your best options, the question is **how to achieve your goals**. The best way is to set up a logical **Action Plan**. If your goal can only be achieved over a period of time, that time span will enable you to check on your progress. For instance, if your goal is getting out of debt (because financial worries are strong Triggering Factors), you might develop an **Action Plan** of reducing your debt by paying all your bills on time, consolidating your debts, making no unnecessary purchases, and keeping a financial ledger. Whatever your choice, an **Action Plan** will help you reach that goal.

With an **Action Plan**, if the going gets tough, you can look back and see how far you've progressed. At the same time, you can assure yourself that your efforts are worth it.

One problem that often arises when we seek solutions is the feeling that there's nothing we can do to make things better. Unfortunately, sometimes this may be true. Yet mostly, we're simply not aware of all the possible options available to us. Or we may be unwilling to take a course of action that offers long-term benefits. Thus, we sometimes get frustrated, and give up.

But there are often reasons for our reluctance to act. We may feel we lack the skills to get things done. Or we may feel the effort will cause anxiety. Yet, when evaluating options, it is important to consider all reasonable alternatives—even if you don't feel ready as yet to put them into action. If you allow yourself to feel helpless, it can lead to a sense of self-defeat or to a feeling that things won't change no matter what you do. If you find yourself feeling helpless, the first step in breaking it is to outline those things you can do **if you are able**. Don't limit your options only to things you feel comfortable doing. Often, experiencing some discomfort in the short run can lead to a valuable long-term payoff.

*   *   *

In summary, the self-help program involves:

PROBLEM IDENTIFICATION:

1. *Identifying* the Triggering Factors *and* Consequences related to your drinking problem.

PROBLEM SOLVING:

2. Listing a set of options that are **feasible alternatives** to problem drinking.

3. **Evaluating each option in terms of its overall outcome**, and in terms of what is necessary to accomplish it.

4. **Deciding which options are best**—with at least one backup plan.

5. **Stating your options as goals** as specifically as possible.

6. **Developing an Action Plan** to accomplish these goals. Allow a reasonable period of time. Your problems did not develop overnight. It is not realistic to think they will disappear overnight.

7. **Monitoring your progress**. If your plan isn't working, try and find out why—and consider alternatives. If your plan is working, take the credit you deserve because changing one's behavior is not easy.

*   *   *

HANDLING NEW PROBLEM-DRINKING SITUATIONS

Although future problems can't be specifically dealt with until they arise, we can consider the **possibility** of them. Generally, you can do this beforehand by following the sample Action Plan described above.

Remember the drawing of Mount Recovery in the first reading. Think of possible dips that might lie ahead. Develop Action Plans to avoid them. There's no sense going downhill, even briefly, if you can find a better path. Scout the trial and make the climb as easy on yourself as possible. Think seriously about Triggering Factors that **might occur** and also what is likely to happen (the Consequences) if you drink to excess. Having done that, you should be able to devise an Action Plan to head off problem drinking in the future.

Of course, you may not foresee every obstacle that lies ahead. It would be great to encounter no obstacles on your hike, but if you do encounter obstacles—dips in the path—how you react to them can be some of the most important decisions you will ever make. Put them in perspective. You can flatten out the dip by **taking early action** (for example, by stopping drinking). The sooner you stop the slide, the quicker you will be back on the trail to Mount Recovery. There are always ways of reducing the impact of problems. **Do not let your problems build up.** Put the incident behind you as a minor setback. And use it as a learning experience: How did the slip happen? And how can you prevent a similar slip from happening again? Even when things don't go right, you can still make the best of the situation. And then put it behind you.

Hopefully, these plans will only be an exercise in thinking ahead, but the possibility of problem drinking always exists. The best way to deal with problems is to **prevent them from occurring—by anticipating them.** But if that doesn't work, you are still not out of options. The quicker you resume your climb, the faster you will reach the summit of Mount Recovery.

* * *

YOUR TURN

Having weighed the **Triggering Factors** and **Consequences** you listed in the first Homework, now is the time to develop realistic **Action Plans** that are most likely to help you. Follow the steps outlined in this reading, then put your chosen options into practice. **Use your own strengths and resources.** You use them in countless situations every day without resorting to excessive drinking. Those same resources are your most effective alternatives.

But an Action Plan is not enough by itself. The way to overcome your drinking problem is by putting the plan into practice. **It's up to you.**

After you have decided upon your Action Plans, complete Homework Assignment 2 and bring it to your next session.

9

Homework Assignments

Homework Assignment 1

At the end of the assessment, Reading 1 and Homework Assignment 1 are given to the client. Homework Assignment 1 (Appendix 9.1) has two parts preceded by a page of general instructions.

Part 1

Homework Assignment 1, Part 1, asks clients to conduct a functional analysis (i.e., evaluation) of their drinking problem by analyzing their three most serious general problem drinking situations. Because clients must perform this task before discussing their problems with the therapist, the completed assignment provides the therapist with an opportunity to evaluate how well the client understands his or her problems and the functional analysis of behavior.

The therapist's role is to work with the client to insure that the answers represent a realistic and relatively complete picture of situations in which the client engages in serious problem drinking. Since there is a range in clients' competence with the task, the therapist will have to provide more assistance to some clients than others. Sometimes a client will not be able to identify three different general problem drinking situations. This occurs infrequently and can mean that the person's drinking is very routinized (e.g., every day after work) or is confined to only one set of circumstances (e.g., when out with particular friends).

If clients have difficulty in identifying triggers and consequences, the therapist can help complete the analysis. One way of proceeding is to ask the client to describe in detail the most recent occurrences of their identified situations. In their descriptions, clients often mention or allude to features that are recognized by therapists and can be probed to determine the triggers and consequences.

There are several other issues that should also be considered by the therapist when reviewing the homework:

- Do the problem descriptions capture the situations in enough detail that the situations can be addressed in a treatment plan?
- Has the client considered the positive consequences (rewards) as well as the negative consequences for each problem-drinking situation?
- Does the salience of negative consequences for any of the problem-drinking situations need to be increased for the client?
- How important is each situation described by the client?
- Are the consequences for each problem-drinking situation particularly negative as compared to other risk situations?
- Does each situation seem appropriately described as one of the client's "most serious" problem drinking situations?
- How frequently does each problem-drinking situation occur? At the bottom of each of the problem-drinking situation forms clients are asked to indicate what percentage of all of their problem drinking situations over the past year occurred in the type of situation described.
- How strong is the client's commitment to avoid problem drinking? The types and numbers of negative consequences identified by clients can aid in evaluating this.
- What types of functions would alternative responses (behavioral options) serve? The types of positive consequences identified by clients can help identify those functions.
- Is the information provided by the client consistent? The therapist should check the correspondence of the homework answers with the assessment data and probe inconsistencies. The probing should be done in a constructive rather than confrontive manner. For example, instead of asking, "Why are the two answers different?," the therapist could say, "I'm trying to make sense of all the information you have given me, and there is one point where I need some clarification. Perhaps you could help me."

Part 2

Homework Assignment 1, Part 2, adds important information about potentially low-risk drinking situations, and it has relevance for deciding whether a nonabstinence goal is feasible. This part of the assignment asks clients to provide information about their most frequent limited-drinking experiences during the past year, with a limited-drinking occasion defined as no more than four standard drinks and no negative consequences. Clients' answers have obvious utility for evaluating the feasibility of a reduced-drinking goal.

For those clients whose limited-drinking occasions are frequent, the contrast between triggers and consequences for problem and non-problem-drinking situations can be used to generate potential strategies for managing high-risk situations (the topic of Homework Assignment 2). Just as certain factors predispose to excessive drinking, other factors may help prevent drinking from becoming excessive. For example, a client may report that he or she never drinks to excess in the presence of certain significant others. Such information can be used in structuring a treatment plan.

The answers to Homework Assignment 1, Part 2, can also be used to identify thought patterns that are inconsistent with behavior. For example, individuals who designate a reduced-drinking goal but also report an absence of any successful limited drinking in the year prior to entering treatment might be asked to provide reasons why that goal makes sense for them. Similarly, individuals who claim to have difficulty identifying situational factors related to their heavy drinking but who also report a substantial amount of successful limited drinking can use distinctions between circumstances associated with the two types of drinking as a starting point for functionally analyzing their heavy drinking.

Finally, it is important to get an idea of how frequently the client has been able to engage in limited drinking successfully. The prognosis for someone who has rarely engaged in limited drinking may be different from that for someone who has frequently engaged in limited drinking (i.e., whose heavy drinking is an occasional event). In this regard, Homework Assignment 1 asks clients to estimate what percent of their total drinking during the past year met the limited-drinking criteria. Both parts of Homework Assignment 1 should be reviewed in terms of the client's Goal Statement, especially if a reduced-drinking goal is chosen.

The vast majority (nearly 90%) of problem drinkers in our studies have reported at least some successful limited-drinking experiences. The list that follows is intended to provide readers with the flavor of clients' descriptions of limited-drinking situations. It presents selected examples of clients' answers to Homework Assignment 1, Part 2. The percentage in parentheses following each description is the client's estimated percentage of total drinking that was composed of limited-drinking situations.

> When I refrain from drinking until after a good meal or with a good meal. (25%)
> When with my children, either baby-sitting or visiting, I always watch my drinking very, very carefully—frequently abstaining totally. Also when driving. (5%)
> At some "ceremonial" event—a birthday, a wedding, a social event that is in some way a "reunion," more than just a party. (95%)

One or two drinks in evening, after supper, baby in bed, housework done, in my own home. (60%)

Usually after meeting my wife—after work—may go out for dinner or usually at home. (5%)

Social occasions—dinners, evening parties, lunch or brunch with friends. (35%)

Drinking at functions, parties where my wife is present. (60%)

Having people over who don't "get drunk." Not wanting to look like one myself. (25%)

When I'm too busy or when I'm with business associates where the situation calls for limited drinking. (75%)

In a social situation with other light or social drinkers—people I'm comfortable with. (20%)

When I'm around people I want to impress as being a light drinker (e.g., relatives). (10%)

Sunday dinner with family—or any evening dinner with family and/or friends. (100%)

Going out to dinner—either at a friend's home or at a restaurant. (50%)

Dinner with my husband; social events. (30%)

Dinner with lover and friends (at house or out). (95%)

Dinner or evening with others. (50%)

Having an evening at a friend's house. (75%)

Drinking during the week with my wife, after dinner, kids in bed, we play a card game. (40%)

Special dinners or functions with my girlfriend. (10%)

At home—just to enjoy a drink with my spouse either listening to music or watching TV. (30%)

In a controlled situation—where others were light or nondrinkers, or determined to maintain control. (20%)

In another's house; when having to drive home; important business lunch. (10%)

Going out with friends or family and being the designated driver. (25%)

Business lunch or high-pressure gathering of business peers. (60%)

Visiting friends with my wife. (20%)

External social situations, mostly family; Sunday/holiday dinner/at certain friends. (2%)

Two points stand out from these examples. First, "social controls" seem to play an important role in limiting drinking; limited drinking often occurs in the presence of particular individuals. Second, limited drinking often occurs in situations where excessive drinking would seriously interfere with task performance (e.g., driving, business functions).

Homework Assignment 2

Homework Assignment 2 (Appendix 9.2) has two parts and is given to clients
with Reading 2.

Part 1

Part 1 provides information for clients about traditional behavioral problem-
solving skills (M. B. Sobell & L. C. Sobell, 1978). It builds on Homework
Assignment 1, Part 1, to give clients experience in using the problem-solving
strategy by asking them to apply that strategy to the problem-drinking situations
they identified in Homework Assignment 1. In brief, for each of their three
major problem-drinking situations identified in Homework Assignment 1,
Part 1, clients are asked to generate a set of options, or positive alternatives
to drinking in that situation, and to evaluate each option in terms of its likely
consequences. Then they are asked to decide upon their best and next best
option for each situation, and to develop an action plan for implementing
each of those options. Examples of clients' options and associated action plans
are presented in Chapter 11.

Discussion of the client's answers to Homework Assignment 2, Part 1,
is usually one of the more time-consuming portions of the treatment sessions.
Although some clients write exemplary answers, others will need some assistance from the therapist in identifying alternatives and evaluating their feasibility. An important point to emphasize to clients when discussing Homework
Assignment 2, Part 1, is that the purpose of the exercise is to give them
experience in using the problem-solving strategy, and that they can use that
strategy to develop plans for dealing with other problem-drinking situations
beyond those identified in the assignments.

A particular challenge in working with problem drinkers is that one
frequently encounters people who report that their problem drinking is primarily positively motivated. Currently, most treatments for alcohol problems are
based on the notion that alcohol abusers' drinking is associated with negative
affective states (i.e., they drink when feeling bad in order to feel less bad).
For these situations, learning behaviors targeted at changing the situation and
alleviating negative feelings might be a way to deal with curbing heavy drinking. However, if the drinking is motivated by a desire to enhance positive
feelings (i.e., drinking when already feeling good to feel even better), changing
the situation may not be effective. One approach that can be used with clients
who report that their drinking is mainly to enhance positive emotional states
is to focus on increasing their motivation for change. This involves (1) increasing the salience of the risk of consequences; (2) looking at what the implica-

tions would be if the consequences actually occurred; and (3) lowering the value of the "high" experience.

Another way of proceeding would be to argue that drinking to "feel even better" is just a rationalization for heavy drinking (Nathan & McCrady, 1986/1987). This argument is at some peril, however, because it lacks an empirical basis (see Wise & Bozarth, 1987). Also, since it is inconsistent with clients' subjective expeiences, it also might lack credibility.

In our view, an approach that is more consistent with clients' perceptions is that they must choose to forgo a pleasurable experience because they cannot afford the long-term costs that might follow if the behavior continues. The client should be asked to generate ideas that could help them forgo the added pleasure associated with excessive drinking when they are in a high-risk situation characterized by positive affect.

While there are probably numerous other techniques that could be used to deal with these high-risk situations in which clients drink when feeling good, they have not been systematically explored. Most research has focused on ways of constructively managing negative affect and stressful situations. The finding that positively motivated drinking is a frequent occurrence for problem drinkers suggests that there is a need to systematically evaluate ways of dealing with heavy drinking associated with positive emotional states.

Part 2

Homework Assignment 2, Part 2, is intended to identify areas of clients' life functioning that may relate to clients' problem drinking. It can form the basis for a discussion exploring clients' personal strengths and resources. The assignment involves completion of a checklist that asks questions about client's life-style. The answers to these questions may provide direction about changes to be made in major areas of their life functioning in order to deal effectively with their drinking problem. The checklist addresses different life circumstances that are sometimes barriers to recovery. The major areas include social relationships, leisure and recreational activities, and availability of alcohol. The checklist is geared for efficiency; the responses provide data that can be discussed during the session.

Discussing the checklist answers with clients also provides a vehicle for exploring how clients deal with various aspects of their lives. Additionally, the checklist provides a basis for a more in-depth analysis of the client's strengths and resources. The focus of the discussion can be on helping clients apply their strengths and resources to dealing with their problem drinking situations.

In identifying strengths and resources, one avenue is to ask clients about times they have succesfully avoided problem drinking in the past. What has worked for them? What has not worked, and for what reasons? Resources that may be available to the individual should be identified. These can include social resources. For example, do some relatives or friends discourage excessive drinking, and could they be enlisted to help the client cope with high-risk situations? Similarly, what social and recreational activities do clients find interesting and satisfying? Could any of these activities be used as alternatives to drinking or to fill time previously spent drinking? Can social situations be arranged so as not to encourage drinking or, at least, so as not to encourage heavy drinking?

The discussion of a client's personal strengths and resources should be nonjudgmental when possible. For example, a client may describe an avoidance strategy that has been used successfully in the past, while the therapist may believe that an assertive response would be preferable. Since clients are being asked to do what they feel comfortable doing, as long as it is effective, a variety of strategies should be entertained.

Some Aids for Completing and Discussing the Homework Assignments

The following are some general guidelines that have been used in training therapists in the guided self-management approach:

• The therapist should stress to the client that the homework assignments are intended to provide examples of a general approach or strategy that can be applied to problem situations. The three situations identified in Homework Assignment 1, Part 1, are not meant to be exhaustive of problem drinking situations. They are examples for clients to use to learn how to analyze their drinking problem. Since the examples have been identified as the client's most serious general problem drinking situations, they will play a prominent role in discussions of how to avoid problem drinking.

• The therapist should not lead clients but rather assist them in identifying antecedents and consequences of their drinking. When possible, the client should identify the relevant variables.

• The therapist should insure that antecedents, consequences, and options are described clearly and specifically.

• The therapist should encourage clients to describe some situations that actually occurred that exemplify the situations described in their answers. This allows the therapist to probe for clarifications and to inquire about possible antecedents and consequences that the client may have overlooked.

• The therapist should explore whether the options are suitable for dealing with the situation (i.e., are they likely to be effective)? Has the full range of possible consequences been considered (e.g., an option may be effective in the short run but have long-term negative consequences)?

• The therapist should examine whether the client's selection of the best and next best option make sense? This question should be considered from the client's perspective.

• The therapist should assess whether the Action Plan is broken down into manageable steps?

• During the discussion of the homework, there should be explicit consideration of how the client's life-style relates to his or her drinking problem (Homework Assignment 2, Part 2, is helpful here). Since drinking has come to play a major role in the person's life, life-style changes may be necessary in order to avoid excessive drinking. At a minimum, the following three life-style areas should be probed:

—Availability of alcohol: Is problem drinking more likely to occur if alcohol is readily available?

—Amount of time spent in drinking or drinking-related activities: If a great deal of time is spent in this manner, clients may need to fill in this time with low-risk activities.

—Relationships with peers, levels of peers' drinking, and social-drinking situations: In some cases, a change in social relationships may be necessary to avoid problem drinking. Likewise, the successful avoidance of problem drinking may bring about some changes in social relationships (e.g., the client may be avoided by heavy-drinking peers).

Aids for Clients

A listing of questions and categories that can be provided to clients to assist them in preparing their homework follows:

Questions

Where and when do you tend to do your most serious problem drinking?

What other people tend to be present on these occasions, and how do they act?

How do you feel before drinking and after you have started drinking?

Is your pattern of drinking different from usual in these situations?

What thoughts are foremost in your mind just before you start drinking?

What do you accomplish by drinking? What purposes does it serve for you?

Some General Categories of Triggers

Your emotional state (e.g., angry, depressed, happy, jealous, sad).

Your physical state (e.g., relaxed, tense, tired, aroused).

Your thoughts (e.g., having to make major decisions, worried about financial problems, bored, work pressures, wanting to go someplace else).

Presence of others (e.g., does your excessive drinking usually occur when certain people are present?).

Having alcohol readily available.

The physical setting (e.g., home, bar, club, sporting event).

Social pressure (e.g., others ask you to have a drink; you are at a party where others are drinking).

Activities (e.g., at work, working at home, playing sports, watching TV, playing cards)

Some General Categories of Consequences

Physical consequences (bodily sensations).

Emotional consequences (mood changes).

Social consequences (how others act toward you).

Material events (e.g., legal charges, financial debts, property damage).

What you are thinking (e.g., feeling guilty; feeling out of control).

In the next chapter, the integration of treatment components is addressed.

APPENDIX 9.1. Homework Assignment 1

THIS ASSIGNMENT HAS TWO PARTS.

BEFORE completing the assignment, you should read "Understanding Your Drinking Problem." It is important that you complete the attached forms and **bring them with you to your next session.** If you forget to fill out the forms, or forget to bring them in, you will still need to complete the forms **before** the session can begin.

Each part of the assignment contains a separate instruction sheet and answer sheets. You are asked to think of various situations that have been associated with your drinking, and to describe what you think triggered your drinking and what you think were the consequences (results) of your drinking.

In the **first part** of the assignment, you are asked to describe three problem-drinking situations that have been associated with your most serious problem drinking.

In the **second part** of the assignment, you are asked to describe the most common type of situation, if any, in the past year when you were able to drink only a small amount of alcohol and did not suffer any negative consequences. If you did not experience such a situation in the past year, write "none" across the answer sheet for the second part of the assignment.

GO ON TO THE FIRST PART OF THE ASSIGNMENT.

Name: _____

PART 1: HOMEWORK ASSIGNMENT 1

One of the best ways to identify factors that have triggered your problem drinking and consequences related to that drinking is to think about **REAL** drinking experiences you have had. In fact, that is what you should do in answering this assignment. Since we want to discuss these experiences with you at your next session, it is important that you bring this completed assignment with you to your next appointment.

Use the attached answer sheets to describe three general types of situations that have been associated with your **MOST SERIOUS** problem drinking.

- For each of the three general types of situations, complete a **separate** copy of the form entitled PROBLEM-DRINKING SITUATION (three copies attached).

On each form:

- Briefly describe the **general nature** of the serious problem-drinking situation. For example, "drinking with friends at a party," "drinking at home after a hard day at work," and so on.

- Then describe the types of **TRIGGERING FACTORS** usually associated with that type of situation. In completing the form, you may find it helpful to refer to the reading "Understanding Your Drinking Problem" and to consider such factors as your physical state, your emotional state, your thoughts, the presence of others and whether they were drinking, the setting, the times, what you were doing when the situation occurred, and so on.

- Next describe the types of **CONSEQUENCES** usually associated with that type of situation. Be sure to consider **both IMMEDIATE Consequences** (things that happened while you were drinking) **and DELAYED Consequences** (things that happened shortly or some time **after** drinking, but were related to the drinking). Also, be sure to consider consequences that were **NEGATIVE or POSITIVE** for you.

- Finally, at the bottom of the form indicate what percentage of your **TOTAL** problem-drinking episodes in the **PAST YEAR** occurred in **that type** of situation.

NOW YOU ARE READY TO COMPLETE THE THREE PROBLEM-DRINKING SITUATION FORMS.

Name: _____

PROBLEM-DRINKING SITUATION # _____

1. Briefly describe **one** of your three **MOST SERIOUS** problem-drinking situations:

_____

_____

_____

_____

_____

2. Describe as specifically as possible the types of **TRIGGERING FACTORS** usually associated with this problem-drinking situation:

_____

_____

_____

_____

_____

(CONTINUE ON BACK OF THIS PAGE IF MORE SPACE IS NEEDED.)

3. Describe as specifically as possible the types of **CONSEQUENCES** usually associated with this problem-drinking situation. Remember to consider **both IMMEDIATE and DELAYED** Consequences and also **NEGATIVE and POSITIVE** Consequences:

_____

_____

_____

_____

_____

(CONTINUE ON BACK OF THIS PAGE IF MORE SPACE IS NEEDED.)

4. How often did this type of situation occur in the PAST YEAR? Of **all** of your problem-drinking episodes over the **past year**, what **percent** of those episodes occurred in **this type** of situation? (For example, if about one out of every three times that you drank excessively it occurred in this situation, you would write 33%).

Write your answer here: _____%

PART 2: HOMEWORK ASSIGNMENT 1

It is also important to know whether there were **any** situations over the **PAST YEAR** in which you were able to drink a **limited amount** (four or fewer drinks) **without experiencing any negative (bad) consequences.**

*   *   *

Because alcoholic beverages vary in their alcohol content, you should use the following definition of 1 standard drink:

1 standard drink is equal to 1½ **oz** of hard liquor/spirits (e.g. whiskey), **OR**
                          5 oz of table wine, **OR**
                          12 oz of beer, **OR**
                          3 oz of fortified wine (port, sherry), **OR**
                          1½ **oz** of liqueur, brandy, or cognac
For example, whether you drank three bottles of beer or three 1½ oz shots of whiskey or three 5-oz glasses of table wine, each case would be considered three standard drinks.

*   *   *

On the attached form titled LIMITED-DRINKING SITUATION, you are asked to first indicate whether at any time during the **past year** (past 12 months) you drank four or fewer standard drinks and did not experience any negative consequences of that drinking. If you indicate that you **never** drank a small amount without problems, then you should not fill out the rest of the form.

However, if over the **PAST YEAR** there were one or more occasions when you drank no more than four standard drinks and you did not experience negative consequences of your drinking, then on the LIMITED-DRINKING SITUATION form you should go on to describe the **MOST COMMON** situation of this sort. Complete the form in the same way as you completed the "Problem-Drinking Situation" forms. That is:

1.   Briefly describe the **most common** situation in which your limited drinking occurred during the past year.
2.   Describe the types of **TRIGGERING FACTORS** usually associated with that type of situation. If you have difficulty identifying specific TRIGGERING FACTORS, simply describe in some detail a typical limited-drinking situation that you actually experienced.
3.   Describe the types of **CONSEQUENCES** usually associated with that type of limited-drinking situation. Remember to include **both** IMMEDIATE and DELAYED Consequences.
4.   Indicate the **percentage of your TOTAL drinking episodes over the PAST YEAR that involved limited drinking** with no negative consequences, **REGARDLESS** of whether the limited drinking occurred in the "most common" situation or in some other type of situation.

Name: _____

LIMITED-DRINKING SITUATION

1. Place a check mark in only **one** of the following boxes:

   ☐ During the **PAST YEAR** (past 12 months), **I NEVER** drank **four or fewer** standard drinks **without experiencing any negative consequences** of my drinking. If you check this alternative, **stop here**; it is not necessary for you to complete the rest of this form.

   ☐ During the **PAST YEAR**, there were **one or more** occasions when I drank **four or fewer** Standard Drinks **and did not experience any negative consequences** from my drinking. If you check this alternative, **go on** to answer the remaining questions on this form.

2. Over the PAST YEAR, in about what **percentage of ALL of your drinking episodes** (including **both** problem-drinking **and** limited-drinking) did you drink **four or fewer standard drinks and experience no negative consequences** of your drinking? (For example, if about one out of every four times that you drank, it involved limited drinking without problems, you would write 25%.)

   Write your answer here: _____ %

3. Briefly describe your **MOST COMMON** limited-drinking situation:

   _____

4. Describe as specifically as possible the types of **TRIGGERING FACTORS** usually associated with this limited-drinking situation. (If you are not able to identify specific Triggering Factors, simply describe in some detail a typical limited drinking situation that you actually experienced.):

   _____

   (CONTINUE ON BACK OF THIS PAGE IF MORE SPACE IS NEEDED.)

5. Describe as specifically as possible the types of **CONSEQUENCES** usually associated with this limited-drinking situation. Remember to consider both IMMEDIATE and DELAYED consequences. (The situation should be associated with no negative consequences. If you are not able to identify any positive consequences, write "none" as your answer.):

   _____

   (CONTINUE ON BACK OF THIS PAGE IF MORE SPACE IS NEEDED.)

APPENDIX 9.2. Homework Assignment 2

Like Homework Assignment 1, this assignment has **TWO** parts.

BEFORE completing the assignment, you should read "Dealing with Your Drinking Problem." As with Assignment 1, you should **bring the completed Homework Assignment 2 to your next appointment**. Otherwise, you will need to complete the assignment before your session can begin.

In the **first part** of the assignment, you are asked to develop **Options** and **Action Plans** for each of the three "Problem-Drinking Situations" that you described in your answers to the previous homework assignment.

In the **second part** of the assignment, you are asked to briefly answer a small set of questions concerning how drinking has fit into your overall **life-style**.

GO ON TO THE FIRST PART OF THE ASSIGNMENT.

Name: _____

PART 1: HOMEWORK ASSIGNMENT 2

This assignment deals with **DEVELOPING OPTIONS AND ACTION PLANS.**

Attached you will find copies of the three "Problem-Drinking Situation" forms that you completed as part of the previous homework assignment. Attached to each of the completed "Problem-Drinking Situation" forms you will also find an OPTIONS form and an ACTION PLAN form.

OPTIONS FORMS

For each of the problem-drinking situations on its attached OPTIONS form **describe at least two,** and preferably more, **positive alternatives** (options) to drinking in that situation.

- Be as **specific** as possible in describing the options.

- All options should be **realistic** (they should be possible), although you may feel that you would have difficulty putting some options into effect.

Next, **for each option** describe its **likely Consequences** (what you think would happen if you successfully used that option instead of drinking).
- Be sure to consider **both** NEGATIVE and POSITIVE Consequences.

- Be sure to consider **both** IMMEDIATE and DELAYED Consequences.

Finally, **taking everything into account** (for example, the likely consequences, the difficulty of putting the option into practice, your own preferences) indicate at the bottom of the OPTIONS form which of those options would be your **first choice** (best option) and which option would be your **second choice** (next best option) for dealing with that problem-drinking situation if it were to occur in the future.

ACTION PLAN FORMS

After you have completed the OPTIONS form for a problem-drinking situation, then go on to complete the ACTION PLAN form for that situation.

- Your Action Plan should describe in some detail **how you could put into practice** your best option and your next best option for that situation.

- You should describe **what things you would need to do** to successfully use each option.

- • Whenever possible, break down the Action Plan into a number of **small steps**. This helps you to be specific, and it also helps you to keep track of your progress toward your goals.

The next page presents an example of a very detailed Action Plan. The Action Plans you develop may or may not be as detailed as the example, depending upon the nature of the problem-drinking situation and the options you select.

Name: _____

EXAMPLE OF A DETAILED "ACTION PLAN"

The following is an example of a very detailed Action Plan for achieving a goal of **getting out of financial debt**. Although this example is a plan for dealing with financial problems rather than for dealing with a problem-drinking situation, the principles for developing an Action Plan are the same in each case:

- The important thing is to **describe what specifically is needed to accomplish the goal.**

- It often helps to break the Action Plan down into **small steps whenever possible.**

Your Action Plans may or may not be as detailed as this example, depending upon the nature of the situation and the option you wish to put into effect.

* * *

ACTION PLAN for gradually getting out of debt:

1. Cancel credit cards.

2. Keep a monthly listing of all bills, their due dates, payment schedule, and up-to-date balance.

3. On payday, make at least some payment on all bills due and handle other related financial matters (for example, respond to past-due notices, call creditors and assure them that I intend to pay off the balance as soon as I am able).

4. Balance checkbook monthly.

5. Work overtime whenever possible to pay off debts more quickly.

6. Allow myself a small amount per month for entertainment or treats so that I do not become discouraged.

7. Use next year's income tax refund, if any, to help pay off my most serious debt.

8. Make a list of debts from which I cross off each debt when it is paid in full.

NOW GO ON TO COMPLETE THE THREE SETS OF "OPTIONS" AND "ACTION PLAN" FORMS WHICH MAKE UP THIS ASSIGNMENT.

Name: _____

OPTIONS

Use this form to describe Options and Likely Consequences for:
Problem-Drinking Situation # _____ (attached)

A. **OPTIONS AND LIKELY CONSEQUENCES:** Below, describe at least two, and preferably more, options and their consequences for this problem-drinking situation.

OPTION # 1: _____

LIKELY CONSEQUENCES OF OPTION # 1: _____

OPTION #2: _____

LIKELY CONSEQUENCES OF OPTION #2: _____

OPTION #3: _____

LIKELY CONSEQUENCES OF OPTION #3: _____

OPTION #4: _____

LIKELY CONSEQUENCES OF OPTION #4: _____

(USE THE BACK OF THIS PAGE TO CONTINUE ANY OF THE ABOVE,
OR TO ADD MORE OPTIONS.)

B. **SELECTING OPTIONS:** From the above options you described for this problem-drinking situation, *taking everything into account:*

   1. Which option would you select as your **best option**?
                                        OPTION # _____

   2. Which option would you select as your **next best option**?
                                        OPTION # _____

NOW GO ON TO COMPLETE THE ACTION PLAN FORM FOR THIS
PROBLEM-DRINKING SITUATION.

Name: _____

ACTION PLAN

Use this form to describe your Action Plan for **Problem-Drinking Situation #__**

For the **best and next best** options for this problem-drinking situation describe an **Action Plan** that would allow you to put the option into effect.

A.   **BEST OPTION:** OPTION # _____ (option selected as "best" on the "Options" form).

ACTION PLAN:

_____

_____

_____

_____

_____

_____

_____

_____

_____

B.   **NEXT BEST OPTION:** Option # _____ (option selected as "next best" on the "Options" form).

ACTION PLAN:

_____

_____

_____

_____

_____

_____

_____

_____

(IF YOU NEED MORE SPACE, CONTINUE ON THE BACK OF THIS PAGE; BE SURE TO LIST THE OPTION NUMBER.)

Name: _____

PART 2: HOMEWORK ASSIGNMENT 2

LIFE-STYLE ASSESSMENT

If you are like many other people who have alcohol problems, your drinking may be strongly related to other aspects of your daily life (for example, the people you spend time with and how you spend your spare time). Sometimes successfully dealing with your drinking problem is helped by EXAMINING how drinking fits into your life. Your answers to the following questions will help clarify whether you should consider making some life-style changes. For each question, **check** either Yes or No. If you answered "yes," you may provide some description in the space preceded by "Describe."

1. Are a great many of your leisure, social, or recreational activities associated with drinking?
   - ☐ (1) Yes Describe: _____
   - ☐ (2) No
2. Do you think you will need to change some of your leisure, social, or recreational activities in order to successfully deal with your drinking?
   - ☐ (1) Yes Describe: _____
   - ☐ (2) No
3. Would not drinking at all, or only drinking small amounts, leave a gap in your daily schedule that will need to be filled in by other activities?
   - ☐ (1) Yes Describe: _____
   - ☐ (2) No
4. Do you sometimes drink just because the alcohol is there, that is, because it is readily available to you?
   - ☐ (1) Yes Describe: _____
   - ☐ (2) No
5. Do you usually drink in the company of others, at least some of whom drink as much or more than you do?
   - ☐ (1) Yes Describe: _____
   - ☐ (2) No
6. Are there some people in whose company you would find it very difficult to not drink or to greatly limit your drinking?
   - ☐ (1) Yes Describe: _____
   - ☐ (2) No
7. Do you have relatives or friends whom you can count on to support your efforts to avoid heavy drinking?
   - ☐ (1) Yes Describe: _____
   - ☐ (2) No
8. Do you think you will need to change any of your relationships with others (e.g., see some people less often) in order to deal with your drinking problem?
   - ☐ (1) Yes Describe: _____
   - ☐ (2) No

10

An Integrated Treatment Program

All of the major components of the guided self-management treatment approach have now been discussed except one—putting the pieces together. As with any approach involving multiple procedures, there is a risk that used individually the procedures will be mechanistic, ineffective, or counterproductive. Also, a "by the numbers" approach to treatment can communicate to the client a sense that the therapist is uncaring or lacks confidence. The extent to which such factors affect treatment outcome has not been studied empirically, but it makes sense that both the client and the therapist should be comfortable with the treatment procedures so that the focus of treatment is on behavior change and not on elements of the treatment process. Thus, how the procedures fit together is an extremely important aspect of the guided self-management approach.

An important element of the integration of treatment components takes place in assessment. In guided self-management, assessment is much more than the gathering of data as a prelude to getting on with the treatment. Assessment *is* the first stage of treatment. As was discussed earlier, providing Reading 1 and Homework Assignment 1 at the end of assessment is intended to capitalize on the self-evaluation started by the assessment process. However, for the formal treatment sessions to get off to a running start, therapists have to do their homework as well. If the therapist does the assessment, this occurs naturally. If someone other than the therapist does the assessment, however, then, prior to meeting with the client, the therapist must carefully review the assessment information and formulate clinical hypotheses based on the assessment material. Although such an approach will not be new for an experienced therapist, such integration and planning is particularly important when conducting brief treatments.

The next chapter presents integrated case examples using actual assessment information. Based on these examples, it will be obvious how assessment information forms the first step in treatment planning. As mentioned earlier, a Clinical Assessment Summary can both help therapists integrate the assessment material and provide an overview of the case during treatment. A Clinical Assessment Summary accompanies each case presented in the next chapter.

The fitting together of the treatment procedures within sessions is the other major integration that is vital to the overall approach. The focus in this chapter will be on integrating the procedures within the conduct of treatment sessions. The importance of this type of integration became apparent when we started to train other therapists in the guided self-management procedures. This was done during a 6-month period when we and the other therapists pilot tested the procedures with clients. While it became clear after seeing a few clients that the procedures were workable, we also realized that utilizing the procedures in any lockstep order would be unreasonable and disconcerting, because it could disrupt the natural flow of the sessions since the therapist might have to interrupt the client in order to adhere to the set sequence of topics.

We found that a more satisfactory degree of structure is for the therapists to ensure that the required procedures for a given session are completed within that session but not necessarily in a required order. This leaves the therapist free to arrange the session to promote continuity between procedures, that is, a smooth transition from topic to topic. It also enables therapists to adapt the approach to their own style and to the needs of individual clients (e.g., some clients easily identify triggers for their heavy drinking, while others require more assistance from the therapist—the procedure described here allows the therapist to allocate as much or as little time to each procedure as necessary). Our experience has been that with a little practice, therapists become quite adept at integrating the treatment procedures and making use of the assessment information.

The Course of Treatment

In clinical practice (in contrast with research), the length of treatment for a given client should be dictated by how long it takes to get through the material, rather than by establishing an arbitrary number of sessions. It is important, however, to examine how much change a client makes over the course of treatment. If a client shows no change or very little change, the lack of progress should be addressed and whether another approach is needed should be determined. In the absence of change, another consideration is whether the client is prepared to make the necessary sacrifices to overcome his or her drinking problem. In such cases, the client's motivational balance can be examined (i.e., factors weighing for and against changing drinking). For a discussion of how to assess a client's motivational balance during treatment, readers are referred to a recent book on this topic (Miller & Rollnick, 1991).

In terms of treatment length, we have used these procedures in studies with varying numbers of sessions: (1) two 90-minute sessions following assessment; (2) four 60-minute sessions following assessment (L. C. Sobell & M. B. Sobell, 1992a); and (3) ten very brief (e.g., 10–15-minute) weekly sessions following assessment, conducted when clients were in a treatment trial combining the guided self-management procedures with an investigational medication intended to reduce urges to drink (Sellers et al., 1991). Across all studies, it has been clear that most problem drinkers are satisfied with and see as appropriate for them a brief self-management cognitively oriented treatment approach that includes goal self-selection.

While there are a limited number of sessions in brief treatments like the guided self-management treatment, one procedure that many therapists have found useful is to schedule the sessions over variable time periods (e.g., every 2 weeks; or the first two sessions once a week with the last two spaced 2 to 3 weeks apart). Such a procedure allows the therapist and client more time to evaluate the client's progress and any problems the client may be experiencing in making changes, yet it retains the cost-effective and minimally intrusive characteristics of the treatment.

Finally, although we have stressed the advantages of flexibility in the delivery of guided self-management treatment, we end this chapter with a suggested ordering of procedures that can be used over four 60-minute sessions as an example of a treatment regimen.

Assessment

- Breath test the client.
- At the end of the assessment, give the client Reading 1 and Homework Assignment 1. Ask the client to complete the homework and bring it to the first session.
- Give the client instructions and logs for self-monitoring alcohol consumption.
- Prior to Session 1, review the assessment information, become familiar with the client's background and presenting problems, and identify areas that need further probing. Review the client's responses to the following assessment instruments:

  —Alcohol Dependence Scale
  —Inventory of Drinking Situations (scores and profile)
  —Timeline Follow-Back drinking history

  —Situational Confidence Questionnaire
  —Goal Statement

Session 1

- Collect Homework 1 and self-monitoring forms.
- Discuss treatment rationale.
- Review with the client his or her understanding of Reading 1.
- Review the client's answers to Homework Assignment 1; probe and augment descriptions as necessary.
- Discuss the client's goal. If the goal is reduced drinking, review recommended guidelines for reduced drinking. If the goal is abstinence, make sure that the rationale is that the client sees this goal as in his or her best interests (i.e., rather than because of a fear that he or she is incapable of reducing drinking).
- Review self-monitoring logs; obtain retrospective Timeline if self-monitoring is not done.
- Briefly review answers to Homework Assignment 1; begin discussion of answers.
- Give the client the Life-Style Assessment (Homework Assignment 2, Part 2) with instructions to bring the completed form to the next session.
- Request that the client continue to maintain self-monitoring record.
- Stress to the client the importance of completing treatment.

Session 2

- Collect completed Life-Style Assessment and self-monitoring logs.
- Review answers to the Life-Style Assessment; probe and augment descriptions as necessary. Discussion should focus on the client's strengths and resources, and on areas where life-style changes may be necessary.
- Discuss the client's personal strengths and resources and how they relate to answers to Homework Assignment 2, Part 2.
- Review self-monitoring records or obtain retrospective Timeline if self-monitoring was not done. Discuss any inconsistencies between the actual drinking and the stated drinking goal (i.e., over the limit, too frequent).
- Finish discussion of answers to Homework Assignment 1.
- Give the client Reading 2 and Homework Assignment 2, Part 1, with instructions to bring the completed assignment to the next session.
- Stress the importance of completing treatment.

Session 3

- Collect Homework Assignment 2, Part 1, and self-monitoring logs.
- Review Reading 2; answer any questions.
- Review self-monitoring logs with respect to the stated treatment goal. If behavior is inconsistent with the goal, discuss how consistency could be achieved.
- Review and discuss answers to Homework Assignment 2, Part 1.
- Stress the importance of completing treatment.

Session 4

- Have the client complete another Goal Statement. Review the statement with the client, as this goal will be the goal for the aftercare or follow-up phase of treatment.
- Collect self-monitoring logs and review in light of treatment goal; discuss inconsistencies.
- Complete discussions of answers to Homework Assignment 2, Parts 1 and 2.
- Advise the client about provisions for further treatment.
- Briefly review the purpose of the treatment program; that is, put the treatment in perspective.
- Conclude formally scheduled treatment sessions.

To this point our discussion of guided self-management treatment has focused on the procedures, their rationale, and their integration. In Chapter 11 we present case examples including assessment and outcome data as well as the clients' actual homework answers. The cases presented are rather typical of the problem drinkers with whom we have worked.

11

Case Examples

In Chapter 6 the assessment instruments that we have found helpful in guided self-management treatment were discussed. One instrument that has considerable clinical utility, the Inventory of Drinking Situations (IDS), identifies situations that present a high risk of heavy drinking. Factor analyses of the IDS, and its sister instrument for measuring of individuals' confidence (self-efficacy) in their ability to resist the urge to drink heavily in various types of situations (Situational Confidence Questionnaire; SCQ), have identified three relatively independent dimensions to clients' reports. These dimensions can be thought of as a Negative Affect dimension, a Positive Affect dimension (often associated with social situations), and a Control Testing dimension (Annis & Graham, 1988; Annis, Graham, & Davis, 1987; Cannon, Leeka, Patterson, & Baker 1990; Isenhart, 1991). In one study (Annis et al., 1987), Positive Affect and Control Testing combined to form a single factor.

Clinically, the IDS dimensions, and especially the relationship of affective situations to drinking, provide a useful shorthand for summarizing case characteristics. One finding that provides support for the use of the IDS profiles is that raters have been able to classify clients' IDS score profiles reliably into categories based on the scales having the highest scores. Furthermore, in most instances the profiles parallel the clients' homework answers (i.e., the high-risk situations identified on clients' homework are also identified on their IDS profile).

The case examples that follow have been selected to exemplify the mix of clients one might expect to encounter in dealing with problem drinkers and to illustrate the range of answers that characterize the homework assignments. Clients' descriptions of their limited-drinking situations are also included to illustrate how problem and nonproblem situations can be contrasted. The case examples include assessment data and homework answers so readers can see how this package of information can be combined into a useful clinical picture. These cases are from clients who participated in guided self-management treatment. Some treatment outcome information is also presented for each case. These clients all were treated using the two-session version of the treatment.

Case 1: Heavy Drinking Related Primarily to Negative Affective States

The client, a 31-year-old self-employed female with a college education, lived with her husband and two children. Figure 11.1 presents the Clinical Assessment Summary for this client. She had no prior history of treatment for alcohol problems, but she reported that her drinking had been a problem for about 10 years. Her Alcohol Dependence Scale (ADS) score of 12 placed her in the first quartile on the ADS norms, well within the group considered problem drinkers. She reported that her heavy drinking consisted mainly of wine when alone. Subjectively, she evaluated her drinking as a Very Minor Problem, which meant that she had not yet suffered any negative consequences. She reported having experienced blackouts and hangovers, and having been unsuccessful in cutting down her drinking.

Her goal at assessment was to reduce her drinking to a maximum of three standard drinks per occasion and to drink less than 1 day per week (recall that a client's goal at assessment does not reflect advice from their therapist or knowledge of recommended guidelines for limited drinking). She planned to confine her drinking to social occasions when she was not in the company of smokers. She felt that her smoking was strongly related to her drinking, and, in addition to wanting to limit her drinking to rare occasions, she also wanted to stop smoking. She planned not to drink at home or when she was alone. By the end of treatment, the client had reduced her goal to no more than two standard drinks per day, but she had increased the frequency to an average of 2 days per week. She also had modified the conditions under which drinking could occur; she indicated she would not drink when alone, when working, or on a weekday evening unless it was as part of a social event at which she felt comfortable with those present.

Figure 11.2 presents an excerpt from this client's Timeline for her drinking 90 days prior to assessment. This excerpt is consistent with her drinking pattern for the year prior to treatment. Her heavier drinking occurred mostly on weekdays and never exceeded 3 days in a row. Although her drinking was not heavy in terms of the absolute amount of alcohol consumed, she tended to consume her drinks over short time periods in the late evening. While her consumption rarely exceeded eight drinks per evening, the blood alcohol concentration she attained as a result of that drinking could have been quite substantial (Kapur, 1991; Watson, Watson, & Batt, 1980).

This client's IDS profile appears in Figure 11.3. The profile is typical of a Negative Affect profile, indicating that the situations in which the client's

Name: _____   Date Completed: _____

CLINICAL ASSESSMENT SUMMARY

ADS Score: _12_   ADS Components: _Hangovers; acute intoxication; blackouts;_
unsuccessfully tried to cut down; difficulty stopping.

Age: _31_   Sex: M (F)   Yrs. Education: _16_   Marital Status: (M/CL) NM S D W

Employment Status: _Part-time, self-employed_ Occupation: _Market researcher_

No. of Alcohol- or Drug-related Arrests: _0_   No. of Jobs lost due to Alcohol or Drug use in past year.: _0_

Ever purposely abstinent: (Y) N   Longest no. mos. purposely abstinent : _3_   Family History of Alc. Problems: (Y)⁻¹ N

Prior A/D treatment: Y (N)   Describe: _____

Problem Self–Appraisal: _Very minor problem – no identified consequences,_
but worries.

Alcohol Consequences: _None identified_

Other Drug Use: _Minimal use cannabis many yrs. past; 1-time use hallucinogens 15 yrs. past_

No. of Yrs. problem drinking: _10_   No. of Yrs. heavy drinking: _1_   No. days morning drinking in past yr.: _0_

Timeline	_174_ No.. of days Abstinent	_104_ No. of days 5 – 9 SDs
Past 360 days	_77_ No. of days 1 – 4 SDs	_5_ No. of days ≥ 10 SDs

Drinking (Patterns, features, or use characteristics): _Drinks about 8 drinks about 4 times per week._
Mostly alone, mostly wine. Has cut down slightly in last 3 months.
(more abstinent and 1-4 SD days).

☐ IDS (heavy use situations in past yr.): _Negative affect profile._

☐ SCQ (vulnerability): _Like IDS._

Goal: _Eventually 3 drinks, less than once a week, only at social_
occasions. At first abstinence while she attempts to
stop smoking.

Additional Observations: _Feels stopping smoking will be essential in_
order to control drinking. Stopped smoking for 2 years
until relapse 6 months ago. Lost 30 pounds 2 years ago.

FIGURE 11.1. Case 1: Clinical Assessment Summary.

	SUN	MON	TUES	WED	THURS	FRI	SAT
							1
F	2	3	4	5	6 0	7 8	8 8
E	9 1	10 8	11 0	12 8	13 0	14 Valentine's Day 8	15 3
B	16 2	17 0	18 8	19 8	20 0	21 0	22 2
	23 0	24 0	25 0	26 8	27 8	28 8	1 1
M	2 3	3 8	4 8	5 0	6 8	7 0	8 Daughter's B'day 5
A	9 4	10 8	11 8	12 8	13 0	14 0	15 0
R	16 1	17 0	18 8	19 8	20 0	21 0	22 4
	23 0	24 0	25 0	26 8	27 8	28 Good Friday 2	29 3
	30 Easter Sunday 3	31 Easter Monday 4	1 8	2 0	3 0	4 0	5 2
A	6 2	7 0	8 8	9 8	10 0	11 8	12 1
P	13 0	14 0	15 0	16 8	17 8	18 0	19 4
R	20 3	21 8	22 0	23 0	24 0	25 6	26 4
	27 3	28 0	29 8	30 0	1 0	2 10	3 0
M	4 0	5 7	6 3	7	8	9	10
A	11 Mother's Day	12	13	14	15	16	17
Y	18	19 Victoria Day	20	21	22	23	24
	25	26	27	28	29	30	31

FIGURE 11.2. Case 1: Timeline for 90 days prior to assessment.

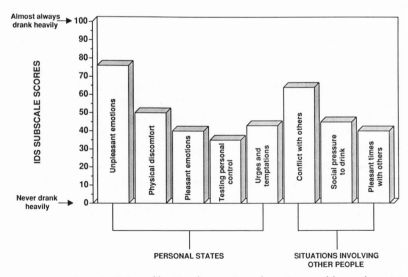

FIGURE 11.3. Case 1: IDS profile. For the version of scoring used here, the minimum possible score is 25.

heavy drinking most frequently occurred were when she felt bad or had been involved in an interpersonal conflict. Such a profile has long been considered typical of the drinking of chronic alcoholics. Over 30 years ago Jellinek (1960b) described the typical drinker on the way to becoming an "alcoholic" as having learned to drink as an inappropriate emotional coping response. While many common therapeutic approaches (e.g., relaxation training; social skills training; stress management; interpersonal process therapy; assertive training) are based on viewing heavy drinking as a way of coping with negative affect, fewer than 20% of the problem drinkers we have evaluated displayed this type of profile.

The client's answers to Homework Assignment 1, Part 1 (identifying her most serious problem drinking situations), were consistent with her IDS profile. She described her most serious problem drinking situation, accounting for approximately 95% of her heavy drinking, as drinking at home in the evening after her chores were done. This situation occurred when she had bad days at work and at home, and when she had too many things to do. Her second most serious problem drinking situation (occurring only 3% of the time) involved drinking in social situations in which she felt ill at ease and uncomfortable. Her third most serious problem drinking situation occurred on only 2% of all occasions and involved being in the company of other heavy drinkers who encouraged and condoned heavy drinking. As shown on her Timeline, she had some occasions of lesser drinking, which she estimated accounted for about 20% of all of her drinking. These limited drinking situations were reported to occur in social situations with light drinkers with whom she felt comfortable.

The situation of drinking at home in the evening after a hard day's work constituted this client's main problem drinking situation. Her proposed ways for dealing with this situation (as noted in her answers to Homework Assignment 2, Part 1) were to develop a reasonable schedule and method of organizing her time, and to develop a healthier life-style. Her action plan for accomplishing these steps included: (1) involve her children in dinner preparation; (2) insist on spending time on her projects; (3) not to let her husband's impulses interfere; (4) get a cleaning service; (5) join a health club and go three times a week; (6) eliminate caffeine; (7) schedule relaxation time from 7:30 to 8:00 PM; and (8) be in bed at 10:00 PM. This treatment plan, developed by the client, is notable for its concreteness and for relating her negative-affect drinking to factors in her life-style. In this case, there was no need to convince the client that getting some help with her chores and joining a health club would be valuable actions to take, she proposed those action steps herself.

Outcome

The client showed distinct improvement over the year following treatment. She greatly increased the number of abstinent days, going from 48% in the year prior to treatment to 79% in the year following treatment. She had no very heavy-drinking days (ten or more drinks) over the follow-up year, whereas prior to treatment 3% of her drinking days had been in that category. Her light-drinking days tripled, going from 21% of all drinking days prior to treatment to 67% following treatment. Although at the end of follow-up she rated her drinking as Not a Problem, and major changes had occurred in her drinking pattern, her subjective perception was that there had been little change in her drinking problem as compared to before treatment.

Case 2: Heavy Drinking Related Primarily to Positive Affective States and Social Pressure Situations

The most common IDS profile produced by the problem drinkers we have treated is reflected in the next two cases. The profile involves heavy drinking primarily associated with positive affective states, which sometimes occurs in social situations. Whereas negative affective state drinkers can be thought of as drinking heavily when they feel bad in order to feel "less bad," positive affective state drinkers can be thought of as drinking heavily when they feel good to feel "even better." This poses a dilemma for the many treatment approaches predicated on the assumption that heavy drinking is an inappropriate way of coping with negative affect. The clinical problem is a classic approach–avoidance conflict pitting the short-term positive consequences of heavy drinking against the risk of short- and long-term negative consequences.

This case involves a male client who was 42 years old when treated. His Clinical Assessment Summary appears in Figure 11.4. He was divorced, had 15 years of education, and lived alone. Unusual for this population, he reported having had a drinking problem for 22 years but had never received treatment. His score on the ADS was 11, but he evaluated his pretreatment drinking as a Very Major Problem, indicating that he had experienced at least two consequences that he considered to be "serious." The consequences he reported included blackouts, major interpersonal and financial problems, and minor vocational problems, including 15 days of missed work in the past year. This latter consequence was at the crux of his seeking treatment: He worked in emergency services where inattention or an incorrect decision could have very serious repercussions. He had discussed the problem with his employer, and they had agreed that he could pursue reducing his drinking, but that if he continued to miss work he would have to become involved in more intensive and almost certainly abstinence-oriented treatment. At assessment his goal was to drink no more than five standard drinks on no more than 3 days per week, and he maintained that goal at the end of treatment despite having been advised that his limit exceeded our recommendation. The key condition he set on his drinking was that he should not drink on nights

Name: _____   Date Completed: _____

CLINICAL ASSESSMENT SUMMARY

ADS Score: _11_   ADS Components: _Acute intoxication ; blackouts; unsuccessfully_
      tried to cut down.; feels can't usually stop.

Age: _42_   Sex: (**M**)   **F**   Yrs. Education: _15_   Marital Status: **M/CL**   **NM**   **S**   (**D**)   **W**

Employment Status: _Full-time_   Occupation: _Emergency services (specific job deleted)_

No. of Alcohol- or Drug-related Arrests: _0_   No. of Jobs lost due to Alcohol or Drug use in past year.: _0_

Ever purposely abstinent: **Y**   (**N**)   Longest no. mos. purposely abstinent : _N.A._   Family History of Alc. Problems: (**Y**)⁻¹ **N**

Prior A/D treatment: **Y**   (**N**)   Describe: _____

Problem Self–Appraisal: _Very major problem._

Alcohol Consequences: _Last 15 days of work; blackouts; interpersonal_
   conflicts; financial problems; health warning.

Other Drug Use: _Cigarettes; sporadic cannabis and hallucinogens use_

No. of Yrs. problem drinking: _22_   No. of Yrs. heavy drinking: _22_   No. days morning drinking in past yr.: _4_

Timeline	_147_ No.. of days Abstinent	_128_ No. of days 5 – 9 SDs
Past 360 days	_0_ No. of days 1 – 4 SDs	_85_ No. of days ≥ 10 SDs

Drinking (Patterns, features, or use characteristics): _No days of ≤ 4 drinks in past year._
   Typically 8-11 drinks about 4-5 days/week. Somewhat more
     frequent on weekends. Mostly beer.

☐ **IDS** (heavy use situations in past yr.): _Good times / social pressure pattern ._

☐ **SCQ** (vulnerability): _Mimics IDS but with social situations the_
       most vulnerable.

Goal: _≤ 5 standard drinks on ≤ 3 days per week. No drinking_
   in evening before a work day. Drink only at parties,
    sporting events, at dinner at a pub with friends.

Additional Observations: _Employer agreed to let him first attempt to_
   reduce his drinking. He will pursue abstinence
   if it doesn't work.

FIGURE 11.4. Case 2: Clinical Assessment Summary.

when he had to work the next day. He planned to confine his drinking to parties, sporting events, or occasions when he had dinner at a pub with friends.

Figure 11.5 displays an excerpt from the client's Timeline drinking report for the 90 days prior to his assessment. A particularly striking feature of the client's heavy drinking reported on the Timeline, but not shown in Figure 11.5, occurred approximately 7 months before entering treatment. At that time the client drank heavily on a daily basis for nearly 3 weeks. Also, during the pretreatment year, 5 drinks were the fewest he ever consumed on a drinking day, and his consumption typically ranged from 8 to 11 drinks per drinking day.

The client's IDS profile, displayed in Figure 11.6, shows three distinct peaks. Two occur for subscales for positive affective states (Pleasant Emotions; Pleasant Times with Others) and one occurs for the Social Pressure subscale. However, examination of the Social Pressure subscale items reveals that several could be categorized as fitting the Pleasant Times with Others subscale (e.g., "When I would be at a party and other people would be drinking").

This profile, referred to as Good Times–Social Pressure, characterized 40% of our problem drinker clients. When a peak on the Testing Control

	SUN	MON	TUES	WED	THURS	FRI	SAT
							1
J	2	3	4	5	6	7	8
U	9	10	11	12	13	14	15
N	16 Father's Day	17	18	19	20	21	22
	23	24	25	26	27 8	28 5	29 10
	30 0	1 Canada Day 0	2 8	3 10	4 9	5 0	6 0
J	7 10	8 0	9 0	10 0	11 0	12 10	13 11
U	14 10	15 9	16 0	17 0	18 0	19 9	20 9
L	21 9	22 10	23 0	24 0	25 0	26 8	27 8
	28 8	29 8	30 8	31 10	1 11	2 0	3 0
A	4 0	5 Civic Holiday 0	6 8	7 8	8 8	9 5	10 10
U	11 0	12 0	13 8	14 0	15 0	16 0	17 0
G	18 10	19 0	20 0	21 0	22 0	23 10	24 11
	25 10	26 9	27 0	28 0	29 0	30 9	31 9
S	1 9	2 Labour Day 10	3 0	4 0	5 0	6 8	7 8
E	8 8	9 8	10 8	11 10	12 11	13 0	14 0
P	15 0	16 0	17 8	18 8	19 8	20 5	21 10
	22 0	23 0	24 8	25	26	27	28
	29	30					

FIGURE 11.5. Case 2: Timeline for 90 days prior to assessment.

subscale occurred with the other peaks, the combined profiles accounted for 49% of all cases. Additionally, across all cases, 30% had profiles characterized by peaks with both negative and positive affective states. Importantly, this means that nearly three quarters of our problem drinker clients had positive affective states as one of the major situations related to their heavy drinking.

This client's Homework Assignment 1, Part 1, was consistent with his IDS profile. His most serious problem drinking situation was going on evenings when he had to work the next day to the local pub with friends or alone and drinking until the pub closed. His second most serious problem drinking situation involved the same behavior but when he did not have to work the next day. He estimated that these two situations accounted for approximately 90% of his problem drinking situations. His third most serious problem drinking situation involved his attending a sporting event or party and drinking until the event or party was over. Finally, he estimated that about 20% of the time when he drank he did not encounter problems. These were occasions he planned in advance.

His treatment plan involved avoiding his heavy-drinking friends and engaging in activities incompatible with heavy drinking. He indicated that he wanted to (1) join a social club so that he could meet new friends; (2) spend less time with old drinking buddies; (3) take a photography course; and (4) become involved in a fitness program. For dealing with party situations,

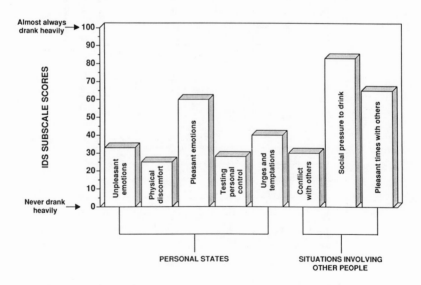

FIGURE 11.6. Case 2: IDS profile. For the version of scoring used here, the minimum possible score is 25.

he planned to go to the party late and drink beverages that would not usually be his first choice.

Outcome

A 1-year pretreatment–posttreatment comparison showed that this client's abstinent days doubled, increasing from 41% to 83% of all days. He only drank heavily (i.e., $\geq$ 10 drinks) on 2% of all drinking days, compared to 40% of all drinking days during the year before treatment. When he drank, however, the mean number of drinks per day was still above recommended limits (it had decreased only slightly from 8.9 drinks to 7.5 drinks per day). At 1 year after treatment he evaluated his drinking as Not a Problem. From the client's perspective, his major problem had been the way his drinking was interfering with his work performance, and it was on this basis that he judged his current drinking as no longer a problem.

Case 3: Heavy Drinking Related Primarily to Positive Affective States

The third case is a variation of the Good Times Drinking profile. The Clinical Assessment Summary for this case appears in Figure 11.7. Although positive affective states are well represented in the client's IDS profile (Figure 11.8), the Social Pressure subscale is not one of the most frequent heavy-drinking situations. The client was a 28-year-old white collar worker who had 15 years of education and lived with his common law spouse. He described himself as having been a problem drinker for 5 years prior to entering the program. Four years prior to his entry into the guided self-management treatment, he had participated in an outpatient treatment program.

The client described himself as primarily a weekend drinker, who typically drank beer, usually with others, and particularly in the company of a friend who drank more than he did. An excerpt from his pretreatment drinking Timeline appears in Figure 11.9 and it illustrates that the majority of his heavy drinking occurred on Fridays and Saturdays. While his total consumption of alcohol could not be described as extremely heavy, he reported interpersonal difficulties related to his drinking, as well as some blackouts, minor vocational consequences, and minor affective consequences. His score on the ADS was 10. He also reported that it was easier for him to moderate his drinking when his wife was nearby.

The client's reports of problem drinking situations on his homework paralleled his IDS profile. He described his most serious problem drinking situation as being at a celebration (e.g., Christmas, parties, weddings, other

Name: _____   Date Completed: _____

CLINICAL ASSESSMENT SUMMARY

ADS Score: __10__   ADS Components: _Blackouts; passed out; tried unsuccessfully_
_____ to stop; gulps.

Age: __28__   Sex: (M) F   Yrs. Education: __15__   Marital Status: (M/CL) NM   S   D   W

Employment Status: __Full-time__   Occupation: __Insurance adjuster__

No. of Alcohol- or Drug-related Arrests: __0__   No. of Jobs lost due to Alcohol or Drug use in past year.: __0__

Ever purposely abstinent: (Y) N   Longest no. mos. purposely abstinent : __1__   Family History of Alc. Problems: (Y) - N

Prior A/D treatment: (Y) N   Describe: _Outpatient counseling 4 yrs. prior - had been almost daily_
                                                                                                              drinker.
Problem Self–Appraisal: _Major problem. Describes self as mainly a weekend_
drinker who typically drinks beer in social situations and
particularly with one heavy drinker friend.

Alcohol Consequences: __Cognitive impairment; minor affective problems;__
interpersonal conflict; minor vocational; occasional blackouts.

Other Drug Use: _Rare use of other drugs, but none recently._

No. of Yrs. problem drinking: __5__   No. of Yrs. heavy drinking: __3__   No. days morning drinking in past yr.: __1__

| Timeline | __242__ No.. of days Abstinent | __34__ No. of days 5 – 9 SDs |
| Past 360 days | __81__ No. of days 1 – 4 SDs | __3__ No. of days ≥ 10 SDs |

Drinking (Patterns, features, or use characteristics): _Weekend pattern mainly with 10 drink_
maximum. Has gradually reduced intake over past year.

☐ IDS (heavy use situations in past yr.): _Good times pattern. Drinks heavily when feeling_
good, with or without others present. No marked social pressure component.
☐ SCQ (vulnerability): _Similar to IDS but also indicates some_
vulnerability in control testing situations.

Goal: _Reduce drinking to ≤ 2 drinks on ≤ 2 days per week,_
with upper limit of 3 drinks. Drink only during meals
when well rested, not at cottage, not in advance of social situations.

Additional Observations: _Has gained some control over his drinking since_
counselling - would like to improve it. Reports when near
his spouse he is more vigilant about keeping control of his drinking.

FIGURE 11.7. Case 3: Clinical Assessment Summary.

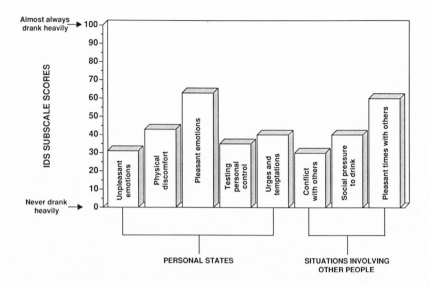

FIGURE 11.8. Case 3: IDS profile. For the version of scoring used here, the minimum possible score is 25.

	SUN	MON	TUES	WED	THURS	FRI	SAT
		1 Canada Day	2	3 O	4 O	5 2	6 4
J	7 O	8 O	9 O	10 O	11 2	12 2	13 4
U	14 O	15 O	16 O	17 O	18 O	19 O	20 2
L	21 O	22 O	23 O	24 6	25 O	26 3	27 3
	28 O	29 6	30 8	31 3	1 O	2 10	3 1
A	4 2	5 Civic Holiday 5	6 5	7 3	8 3	9 3	10 O
U	11 O	12 aline 2	13 O	14 O	15 O	16 3	17 3
G	18 O	19 O	20 O	21 1	22 O	23 6	24 5
	25 O	26 O	27 O	28 O	29 3	30 8	31 3
S	1 4	2 Labour Day O	3 O	4 O	5 O	6 3	7 4
E	8 O	9 O	10 O	11 1	12 O	13 3	14 8
P	15 O	16 O	17 O	18 O	19 O	20 2	21 6
	22 O	23 O	24 O	25 3	26 O	27 1	28 3
	29 2	30 O					

FIGURE 11.9. Case 3: Timeline for 90 days prior to assessment.

large gatherings). He estimated that such situations accounted for about 25% of his problem drinking. His second most serious situation involved "just sitting around on weekends, sometimes working, sometimes not." While this situation accounted for about half of his problem drinking, it was not his "most serious" problem drinking situation. Finally, he reported that about 10% of his problem drinking situations occurred on nights after work, when he had cocktails and dinner and returned home late.

Approximately 80% of all of his drinking situations involved small amounts of alcohol with no adverse consequences (e.g., business lunches, dinner at a restaurant, meeting with friends). Several such instances were apparent on his Timeline. This case illustrates that some problem drinkers exhibit good control much of the time when they drink. This client's history suggests that he would be a poor match for traditional alcohol treatment programs.

The client's treatment goal at assessment (before contact with the therapist) was to reduce his drinking to an average intake of two drinks on about 2 days per week, allowing himself three drinks on occasion. He planned to drink only when he was well rested and only during, not after, a meal. He planned not to drink when at his cottage, previously a favorite location for drinking with friends. He also planned not to drink in advance of social situations, particularly when he felt excited or exhilarated.

By the end of his second treatment session, the client had maintained the same limits on his drinking as he had set at assessment, except that his upper limit for special occasions was raised from three drinks to four drinks. He also modified the conditions under which he would drink. According to the new plan, he allowed himself only one drink with meals. But if he waited 3 hours after the meal, then he could have another drink. He also decided that he would only drink if he was actively doing something else at the same time, and that he would space his drinks at least 1 hour apart. In terms of situations where he would not drink, he expanded these to include when he was idle in the evening, when he might have to drive, when he was doing heavy labor, when he had not eaten, and when he felt very excited.

The client devised a multifaceted treatment plan that called for him to be prepared to miss a little excitement and enjoyment. In return, he felt his relationship with his spouse would improve, that their conversations would be better, and that his spouse would enjoy herself more. He felt that planning was very important, and he intended to schedule his evenings differently. In particular, he planned to structure his evenings with prearranged events, such as dinner and the theater with family or friends who were not heavy drinkers. He also decided he would set his drinking limit and let his wife know about it in advance. He felt that it was important to provide himself some external reason to limit his drinking. Thus he decided that if he gave himself responsibility for tasks such as driving home from or taking pictures at the event, this would help him limit his drinking (though the wisdom of risking driving while intoxicated, if he were to drink past his limit, is dubious). Other aspects of his treatment plan dealt more directly with drinking style. These included not having a drink immediately upon arrival at an event, drinking diluted drinks (e.g., light beer), and alternating nonalcoholic with alcoholic drinks. Finally, he determined that while at an event he should spend as much time as possible with his wife and that they should set a time limit on their attendance.

Outcome

The client's 1-year follow-up indicated a positive outcome. Compared to the year prior to treatment, his abstinence days decreased from 67% to 56%. His heavy-drinking days diminished from 3% to none, and the proportion of his total drinking days that were light-drinking days (≤ 4 drinks) increased from 22% to 97%. His mean number of drinks per drinking day decreased from 3.9 to 2.3. Finally, whereas prior to treatment he subjectively evaluated the severity of is drinking problem as Major (indicating one "serious" conse-quence), at 1 year following treatment he evaluated his problem as Very Minor, which was defined as worrying about the drinking, but not having experienced any adverse consequences.

Case 4: Heavy Drinking Related to Testing Personal Control

Testing Personal Control stands out in statistical analyses of the IDS as a relatively independent dimension of heavy-drinking situations. In practice, however, a peak on the Testing Personal Control subscale is usually associated with an affective profile. This next case presents a typical case in which a peak on Testing Personal Control is prominent. There are associated peaks on the two positive-affective and the social pressure subscales.

The client was a 35-year-old male with 20 years of education, who was unemployed at the time he entered treatment. His Clinical Assessment Summary appears in Figure 11.10. He was married with no children. He reported that he had been a heavy drinker, typically consuming more than five drinks on a drinking occasion for about 15 years prior to entering treatment. However, he stated that his drinking had only been a "problem" for the 5 years prior to treatment entry. He had never received any prior alcohol treat-ment. His ADS score was 17, higher than the group mean (13) for problem drinkers we have treated with guided self-management but still below the 50th percentile on norms for the ADS. He reported multiple consequences of his drinking, including physical aggression, complaints from his supervisor

Name: _____   Date Completed: _____

CLINICAL ASSESSMENT SUMMARY

ADS Score: _17_   ADS Components: _Hangovers; acute intoxication; blackouts;_
unsuccessful attempts to cut down; gulps; difficulty stopping.

Age: _35_   Sex: (M)   F   Yrs. Education: _20_   Marital Status: (M/CL)   NM   S   D   W

Employment Status: _Unemployed_   Occupation: _Civil Servant_

No. of Alcohol- or Drug-related Arrests: _0_   No. of Jobs lost due to Alcohol or Drug use in past year.: _0_

Ever purposely abstinent: Y   (N)   Longest no. mos. purposely abstinent : _N.A._   Family History of Alc. Problems: (Y)⁻¹ N

Prior A/D treatment: Y   (N)   Describe: _____

Problem Self–Appraisal: _Very major problem._

Alcohol Consequences: _Cognitive impairment; interpersonal conflict;_
physical aggression; work jeopardy; minor financial.

Other Drug Use: _None in recent years. Some occasion. use of cannabis; LSD many yrs ag_

No. of Yrs. problem drinking: _5_   No. of Yrs. heavy drinking: _15_   No. days morning drinking in past yr.: _0_

Timeline	_280_ No.. of days Abstinent	_7_ No. of days 5 – 9 SDs
Past 360 days	_36_ No. of days 1 – 4 SDs	_37_ No. of days ≥ 10 SDs

Drinking (Patterns, features, or use characteristics): _Isolated days of 10-15 drinks, usually on_
weekdays. Drinks mostly beer, mostly with others — some heavier
drinkers. Greatly increased number of light drinking days in past month.

☐ **IDS** (heavy use situations in past yr.): _Control testing peak, with slight_
elevations at affective scales.

☐ **SCQ** (vulnerability): _Shows same pattern as IDS._

Goal: _Goal at assessment exceeds recommendations. Desires_
occasional (less than weekly) consumption of 5 drinks and
sometimes 10, but only with his family.

Additional Observations: _Wants to avoid drinking at bars and_
sporting events.

FIGURE 11.10. Case 4: Clinical Assessment Summary.

when he had been working, blackouts, hangovers, and minor financial and interpersonal problems. The vast majority of his drinking was beer. An excerpt from his Timeline, displayed in Figure 11.11, illustrates that compared to other clients in the study his pattern tended to be bimodal, involving occasional days of low consumption (typically one or two drinks) or very high consumption. Since his heavy drinking almost always occurred on single isolated days, such a pattern can hardly be referred to as a "binge" pattern.

As already mentioned, this client's IDS profile, shown in Figure 11.12, has Testing Control as the most prevalent heavy-drinking situation. This was accompanied by peaks on the Pleasant Emotions, Pleasant Times with Others, and Pressure from Others subscales. An unusual feature of this case is that the client's IDS profile differed considerably from his profile on the SCQ. The client's SCQ profile appears as Figure 11.13 and illustrates that the client felt particularly vulnerable in control testing situations. An example of an item from the Testing Personal Control subscale of the IDS and SCQ is "If I would wonder about my self-control over alcohol and would feel like having a drink to try it out."

The types of high-risk situations the client identified in his homework assignments involved primarily affective (both positive and negative) and social occasions, with few explicit references to control testing. He described his

	SUN	MON	TUES	WED	THURS	FRI	SAT
			1	2	3	4	5
A	6	7	8	9	10 0	11 0	12 0
P	13 0	14 0	15 10	16 0	17 2	18 0	19 0
R	20 0	21 0	22 2	23 2	24 0	25 0	26 0
	27 0	28 2	29 0	30 0	1 1	2 0	3 0
M	4 0	5 0	6 10	7 5	8 0	9 0	10 0
A	11 Mother's Day 0	12 10	13 0	14 5	15 0	16 0	17 0
Y	18 0	19 Victoria Day 0	20 0	21 5	22 0	23 0	24 0
	25 0	26 0	27 20	28 0	29 0	30 0	31 0
J	1 0	2 0	3 0	4 0	5 2	6 2	7 10
U	8 2	9 2	10 2	11 2	12 2	13 10	14 2
N	15 Father's Day 2	16 0	17 2	18 0	19 2	20 2	21 0
	22 0	23 0	24 15	25 0	26 0	27 0	28 0
	29 0	30 0	1 Canada Day 0	2 0	3 0	4 1	5 0
J	6 0	7 0	8 0	9	10	11	12
U	13	14	15	16	17	18	19
L	20	21	22	23	24	25	26
	27	28	29	30	31		

FIGURE 11.11. Case 4: Timeline for 90 days prior to assessment.

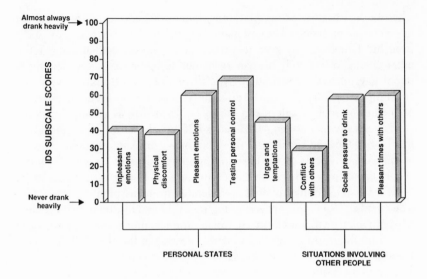

FIGURE 11.12. Case 4: IDS profile. For the version of scoring used here, the minimum possible score is 25.

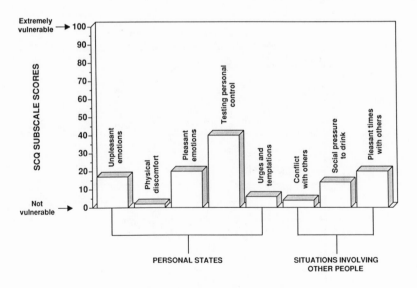

FIGURE 11.13. Case 4: SCQ profile.

most serious problem drinking situation, accounting for about 90% of his problem drinking, as getting drunk at the local bar. This tended to occur when he dropped into the bar after having been somewhere else (e.g., often following a sporting event) or started to drink too early in the day due to boredom (he was unemployed). His second most serious problem drinking situation (5% of his problem drinking situations) was drinking with friends at bars other than his local bar. This tended to be after spending an evening curling (the sport) with friends from his former job. In describing this situation, the client alluded to control testing, "Just getting together for a drink; 2 drinks turn into 5, 10, 15." His third problem drinking situation was a one-time occurrence. It took place at a large party related to his former job that he was expected to attend; his wife did not accompany him. In describing his non-problem-drinking situations (estimated as constituting about 60% of all drinking occasions), he reported functions or parties at which his wife was present. He identified the key factor in these situations as drinking with his wife and her friends.

The major feature of this client's self-developed treatment plan was avoiding drinking in bars, particularly his local bar. He felt the need to spend more time at home, to engage in more activities with his wife, and to participate more in sports. Acknowledging that there still might be occasions when he would go to a bar, he planned not to go there alone and to drink only in the company of close friends and family. He felt special efforts would be needed to deal with his tendency to drink in bars with friends after a sporting event. He felt it would help in dealing with such situations if he limited his attendance to the game itself, joined a league, and structured commitments (e.g., to meet his wife) within an hour after the event. Also, he felt it would be important to let his friends who played sports with him know that he would not be drinking. Finally, he planned that if an event should occur (e.g., a large party) where he felt uncomfortable, he would assess the situation beforehand and decide whether he should attend, bring his wife if he attended, and structure his time to arrive late and leave early. He also felt it would be better to attend small house parties with close friends than to attend large gatherings.

His goal at assessment was to reduce his drinking to no more than five drinks on average, to drink no more than ten drinks on an upper-limit day, and not to drink every day. He specified that he would drink only when family members were present. At the second treatment session, he modified these objectives to drinking no more than three drinks on a drinking day and to drinking on average less than once a week. One day per month he allowed himself four drinks as his upper limit. The conditions under which he would allow himself to drink continued to require the presence of family members, but he added that he would on rare occasions drink with friends. He further specified that he planned to abstain entirely for the first 3 months after treatment. Over the course of treatment, which took about 5 weeks, he was abstinent.

Outcome

This client's outcome results are instructive. Abstinent days typified the client's drinking in the year before and after treatment, increasing from 78% pretreatment to 89% posttreatment. Considering just those days when the client did drink, his proportion of drinking days when he drank 4 or fewer drinks stayed relatively constant, going from 45% pretreatment to 41% posttreatment. His days of heavy drinking (≥10 drinks), however, showed a marked decrease from 46% of all drinking days in the pretreatment year to 10% in the posttreatment year. His mean drinks per drinking day fell from 7.2 pretreatment to 5.2 posttreatment.

Although the amount of alcohol he consumed per drinking day at follow-up was clearly above our recommended level, a closer look at the clients' outcome data puts these results in perspective. The proportion of drinking days that were heavy drinking can be misleading unless one bears in mind the total number of days when any drinking occurred. For example, if a client drank on only 2 days posttreatment and drank heavily on one of those days, the client would technically have engaged in heavy drinking 50% of his or her drinking days. However, heavy drinking would only have occurred on one day during the entire year—an excellent outcome. In the present case, it should be noted that the vast majority of days in the posttreatment year were abstinent. Thus, in terms of the actual number of days of heavy drinking, there were 37 such days in the pretreatment year, but only 4 in the posttreatment year, representing a near elimination of days of extremely heavy intake. Lastly, at assessment he rated the severity of his drinking problem as Very Major, meaning that he had expeienced at least two drinking-related consequences that he felt were "serious." At the 1-year follow-up, he rated the severity of is problem for the posttreatment year as Minor, meaning that he had experienced some consequences, but none that he considered serious. The main outcome, therefore, was a drastic reduction in the number of heavy-drinking days.

Case 5: Heavy Drinking Across Most Situations

A relatively flat IDS profile can be thought of as undifferentiated, since it lacks distinct peaks among the subscale scores, although undifferentiated profiles that differ in overall elevation may also differ in their clinical relevance. For example, an undifferentiated but generally low profile might indicate a person for whom there are not many situational determinants of heavy drinking (or for whom the situational determinants of drinking, if any, are not assessed by the IDS) and who rarely drinks heavily. Such a profile could reflect a person who now and then drinks too much. In our experience, however, an undifferentiated profile that has a high elevation (high subscale scores) is likely to reflect a more serious case, where drinking is quite frequent and has come to pervade many aspects of a person's life (i.e., has become a generalized response). Although we have found undifferentiated profiles to be infrequent among problem drinkers, the following case is presented to illustrate the clinical features likely to accompany a flat, elevated profile.

The client was a 42-year-old married female with 20 years of education who worked as an accountant. Figure 11.14 presents her Clinical Assessment Summary. When she entered treatment she reported that she had drank five or more drinks per occasion for 24 years prior to entering treatment but that her drinking had only been a problem for her for the 4 years prior to treatment. Her ADS score was 21, the highest score that could qualify for the study. She reported consequences of blackouts, loss of coordination, hangovers, missed work, affective impairment when she combined drinking with the use of cannabis, and failed attempts at cutting down. She described her style as a steady drinker who drank mostly liquor and primarily when alone. She had not been in treatment previously. Her treatment goal at assessment and at the end of treatment was abstinence.

The excerpt from her Timeline shown in Figure 11.15 is representative of her drinking for the pretreatment year and shows a pattern of typically drinking six or seven drinks on 5 days per week. Her IDS profile, which appears as Figure 11.16, reflects the undifferentiated general elevation discussed earlier. In Homework Assignment 1 she described her most serious problem drinking situation as when she was alone at home. She estimated that such situations constituted about 75% of all of her problem drinking episodes. The major variation in situations was that on weekdays she began drinking later in the evenings, whereas on weekends she started earlier. She described her second most serious type of problem drinking situation as getting drunk at parties or when visiting with friends, which accounted for about 15% of her problem drinking occasions. The third problem drinking situation was when she was thinking about her mother. She reported that such circumstances were associated with about 10% of her problem drinking and that it was a virtual certainty that she would drink heavily in such situations. Interestingly, she reported that on rare occasions (2% of all drinking occasions) she was able to limit her drinking to small amounts without adverse consequences. Such situations were limited to her work environment (e.g., office Christmas party, business lunch).

With such clients it is important to discuss the role that conditioning, or habit strength, is likely to play as they attempt to change their behavior.

Name: _____   Date Completed: _____

CLINICAL ASSESSMENT SUMMARY

ADS Score: _21_   ADS Components: _Blackouts; loss of coordination; some_ _sickness next day; tried to cut down and failed._

Age: _42_   Sex: M (F)   Yrs. Education: _20_   Marital Status: (M/CL) NM S D W

Employment Status: _Full-time_   Occupation: _Accountant_

No. of Alcohol- or Drug-related Arrests: _0_   No. of Jobs lost due to Alcohol or Drug use in past year.: _0_

Ever purposely abstinent: (Y) N   Longest no. mos. purposely abstinent : _1_   Family History of Alc. Problems: (Y) -2 N

Prior A/D treatment: Y (N)   Describe: _____

Problem Self–Appraisal: _Major problem. Describes self as steady drinker_ _who mostly drinks liquor when alone._

Alcohol Consequences: _3 days missed work; cognitive impairment;_ _affective problems when combines drinking with cannabis;_ _some blackouts._

Other Drug Use: _Prescribed Atarax. Occasional cannabis, but doesn't see it as problem._

No. of Yrs. problem drinking: _4_   No. of Yrs. heavy drinking: _24_   No. days morning drinking in past yr.: _0_

Timeline	_100_ No.. of days Abstinent	_256_ No. of days 5 – 9 SDs
Past 360 days	_4_ No. of days 1 – 4 SDs	_0_ No. of days ≥ 10 SDs

Drinking (Patterns, features, or use characteristics): _Consistent moderately heavy intake_ _with a few abstinent days thrown in lately. Now focusing_ _more on weekends._

☐ IDS (heavy use situations in past yr.): _Fairly flat profile – not much_ _differentiation._

☐ SCQ (vulnerability): _Reports self as most vulnerable in control testing_ _situations and when affectively aroused (positive or negative)._

Goal: _Abstinence._

Additional Observations: _Quit smoking 13 years prior. Resolved drug_ _problem 18 years prior._

FIGURE 11.14. Case 5: Clinical Assessment Summary.

	SUN	MON	TUES	WED	THURS	FRI	SAT
		1 Canada Day	2	3	4	5	6
J	7	8	9 *6*	10 *6*	11 *6*	12 *6*	13 *6*
U	14 *6*	15 *6*	16 *6*	17 *6*	18 *6*	19 *6*	20 *6*
L	21 *6*	22 *6*	23 *6*	24 *6*	25 *6*	26 *6*	27 *6*
	28 *6*	29 *0*	30 *5*	31 *0*	1 *0*	2 *6*	3 *6*
A	4 *7*	5 Civic Holiday *5*	6 *5*	7 *0*	8 *0*	9 *6*	10 *6*
U	11 *7*	12 *5*	13 *5*	14 *0*	15 *0*	16 *6*	17 *6*
G	18 *7*	19 *5*	20 *5*	21 *0*	22 *0*	23 *6*	24 *6*
	25 *7*	26 *5*	27 *5*	28 *0*	29 *0*	30 *7*	31 *7*
S	1 *6*	2 Labour Day *6*	3 *7*	4 *0*	5 *7*	6 *0*	7 *6*
E	8 *6*	9 *0*	10 *6*	11 *0*	12 *6*	13 *0*	14 *6*
P	15 *6*	16 *0*	17 *6*	18 *7*	19 *0*	20 *0*	21 *3*
	22 *0*	23 *6*	24 *0*	25 *0*	26 *7*	27 *4*	28 *5*
	29 *0*	30 *0*	1 *0*	2 *8*	3 *0*	4 *4*	5 *1*
O	6 *0*	7	8	9	10	11	12
C	13	14 Thanksgiving	15	16	17	18	19
T	20	21	22	23	24	25	26
	27	28	29	30	31 Halloween		

FIGURE 11.15. Case 5: Timeline for 90 days prior to assessment.

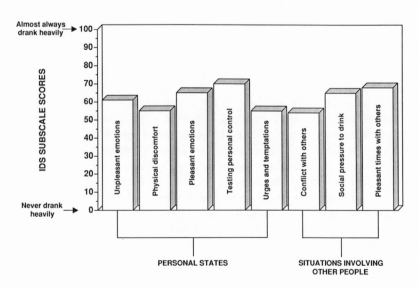

FIGURE 11.16. Case 5: IDS profile. For the version of scoring used here, the minimum possible score is 25.

Clients who have a regularized, if not ritualized, pattern of consumption can readily understand that it should be expected that there will be a strong habit component to their drinking. This can lead to a discussion that in breaking any habit, not just drinking, temporary discomfort should be expected to accompany the change. The client should understand that the discomfort does not have a mystical basis. Rather, there will be problems such as are associated with changing any well-practiced behavior pattern. The client can be asked to remember some habit that he or she wanted to break at one time and to focus in particularly on how the discomfort subsided over time. This exercise is intended to reinforce the point that it is natural to feel discomfort at changing a well-practiced behavior and that to some extent success at changing the pattern will require tolerating the discomfort until "not engaging in the behavior" becomes the new normal state.

In terms of the client's self-devised treatment plan, she felt it was essential that she make new friends and get out of the house so that she would not be alone at home. She met two new friends over the course of treatment and intended to get out of the house or to invite friends over at least one night per week. She also thought it would be helpful to ask her spouse to do things with her on weekends. To fill her time at home, she planned to buy a sewing machine and begin projects (e.g., Christmas gifts, house redecorating). She also accepted the nomination to become the vice-president of a club to which she belonged. She felt that having to prepare for speaking engagements would occupy her time and make drinking more difficult. Finally, she planned to speak with a wardrobe consultant and to take a makeup course to increase her self-esteem and confidence. She stated: "You don't have to look 'dated.'"

Outcome

Except for 1 day early in treatment the client was abstinent throughout the course of treatment. After treatment, her drinking was greatly diminished for the posttratment year compared to the pretreatment year: She went from 28% abstinent days during the pretreatment year to 96% abstinent days during the year following treatment. Her light drinking (1–4 drinks) increased from 1% pretreatment to 56% of all drinking days. As for heavy-drinking days ($\geqslant 10$ drinks), she had none in the pretreatment year, while these constituted 7% of her drinking days in the posttreatment year. While her mean drinks per drinking day decreased from 6.1 pretreatment to 4.0 posttreatment, the more impressive change was in her actual drinking days. They declined from 260 days in the year prior to treatment to a posttreatment year total of 14 days (about one drinking day per month). Finally, while she had evaluated her drinking as a Major Problem (negative consequences, of which at least one was "serious") prior to treatment, she rated it as Not a Problem at the 1-year follow-up.

This chapter was intended to provide readers with an overview of the types of clients for whom this treatment approach was developed and to highlight the abilities that the clients themselves ought to bear in dealing with their problems. The examples presented here were not selected as the "best," but rather to exemplify different types of IDS profiles. These examples clearly illustrate that problem drinkers not only can take responsibility for dealing with their own problems, but that they can be quite creative and ingenious.

12

Outcomes and Afterthoughts

Because this book is a treatment manual and not a scientific report, it does not contain detailed treatment outcome data about the guided self-management treatment approach with problem drinkers. Some discussion of those findings is relevant, however, and is included to the extent that it is instructive or raises important clinical issues. The findings discussed here derive from our evaluation of a two-session (90 minutes each) version of the treatment.

While the guided self-management approach has been evaluated in one major study, other studies have also evaluated variations of this approach (L. C. Sobell & M. B. Sobell, 1992a; Romach et al., 1991; Sobell, Sobell, & Leo, 1990; Sellers et al., 1991). It is important to note that many of the current treatment components have previously been well validated in other behavioral treatments. Functional analysis, for example, is a cornerstone of behavioral treatments for alcohol problems. In many ways, the guided self-management approach can be viewed as a standard behavioral treatment with a strong motivational component. In evaluating the treatment it is important to examine outcomes and to take note of clients' perceptions of the appropriateness of the approach as well as the therapists' comfort in delivering the procedures. Since it is common in the alcohol field to find few substantial differences in effectiveness between methods (when pretreatment status of clients and other potentially confounding factors are controlled), matters such as attractiveness to clients and cost effectiveness are important determinants of treatments of choice.

Three types of findings will be discussed: (1) treatment outcome data—how clients fared during and after treatment; (2) interviews conducted with former clients about their views of the treatment; and (3) interviews conducted with therapists who used the treatment. Each perspective contributes to the total picture of what happened to clients who participated in a guided self-management treatment. The findings presented are from the major evaluative study of the approach.

154

The Topography of Outcomes

The outcomes of clients treated by the guided self-management approach are generally consistent with findings for other behavioral treatments with problem drinkers (Sobell, Sobell, & Leo, 1990). For example, in the year following treatment, the total number of drinks consumed was reduced by approximately 54%. There were significant increases in the number of abstinent days and the number of days of drinking four or fewer drinks, and there was a significant decrease in heavy-drinking days (i.e., ten or more drinks). Nevertheless, ideal outcomes were relatively rare. As an example, in most cases there were at least a few days of drinking beyond the recommended limits. In terms of consequences, they were greatly diminished, although some still occurred. Overall, this study found major reductions in drinking and significant improvements in functioning.

The differences in drinking took place over the course of treatment, and the average length of time from assessment until the end of the second treatment session was about 5 weeks. The changes were then sustained and even improved somewhat over the first year of follow-up. Clients' subjective judgments of how they fared were similar to their outcome data. These data are graphically displayed in Figure 12.1. This figure portrays clients' ratings of their drinking problem severity for the year prior to treatment and the year following treatment using the categories described in Table 3.2 (see p. 24).

Figure 12.1 shows that the treatment outcomes for all clients can be described as improved. There is a clear and major shift along the dimension of problem severity. Thus, while before treatment the vast majority of clients classified their drinking problem as Major or Very Major, after treatment most clients classified their drinking problem as Minor and about a quarter dscribed themselves as problem free (a rating of Very Minor was operationally defined as having experienced no negative consequences).

Our major evaluative study found that the inclusion of relapse prevention components in the treatment did not confer any advantage in terms of treatment outcome (Sobell, Sobell, & Leo, 1990). Moreover, data from the study indicated that only 10% of the clients reported that they tended to drink heavily on the day following a day of heavy drinking (i.e., they did not drink in a manner that conforms to explanation by the relapse prevention model). Despite the findings, all therapists felt it was awkward to conduct the treatment without mentioning relapse prevention issues, and clients who received the relapse prevention version of the treatment saw those components as valuable. Considering that there was no difference in the amount or intensity of treatment when cognitive relapse prevention procedures were incorporated, it is recommended that they be retained. However, therapists should be careful in how the likelihood of relapse is communicated to clients. Problem drinker clients should not be led to expect that relapse is so common as to be nearly inevitable. The emphasis should be placed on maintaining commitment to change even if setbacks occur. The aspect of relapse prevention that is most consistent with a motivational intervention is the importance of remaining committed to recovery over time.

In terms of treatment goals, very little change occurred over the course of follow-up. About 10% to 20% of clients changed their goal sometime between the assessment and the end of the first year of follow-up. Of these, about one third changed from abstinence to a reduced-drinking goal, and the remainder changed from reduced-drinking to an abstinence goal.

Level of education emerged as a factor in two ways. First we found that better-educated clients preferred a goal of reduced drinking. Those clients who selected a reduced-drinking goal at assessment were significantly better educated (mean education = 15.3 years) than those who selected abstinence (mean education = 12.8 years). Second, we found that better-educated clients

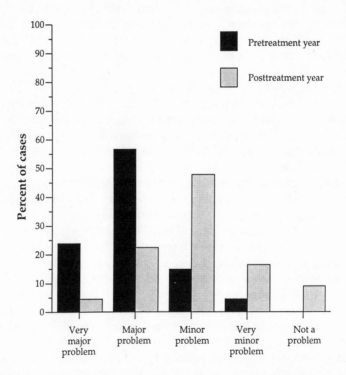

FIGURE 12.1. Clients' ratings of problem severity in their pretreatment year and posttreatment year. Note that a rating of "Very Minor Problem" means that the individual had not experienced any negative consequences of drinking but worried about his or her drinking.

preferred to choose their goal. In another study we conducted (Sobell, Sobell, Bogardis, Leo, & Skinner, 1992), clients with at least some university education were significantly more likely to prefer to select their own goal (78%) compared to clients with less education (51% preferred goal self-selection). This suggests that a program such as guided self-management may have particular appeal to better-educated problem drinkers.

About half of the clients in the guided self-management treatment reported at their 2-year follow-up interview that the amount of treatment had been sufficient and that the overall outcome of the treatment was quite positive. The rest felt that the 2-session treatment had been too brief, and about the same number reported they had sought further treatment after their second session. An analysis comparing the drinking of clients who did not seek further treatment with those who did found some differences between the groups. Those who sought further treatment had lower levels of abstinence prior to treatment and smaller increases in abstinence days than those who did not seek further treatment. Also, while the percentage of heavy-drinking days (i.e., ten or more drinks) prior to treatment did not differ between the groups, those who did not seek treatment showed a marked decrease in heavy drinking after treatment compared to little change for those who sought additional treatment.

Those clients who sought further treatment most frequently received that treatment at the same agency that had provided the formal guided self-management treatment, and they uniformly reported that the additional sessions were "helpful." Attendance at Alcoholics Anonymous meetings, even when sporadic, was reported as the next most helpful additional treatment.

That about half of the clients felt that their brief treatment experience was sufficient suggests that a substantial number of problem drinkers respond well to a brief self-managment oriented approach. The use of a brief self-management treatment for persons whose problems are not severe and who are accepting of the approach is a sensible "front end" approach to providing services for problem drinkers. That about half of the clients felt that they needed additional treatment communicates that it is also important to provide supplementary services for these clients.

Client Perceptions of Guided Self-Management

An important but seldom investigated aspect of most treatments is how they are perceived by clients. Part of the 2-year follow-up interview for the guided self-management treatment asked clients to evaluate various components of their treatment. If a client did not recall a component, they were reminded of it before being asked for an evaluation.

Treatment Components

Clients' recall of procedures and aspects of the treatment varied from component to component. The best-recalled components were the homework assignments (recalled by 92%) and the use of self-selected goals (91%). Both of these components involved clients actively completing forms. Recall of other aspects of the treatment (e.g., number of sessions, identifying triggers) was somewhat lower (70% to 80%). However, only 21% recalled that the treatment was specifically designed for problem drinkers. And of those treated with the relapse prevention version of the treatment, only 23% recalled the emphasis on a long-term perspective on recovery, and only 47% recalled that slips should be construed constructively.

Clients were asked to rate the helpfulness of each component. All components were evaluated as helpful by at least a majority (55% to 85%) of the clients interviewed. One component, however, stood out among all others: The therapists were rated as helpful by 84% of all clients. The two components with the lowest helpfulness ratings were the readings (55%) and the follow-up (56%).

Clients' Outcome Attributions

An important question for motivational interventions concerns clients' attributions about what they feel contributed to their outcome. Clients were asked to comment about whether and to what extent (i.e., Very Much, Somewhat, or Not at All) each of the following contributed to their outcome: themselves, the treatment program, their therapist, and other factors ("things outside of treatment that occurred in your life"). Consistent with a motivational intervention, 73% of the clients stated that they had contributed Very Much to their outcome, whereas 41% rated the treatment as having contributed Very Much, and 33% said that their therapist contributed Very Much to their outcome.

Almost half (48%) of the clients rated other factors as having contributed Very Much to their outcome. Clients' descriptions of other factors were more often reported as positive than negative factors. Three types of positive factors emerged. The most prevalent factor was social support. This finding is consistent with studies of natural recovery (recovery without treatment), where the most prominent factor reported as helping persons maintain their recoveries has been support by their spouse, family, and friends (Sobell, Sobell, & Toneatto, 1992; Sobell, Sobell, Toneatto, & Leo, in press). The other two types of positive other factors contributing very much to clients' reports of outcome were additional treatment and changes in circumstances. Table 12.1 provides a summary of these positive other factors.

TABLE 12.1. Positive Other Factors Contributing Very Much to Clients' Reports of Outcome

---

Social Support
  Continued encouragement from their spouse
  Verbal admonitions to stop drinking by family
  Support from friends in the form of not encouraging drinking
  Desire of the client to maintain a relationship by resolving drinking problem
Additional Treatment
Changes in Circumstances
  Job circumstances (e.g., changed from one job to another; positive changes at work)
  Marital status (e.g., divorced from a bad marriage)
  Other (e.g., became more settled by having a baby; bought a house; made new
    friends; went back to school)

A small number of negative influences were also identified. These focused on marital problems (e.g., divorce, separation, custody problems).

Again, the most important point about clients' attributions is that three quarters saw themselves as Very Much responsible for their outcome. This is very consistent with a motivational treatment.

Goal Self-Selection

Clients were asked whether choosing their own goal was a Good Thing or a Bad Thing. Eighty-one percent of the clients felt that being able to choose their own goal was a Good Thing. The main reasons given by clients for this were: (1) resistance to having decisions forced on them; (2) that they felt more motivated to achieve a self-set goal; (3) that they liked to take responsibility for decisions affecting themselves; and (4) that self-selection was a realistic procedure in that they had ultimate responsibility for their behavior. Examples of clients' responses (some paraphrased and some verbatim) to the open-ended inquiry about why they said choosing their own goal was a Good Thing follow:

- "Can set reasonable goal which I can achieve, accomplish."
- Individuals must ultimately assume responsibility to control their drinking, a good initial step.
- May not be as motivated to listen to other's advice.
- "Wouldn't stick to goals if they were forced on me; you have to make up your own mind."
- "Placed responsibility on me."
- "You're your own boss; not being told what to do."

- Suited the type of person she is—wouldn't respond to someone else telling her what to do—responsibility was up to her to meet her own goals.
- "Up to you to be able to stop yourself; no one else can tell you what to do."
- "Feel you're in control, able to set own limits."
- Doesn't take well to someone telling her what to do; felt that self-determination was the only approach.
- "Not so much choosing, as a realistic goal was coached out of me. I would have to change whole personality type to accept external goals and values."
- Liked having the freedom of choice (with advice). Type of person who has personal integrity such that if he makes a commitment (to himself, especially) he would strive to achieve it.
- "Because if you see a goal not working, then you have the ability to change it versus being told there's only one way to go."

A few clients rated goal self-selection as a Bad Thing. These clients responded that they had decided they needed a more direct approach because they either felt unable to exercise control over their behavior or felt they might make a poor decision, especially early in treatment.

Clients were also asked what types of people should choose their own treatment goals and what types of people should have their goals assigned by their therapist. Clients described good candidates for goal self-selection as persons who have less-severe drinking problems, have more self-determination, are highly motivated, are used to working earnestly toward goals, are honest with themselves, who have a history of prior control, and who have resources to call upon. Examples of clients' responses (some paraphrased and some verbatim) to the question about what types of individuals should choose their own treatment goals follow:

- "Those that are honest with themselves and who know what their limits are."
- "Those with their physical and mental health and some external resources."
- "Less acute, milder drinking problems; capable of running their lives, making decisions more."
- "Clients who are able to deal with working toward goals."
- Those who are in early stages and might be able to work toward a moderation goal.
- People that can self-manage, who have motivation, and are not severely dependent.
- "Someone who is accustomed to making their own choices, if they've decided they have a problem."

- "People who have less-severe problems; depends how good people are at controlling their drinking."
- Still have some "support," e.g., emotional, financial, going for them.
- "Ones who aren't as dependent or people who have more self-determination."
- People who have the resources or strengths to set their own goals and work toward achieving them.

The types of persons that our clients thought should have their goals assigned by the therapist were in many ways the opposite of those they thought should select their own goals. Those seen as appropriate for therapist goal assignment were described as more severely dependent, unable to take care of themselves, in need of strong direction, and low in willpower, support, or ability to help themselves. Rather than focusing on a perceived inability to control drinking as the major feature dictating which type of individual should have their goals assigned by the therapist, many of the statements described persons who are responsive to authority and look to others for direction. Examples of clients' descriptions (some paraphrased and some verbatim) of features of individuals who should have their treatment goals set by the therapist follow:

- More severe alcohol problem; more negative effects of drinking; unable to take care of themselves.
- "Depends on pattern—long history of alcoholism—difficult stopping—unrealistic."
- "People who need someone in authority."
- "Repeat clients [i.e., in treatment] who have shown that they are unable to work towards self-set goals."
- "Those whose physical and mental health is severely damaged and have no motivation or skills in language, job, society."
- "Self-admitted alcoholics."
- "Those who are habitual drinkers or have severe problems."
- Severely dependent clients and those without outside support or resources (e.g., no job, family).
- "People who like to fool themselves."
- "People who lack self-control and have a severe drinking problem—severity."
- "People that need more direction."
- "People accustomed to taking other peoples' definitions of themselves."
- "People more comfortable in authoritarian situations."
- "Very severely dependent people who may not be able to deal with their problem without someone else telling them what to do."
- People who don't have any "support."

- "People who aren't able to set goals and need an authoritative voice to tell them what to do."
- "People who want to be told what to do; who need authoritative influence."

Improving Guided Self-Management

Nearly all (97%) of the clients interviewed said that the guided self-management treatment should continue to be available. When asked how the treatment could be improved, the most frequent recommendation was that additional treatment should be provided, although this was often mentioned in terms of "aftercare" sessions with the therapist. Examples of the comments by clients (some paraphrased and some verbatim) about ways to improve the treatment follow:

- "Regular support group with staff would have been helpful but not in terms of the AA approach"—dislikes AA philosophy and setup.
- More follow-up with therapist.
- Feels that group sessions would be helpful, i.e., sharing experiences with others trying to abstain from or control their drinking. "Like AA but not rigid."
- More treatment sessions.
- "For interested clients, teach them about the medical effects of alcohol on their bodies and to recognize effects of alcohol."
- More therapist contact, e.g., phone contact during follow-up to see how client is doing.
- Should be stressed that this program is no guarantee, i.e., "that it is not for everyone and that there are other treatment options if this program wasn't working."
- Interaction with another person, i.e., clients, to exchange experiences. "Lets you know you're not alone; comparison as a motivator."
- More flexibility in terms of amount of treatment contact, depending on the individual's needs.
- More contact with therapist and with follow-up.
- More structured, more motivational, more directive treatment.

Other Observations

Clients were given an opportunity to make additional comments if they wished. Comments selected because they are particularly meaningful in relation to the nature of the intervention follow:

- [Therapist] was very helpful. Remembers that she did more listening than speaking, letting client talk herself out, facing up to problems that she may not have wanted to admit. Very happy about what the program did for her. Although she had some slips in the beginning, she is now abstinent with no desire to drink, realizing she was the only one who could make changes in her life.

- "Analytical approach" [identifying problem situations and triggers and how to deal with them] suited his way of dealing with his life. Also liked the "soft sell" of the program, that is, not labeling patient as an "alcoholic" but talking in terms of negative consequences and how to deal with problems. Liked the emphasis that recovery wasn't black and white (success/failure), that slips may occur and not to overdramatize it and not to give up.

- The staff were nonjudgmental. Feels that the program didn't work for her. Perhaps she lacked enough motivation to change "on her own." Efforts to stick to drinking goals took too much effort. Found goals to be somewhat artificial. Realized that abstinence may be the only way for her because even having one drink after abstinence can lead to overindulging.

- "It helped me realize that total abstinence was my only hope."

- Program wasn't intensive, which fit his life-style—work schedule, problem-solving approach.

- It suited her life-style, cognitive style. She likes to be in control, analyzes things in her life, and likes things orderly. The fact that from the first step of filling out questionnaires in assessment, which helped her see patterns in her drinking, to being able to set goals that matched her view that responsibility was on her, to the emphasis of doing it on her own, and the nonjudgmental approach of everyone that she came into contact with, which suited her view of wanting to be in control and not having others tell her what to do—"all this was very good." She commented that not many people know about [the facility], and many people like herself would probably not pursue treatment because of stigma and of "alcoholism" and only knowing about treatment for severely dependent people, "alcoholics."

- Felt that this program was geared toward the middle class with their associated beliefs, toward a self-assertive "pull up your bootstraps" [sic] type of person and, therefore, not appropriate for people who are more passive. He described himself as taking a more "passive random" approach to life and the structured behavioral assertive orientation did not appeal to or fit in with his way of living.

- Filling out the questionnaires and homework assignments was good because you put the problem down on paper and you can look at it. "You see things that you normally wouldn't be aware of just experiencing the problem."

- Liked how the program was tailored to her individual needs, and the problem-solving strategy suited her. What was very helpful but difficult to do were the homework assignments. To have to write things down and have it in front of her was enlightening. Exactly what she needed to deal with her problem.

• Nonjudgmental. Had a friend who went to [another facility] and was told by their staff that he didn't have a drinking problem and therefore wasn't eligible for treatment. He liked the fact that [this facility] didn't do that and was able to help him even if his problem wasn't deemed "serious."

• Best part of the program was being able to talk to [her therapist] about her drinking without feeling that [the therapist] was being judgmental or without being afraid of censure. The cognitive approach was compatible with the way she thinks, and she appreciated the fact that the program treated her with respect, that is, that she was intelligent and resourceful enough to deal with her drinking.

• The treatment program provided a framework for dealing with his problem that was very compatible with the way he manages his life and business, that is, using problem-solving strategies, setting objectives for himself to achieve.

• Did not see how others in the program could manage to deal with their problems on their own (self-management), as she found it very difficult. She said perhaps if a person had a good "support" system (e.g., friends and family), they could do it. Since she didn't have that kind of support, she found it difficult.

Therapist Perceptions of Guided Self-Management

A final perspective on guided self-management treatment comes from the therapists who conducted the treatment. Four therapists who were involved in a treatment study were interviewed. Our own views are also relevant because we were among the therapists who conducted the treatment with these clients. The interview questions and answers are summarized below.

The therapists were unanimous in their recollections that prior to the study they had concerns that the treatment might not be sufficient. This concern, however, was addressed by allowing clients to request further treatment after the required sessions had been completed. The therapists also noted that the clients differed somewhat from the regular flow of outpatient clients in that their problems were less severe and that they were more socially stable.

Therapists' Impressions

As with the clients, therapists were asked to evaluate the helpfulness of the various instruments and procedures. The assessment instruments that received the highest ratings by the therapists were the Inventory of Drinking Situations, which was described as accelerating treatment planning, and the Clinical Assessment Summary, which provided a quick reference to the essential features of the case. The Goal Statement, which was also rated highly, was seen as helping clients take responsibility for setting their own goals. The drinking Timeline was evaluated as providing a longitudinal picture of the client's drinking: In one display the Timeline captured drinking levels, patterns, and trends over time and often had notations about life events related to the drinking. The Timeline was seen as helpful to clients in terms of illustrating patterns in their drinking and calling their attention to the extent of their drinking.

With regard to treatment components, the readings, especially the diagram of Mount Recovery, were highly rated. The procedure of goal self-selection was also seen as very valuable. One therapist described completion of the Goal Statement as a "ritual of commitment and self-review." The availability of further treatment after the second session was seen as an essential "safety net." Two other highly regarded treatment components were the relapse prevention procedures and the problem-solving guidelines. One therapist described the problem-solving guidelines as making the cost of changing clear to clients.

When therapists were asked to identify three components that they liked most about the approach and procedures of the program, they identified: (1) the readings, homework, and Goal Statement; (2) that the treatment was tailored to persons who were not severely dependent and was oriented toward clients taking responsibility for managing their own affairs; and (3) that the treatment was practical and straightforward.

Therapists were also asked to identify three components of the program that they disliked most. Much of the concern here focused on the brevity of treatment (the 2-session treatment model). The therapists also noted that it was difficult to complete the required procedures in the allotted time for clients who had other concerns (e.g., marital problems). Some of the unhappiness with the shortness of the treatment was related to the treatment's lack of focus on maintenance of change. However, it is important to note that these criticisms of the treatment relate in part to the necessity of standardizing procedures in a treatment research study; in clinical practice procedures can be modified to fit the needs of each case.

Almost all the therapists felt that it would be beneficial to extend the treatment to three or four sessions. It was suggested that a few maintenance (aftercare) appointments be scheduled at the end of the second session that could be subsequently canceled by the client if he or she felt that he or she did not need them. The thinking was that the prescheduling would allow clients access to further treatment without having to make a request for it.

Therapists were also asked to suggest which types of clients they thought would do well with the guided self-management approach. In general, they felt that well-motivated, socially stable, low-dependence drinkers would be the best candidates. They also felt that the client's educational level was important and availability of supports (e.g., from significant others) were important, and that the person should perceive "choice" as possible and desirable.

All but one therapist, who was no longer working in the alcohol field, responded that they had occasion to utilize guided self-managment procedures or materials since the completion of the study. Interestingly, despite being unaware of the results when interviewed, they had a view of the treatment that was consistent with the outcome results. They thought that the approach worked well with some but not all of the clients. They thought that for almost all of the clients in the study it was a good way to start treatment, with access to further treatment being an essential backup provision for those who were not able to change their behavior sufficiently from a brief intervention.

Finally, the therapists noted that clients' ability to analyze their drinking and develop a treatment plan varied considerably. As a result therapists needed to be flexible in the extent to which they devoted time to these matters in the sessions.

On Implementing Guided Self-Management Treatment in Clinical Practice

As with treatment approaches for other types of problems, it is important for therapists to recognize that there are a variety of potentially effective treatment strategies and procedures that constitute their overall therapeutic armamentarium, with the approach to any specific case determined by the particular features of that case. Considered in this way, guided self-management is a good first treatment of choice for some people. It is low cost, minimally intrusive, and consistent with maintaining or increasing clients' self-esteem. It also is clear that many problem drinkers are quite satisfied with a self-management, cognitively oriented treatment approach that includes goal self-selection. As we stated earlier, there will be some problem drinkers who do not do well with such an approach, even though they might begin the treatment thinking that it would be a good match. Thus, clients' functioning should be monitored after the formal sessions are completed, and additional or alternative treatment should be available for those who continue to have problems.

Although our research found no advantage for including relapse prevention as part of the treatment, it is notable that the therapists found it awkward to conduct therapy without it. However, those clients who received guided self-management without the relapse prevention components did not perceive the treatment as awkward. From the standpoint of clinical practice, it seems reasonable to inform clients that the road to recovery might well have its ups and downs. Thus, we still recommend inclusion of the relapse prevention components and have presented the treatment that way in this book.

In summary, our presentation of guided self-management treatment has focused on how to conduct the treatment in community treatment settings rather than in research projects. There is no rigorous order to the procedures, no requirement that all procedures be used or used in the same intensity with each client, and no arbitrary specification of how many sessions are necessary. Guided self-management is a motivational intervention where the aim is to enable clients to solve their own problems. Motivational interventions are a recent development among treatments for alcohol problems (Miller & Rollnick, 1991), and as such there is abundant room for further innovations. The essential thing is that clinicians keep in mind the principle of helping clients help themselves.

References

Adams, L. D., & Henley, J. R. (1977). Measuring various drug use dimensions with a calendar method. *International Journal of the Addictions, 12,* 423–427.

Alden, L. (1988). Behavioral self-management controlled drinking strategies in a context of secondary prevention. *Journal of Consulting and Clinical Psychology, 56,* 280–286.

Allsop, S., & Saunders, B. (1989a). Relapse: A critique. In M. Gossop (Ed.), *Relapse and addictive behaviors* (pp. 249–277). New York: Tavistock/Routledge.

Allsop, S., & Saunders, B. (1989b). Relapse and alcohol problems. In M. Gossop (Ed.), *Relapse and addictive behaviour* (pp. 11–40). New York: Tavistock/Routledge.

American Psychiatric Association. (1987). *Diagnostic and statistical manual of mental disorders* (3rd ed., rev.). Washington, DC: Author.

Annis, H. M. (1986a). Is inpatient rehabilitation of the alcoholic cost effective? Con position. *Advances in Alcohol and Substance Abuse, 5,* 175–190.

Annis, H. M. (1986b). A relapse prevention model for the treatment of alcoholics. In W. R. Miller & N. Heather (Eds.), *Treating addictive behaviors: Processes of change* (pp. 407–435). New York: Pergamon Press.

Annis, H. M., & Davis, C. S. (1988a). Assessment of expectancies. In D. M. Donovan & G. A. Marlatt (Eds.), *Assessment of addictive behaviors* (pp. 84–111). New York: Guilford Press.

Annis, H. M., & Davis, C. S. (1988b). Self-efficacy and the prevention of alcoholic relapse: Initial findings from a treatment trial. In T. Baker & D. Cannon (Eds.), *Assessment and treatment of addictive behaviors* (pp. 88–112). New York: Praeger.

Annis, H. M., & Graham, J. M. (1988). *Situational Confidence Questionnaire (SCQ 39): User's guide.* Toronto: Addiction Research Foundation.

Annis, H. M., Graham, J. M., & Davis, C. S. (1987). *Inventory of Drinking Situations (IDS) User's Guide.* Toronto: Addiction Research Foundation.

Atkinson, R. M., Tolson, R. L., & Turner, J. A. (1990). Late versus early onset problem drinking in older men. *Alcoholism: Clinical and Experimental Research, 14,* 574–579.

Babor, T. F., Kranzler, H. R., & Lauerman, R. J. (1987). Social drinking as a health and psychosocial risk factor. Anstie's limit revisited. In M. Galanter (Ed.),

169

Recent developments in alcoholism (Vol. 5, pp. 373–402). New York: Plenum Press.

Babor, T. R., Ritson, E. B., & Hodgson, R. J. (1986). Alcohol-related problems in the primary health care setting: A review of early intervention strategies. *British Journal of Addiction, 81,* 23–46.

Babor, T. F., Stephens, R. S., & Marlatt, G. A. (1987). Verbal report methods in clinical research on alcoholism: Response bias and its minimization. *Journal of Studies on Alcohol, 48,* 410–424.

Baker, T. B., Morse, E., & Sherman, J. E. (1987). The motivation to use drugs: A psychobiological analysis of urges. In C. Rivers (Ed.), *The Nebraska symposium on motivation: Alcohol use and abuse* (pp. 257–323). Lincoln, NE: University of Nebraska Press.

Bandura, A. (1969). *Principles of behavior modification.* New York: Holt, Rinehart & Winston.

Bandura, A. (1977). Self-efficacy: Toward a unifying theory of behavioral change. *Psychological Review, 84,* 191–215.

Bandura, A. (1986). *Social foundations of thought and action: A social cognitive theory.* Englewood Cliffs, NJ: Prentice-Hall.

Beck, A. T. (1976). *Cognitive therapy and the emotional disorders.* New York: International Universities Press.

Beck, A. T. (1991). Cognitive therapy: A 30-year retrospective. *American Psychologist, 46,* 368–375.

Birke, S. A., Edelmann, R. J., & Davis, P. E. (1990). An analysis of the abstinence violation effect in a sample of illicit drug users. *British Journal of Addiction, 85,* 1299–1307.

Booth, P. G., Dale, B., & Ansari, J. (1984). Problem drinkers' goal choice and treatment outcome: A preliminary study. *Addictive Behaviors, 9,* 357–364.

Cahalan, D. (1970). *Problem drinkers: A national survey.* San Francisco: Jossey-Bass.

Cahalan, D. (1987). Studying drinking problems rather than alcoholism. In M. Galanter (Ed.), *Recent developments in alcoholism* (Vol. 5, pp. 363–372). New York: Plenum Press.

Cahalan, D., & Room, R. (1974). *Problem drinking among American men.* New Brunswick, NJ: Rutgers Center of Alcohol Studies.

Cannon, D. S., Baker, T. B., Gino, A., & Nathan, P. E. (1986). Alcohol-aversion therapy: Relation between strength of aversion and abstinence. *Journal of Consulting and Clinical Psychology, 54,* 825–830.

Cannon, D. S., Leeka, J. K., Patterson, E. T., & Baker, T. B. (1990). Principal components analysis of the inventory of drinking situations: Empirical categories of drinking by alcoholics. *Addictive Behaviors, 15,* 265–269.

Carver, C. S., & Dunham, R. G. (1991). Abstinence expectancy and abstinence among men undergoing inpatient treatment for alcoholism. *Journal of Substance Abuse, 3,* 39–57.

Chaney, E. F., O'Leary, M. R., & Marlatt, G. A. (1978). Skill training with alcoholics. *Journal of Consulting and Clinical Psychology, 46,* 1092–1104.

Chapman, P. L. H., & Huygens, I. (1988). An evaluation of three treatment programmes for alcoholism: An experimental study with 6- and 18-month follow-ups. *British Journal of Addiction, 83,* 67–81.

Chick, J., Lloyd, G., & Crombie, E. (1985). Counselling problem drinkers in medical wards: A controlled study. *British Medical Journal, 290,* 965–967.

Chick, J., Ritson, B., Connaughton, J., Stewart, A., & Chick, J. (1988). Advice versus extended treatment for alcoholism: A controlled study. *British Journal of Addiction, 83,* 159–170.

Collins, R. L. (1993). Women's issues in alcohol use and smoking. In J. S. Baer, G. A. Marlatt, & R. J. McMahon (Eds.), *Addictive behaviors across the life span: Prevention, treatment, and policy issues* (pp. 274–306). New York: Sage.

Condiotte, M. M., & Lichtenstein, E. (1981). Self-efficacy and relapse in smoking cessation programs. *Journal of Consulting and Clinical Psychology, 49,* 648–658.

Connors, G. J., Tarbox, A. R., & Faillace, L. A. (1992). Achieving and maintaining gains among problem drinkers: Process and outcome results. *Behavior Therapy. 23,* 449–474.

Cook, C. C. H. (1988a). The Minnesota Model in the management of drug and alcohol dependency: Miracle, method or myth? Part I. The philosophy and the programme. *British Journal of Addiction, 83,* 625–634.

Cook, C. C. H. (1988b). The Minnesota Model in the management of drug and alcohol dependency: Miracle, method or myth? Part II. Evidence and conclusions. *British Journal of Addiction, 83,* 735-748.

Cummings, C., Gordon, J. R., & Marlatt, G. A. (1980). Relapse: Prevention and prediction. In W. R. Miller (Ed.), *Addictive behaviors* (pp. 291–321). New York: Pergamon Press.

Davidson, R. (1987). Assessment of the alcohol dependence syndrome: A review of self-report screening questionnaires. *British Psychological Society Bulletin, 26,* 243–255.

Davidson, R., & Raistrick, D. (1986). The validity of the short alcohol dependence data (SADD) questionnaire: A short self-report questionnaire for the assessment of alcohol dependence. *British Journal of Addiction, 81,* 217–222.

Davies, A. D. M. (1968). The influence of age on trail making test performance. *Journal of Clinical Psychology, 24,* 96–98.

Devgun, M. S., & Dunbar, J. A. (1990). Alcohol consumption, blood alcohol level and the relevance of body weight in experimental design and analysis. *Journal of Studies on Alcohol, 51,* 24–28.

Edwards, G. (1980). Alcoholism treatment: Between guesswork and certainty. In G. Edwards & M. Grant (Eds.), *Alcoholism treatment in transition* (pp. 307–320). London: Croom Helm.

Edwards, G. (1986). The alcohol dependence syndrome: A concept as stimulus to enquiry. *British Journal of Addiction, 81,* 171–184.

Edwards, G., & Gross, M. M. (1976). Alcohol dependence: Provisional description of a clinical syndrome. *British Medical Journal, 1,* 1058–1061.

Edwards, G., Gross, M., Keller, M., Moser, J., & Room, R. (Eds.). (1977). *Alcohol-related disabilities* (WHO Offset Publication No. 32). Geneva: World Health Organization.

Edwards, G., & Guthrie, S. (1967). A controlled trial in inpatient and outpatient treatment of alcohol dependency. *Lancet, 1,* 555–559.

Edwards, G., Orford, J., Egert, S., Guthrie, S., Hawker, A., Hensman, C., Mitcheson, M., Oppenheimer, E., & Taylor, C. (1977). Alcoholism: A controlled trial of "treatment" and "advice." *Journal of Studies on Alcohol, 38,* 1004–1031.

Elal-Lawrence, G., Slade, P. D., & Dewey, M. E. (1986). Predictors of outcome type in treated problem drinkers. *Journal of Studies on Alcohol, 47,* 41–47.

Eriksen, L., Björnstad, S., & Götestam, K. G. (1986). Social skills training in groups for alcoholics: One-year treatment outcome for groups and individuals. *Addictive Behaviors, 11,* 309–329.

Fillmore, K. (1974). Drinking and problem drinking in early adulthood and middle age. *Quarterly Journal of Studies on Alcohol, 35,* 819–840.

Fillmore, K. M. (1988). *Alcohol use across the life course: A critical review of 70 years of international longitudinal research.* Toronto, Ontario: Addiction Research Foundation.

Fillmore, K. M., & Midanik, L. (1984). Chronicity of drinking problems among men: A longitudinal study. *Journal of Studies on Alcohol, 45,* 228–236.

Fingarette, H. (1988). *Heavy drinking: The myth of alcoholism as a disease.* Berkeley, CA: University of California Press.

Finney, J. W., & Moos, R. H. (1986). Matching patient with treatments: Conceptual and methodological issues. *Journal of Studies on Alcohol, 47,* 122–134.

Flying and alcohol do not mix. (1990, March 19). *Newsweek,* p. 27.

Foy, D. W., Miller, P. M., Eisler, R. M., & O'Toole, D. H. (1976). Social skills training to teach alcoholics to refuse drinks effectively. *Journal of Alcohol Studies, 37,* 1340–1345.

Foy, D. W., Nunn, L. B., & Rychtarik, R. G. (1984). Broad-spectrum behavioral treatment for chronic alcoholics: Effects of training controlled drinking skills. *Journal of Consulting and Clinical Psychology, 52,* 218–230.

Gordis, E. (1987). Accessible and affordable health care for alcoholism and related problems: Strategy for cost containment. *Journal of Studies on Alcohol, 48,* 579–585.

Gordis, E., Dorph, D., Sepe, V., & Smith, H. (1981). Outcome of alcoholism treatment among 5578 patients in an urban comprehensive hospital-based program: Application of a computerized data system. *Alcoholism: Clinical and Experimental Research, 5,* 509–522.

Gorman, D. M., & Peters, T. J. (1990). Types of life events and the onset of alcohol dependence. *British Journal of Addiction, 85,* 71–79.

Graber, R. A., & Miller, W. R. (1988). Abstinence or controlled drinking goals for problem drinkers: A randomized clinical trial. *Psychology of Addictive Behaviors, 2,* 20–33.

Hall, S. M., Havassy, B. E., & Wasserman, D. A. (1990). Commitment to abstinence and acute stress in relapse to alcohol, opiates, and nicotine. *Journal of Consulting and Clinical Psychology, 58,* 175–181.

Hall, W., & Heather, N. (1991). Issue of statistical power in comparative evaluations of minimal and intensive controlled drinking interventions. *Addictive Behaviors, 16,* 83–87.

Hansen, J., & Emrick, C. D. (1983). Whom are we calling "alcoholic"? *Bulletin of the Society of Psychologists in Addictive Behaviors, 2,* 164–178.

Harris, K. B., & Miller, W. R. (1990). Behavioral self-control training for problem drinkers: Components of efficacy. *Psychology of Addictive Behavior, 4,* 82–90.

Hasin, D. S., Grant, B., & Endicott, J. (1990). The natural history of alcohol abuse: Implications for definitions of alcohol use disorders. *American Journal of Psychiatry, 147,* 1537–1541.

Hawkins, J. D., Catalano, R. F., Jr., & Wells, E. A. (1986). Measuring effects of a skills training intervention for drug abusers. *Journal of Consulting and Clinical Psychology, 54,* 661–664.

Heather, N. (1989). Psychology and brief interventions. *British Journal of Addiction, 84,* 357–370.

Heather, N. (1990). Brief intervention strategies. In R. K. Hester & W. R. Miller (Eds.), *Handbook of alcoholism treatment approaches: Effective alternatives* (pp. 93–116). New York: Pergamon Press.

Heather, N., Kissoon-Singh, J., & Fenton, G. W. (1990). Assisted natural recovery from alcohol problems: Effects of a self-help manual with and without supplementary telephone contact. *British Journal of Addiction, 85,* 1177–1185.

Heather, N., & Robertson, I. (1983). *Controlled drinking* (2nd ed.). New York: Methuen.

Heather, N., Robertson, I., MacPherson, B., Allsop, S., & Fulton, A. (1987). Effectiveness of a controlled drinking self-help manual: One-year follow-up results. *British Journal of Clinical Psychology, 26,* 279–287.

Heather, N., Whitton, B., & Robertson, I. (1986). Evaluation of a self-help manual for media-recruited problem drinkers: Six-month follow-up results. *British Journal of Clinical Psychology, 25,* 19–34.

Hester, R. K., & Miller, W. R. (1990). Self-control training. In R. K. Hester & W. R. Miller (Eds.), *Handbook of alcoholism treatment approaches: Effective alternatives* (pp. 141–149). New York: Pergamon Press.

Hill, S. Y. (1985). The disease concept of alcoholism: A review. *Drug and Alcohol Dependence, 16,* 193–214.

Hilton, M. (1987). Drinking patterns and drinking problems in 1984: Results from a general population survey. *Alcoholism: Clinical and Experimental Research, 11,* 167–175.

Hilton, M. E. (1991). A note on measuring drinking problems in the 1984 national alcohol survey. In W. B. Clark & M. E. Hilton (Eds.), *Alcohol in America: Drinking practices and problems* (pp. 51–70). Albany: State University of New York Press.

Hingson, R., Mangione, T., Meyers, A., & Scotch, N. (1982). Seeking help for drinking problems: A study in the Boston metropolitan area. *Journal of Studies on Alcohol, 43,* 273–288.

Holden, C. (1987). Alcoholism and the medical cost crunch. *Science, 235,* 1132–1133.

Hunt, G. M., & Azrin, N. H. (1973). A community-reinforcement approach to alcoholism. *Behaviour Research and Therapy, 11,* 91–104.

Hunt, W. A., Barnett, L. W., & Branch, L. G. (1971). Relapse rates in addiction programs. *Journal of Clinical Psychology, 27,* 455–456.

Institute of Medicine. (1990). *Broadening the base of treatment for alcohol problems.* Washington, DC: National Academy Press.

Isenhart, C. E. (1991). Factor structure of the Inventory of Drinking Situations. *Journal of Substance Abuse, 3,* 59–71.

Ito, R. J., Donovan, D. M., & Hall, J. J. (1988). Relapse prevention in alcohol aftercare: Effects on drinking outcome, change process, and aftercare attendance. *British Journal of Addiction, 83,* 171–181.

Jastak, J. F., & Jastak, S. (1965). The Wide Range Achievement Test manual. Wilmington, DE: Jastak.

Jellinek, E. M. (1946). Phases in the drinking histories of alcoholics. *Quarterly Journal of Studies on Alcohol, 7,* 1–88.

Jellinek, E. M. (1952). Phases of alcohol addiction. *Quarterly Journal of Studies on Alcohol, 13,* 673–684.

Jellinek, E. M. (1960a). Alcoholism, a genus and some of its species. *Canadian Medical Association Journal, 83,* 1341–1345.

Jellinek, E. M. (1960b). *The disease concept of alcoholism.* New Brunswick, NJ: Hillhouse Press.

Kanas, T. E., Cleveland, S. E., Pokorny, A. D., & Miller, B. A. (1976). Two contrasting alcoholism treatment programs: A comparison of outcomes. *International Journal of the Addictions, 11,* 1045–1062.

Kantorovich, N. V. (1929). An attempt at association reflex therapy in alcoholism. *Novoe u refleksologii i fiziologii nervnoi sistemy, 3,* 435–447.

Kapur, B. H. (1991). CBAC: Computerized Blood Alcohol Concentration a computer model as a clinical and educational tool. *Annales de Biochimie Clinique du Québec, 30,* 36–39.

Kazdin, A. E., & Bass, D. (1989). Power to detect differences between alternative treatments in comparative psychotherapy outcome research. *Journal of Consulting and Clinical Psychology, 57,* 138–147.

Killen, J. D., Fortmann, S. P., Newman, B., & Varady, A. (1990). Evaluation of a treatment approach combining nicotine gum with self-guided behavioral treatments for smoking relapse prevention. *Journal of Consulting and Clinical Psychology, 58,* 85–92.

Kissin, B. (1983). The disease concept of alcoholism. In R. G. Smart, F. B. Glaser, Y. Israel, H. Kalant, R. E. Popham, & W. Schmidt (Eds.), *Research advances in alcohol and drug problems* (Vol. 7, pp. 93–126). New York: Plenum Press.

Kissin, B., Platz, A., & Su, W. H. (1970). Social and psychological factors in the treatment of chronic alcoholism. *Journal of Psychiatric Research, 8,* 13–27.

Kristenson, H. (1987). Alcohol dependence and problem drinking in urban middle aged men. *Alcohol and Alcoholism, 1,* 601–606.

Kristenson, H., Öhlin, H., Hultén-Nosslin, M. B., Trell, E., & Hood, B. (1983). Identification and intervention of heavy drinking in middle-aged men: Results and follow-up of 24–60 months of long-term study with randomized controls. *Alcoholism: Clinical and Experimental Research, 7,* 203–209.

Kristenson, H., Trell, E., & Hood, B. (1981). Serum-γ-glutamyltransferase in screening and continuous control of heavy drinking in middle-aged men. *American Journal of Epidemiology, 114,* 862–872.

Kuchipudi, V., Hobein, K., Flickinger, A., & Iber, F. L. (1990). Failure of a 2-hour motivational intervention to alter recurrent drinking behavior in alcoholics with gastrointestinal disease. *Journal of Studies on Alcohol, 51,* 356–360.

Larimer, M. E., & Marlatt, G. A. (1990). Applications of relapse prevention with moderation goals. *Journal of Psychoactive Drugs, 22,* 189–195.

Lazarus, A. A. (1965). Towards the understanding and effective treatment of alcoholism. *South African Medical Journal, 39,* 736–741.

Lloyd, G., Chick, J., Crombie, E., & Anderson, S. (1986). Problem drinkers in medical wards: Consumption patterns and disabilities in newly identified male cases. *British Journal of Addiction, 81,* 789–795.

Lovibond, S. H., & Caddy, G. (1970). Discriminated aversive control in the moderation of alcoholics' drinking behavior. *Behavior Therapy, 1,* 437–444.

Mahalik, J. R., & Kivlighan, D. M., Jr. (1988). Self-help treatment for depression: Who succeeds? *Journal of Counseling Psychology, 35,* 237–242.

Mahoney, M. J., & Lyddon, W. J. (1988). Recent developments in cognitive approaches to counseling and psychotherapy. *Counseling Psychologist, 16,* 190–234.

Mandell, W. (1983). Types and phases of alcohol dependence. In M. Galanter (Ed.), *Recent developments in alcoholism* (Vol. 3, pp. 415–448). New York: Plenum Press.

Marlatt, G. A. (1978). Craving for alcohol, loss of control, and relapse. In P. E. Nathan, G. A. Marlatt, & T. Løberg (Eds.), *Alcoholism: New directions in behavioral research and treatment* (pp. 271–314). New York: Plenum Press.

Marlatt, G. A. (1983). The controlled-drinking controversy: A commentary. *American Psychologist, 38,* 1096–1110.

Marlatt, G. A., & Gordon, J. R. (Eds.). (1985). *Relapse prevention.* New York: Guilford Press.

McCrady, B., Longabaugh, R., Fink, E., Stout, R. L., Beattie, M., & Ruggieri-Authelet, A. (1986). Cost effectiveness of alcoholism treatment in partial hospital versus inpatient settings after brief inpatient treatment: 12-month outcomes. *Journal of Consulting and Clinical Psychology, 54,* 708–713.

McKay, J. R., O'Farrell, T. J., Maisto, S. A., Connors, G. J., & Funder, D. C. (1989). Biases in relapse attributions made by alcoholics and their wives. *Addictive Behaviors, 14,* 513–522.

McLachlan, J. F. C., & Stein, R. L. (1982). Evaluation of a day-clinic for alcoholics. *Journal of Studies on Alcohol, 43,* 261–272.

Mendelson, J. H., LaDou, J., & Solomon, P. (1964). Experimentally induced chronic intoxication and withdrawal in alcoholics: Part 3. Psychiatric findings. *Quarterly Journal of Studies on Alcohol, 25*(Suppl. 2), 40–52.

Miller, W. R. (1977). Behavioral self-control training in the treatment of problem drinkers. In R. B. Stuart (Ed.), *Behavioral self-management: Strategies, techniques and outcomes* (pp. 154–175). New York: Brunner/Mazel.

Miller, W. R. (1983). Motivational interviewing with problem drinkers. *Behavioral Psychotherapy, 11,* 147–172.

Miller, W. R. (1985). Motivation for treatment: A review with special emphasis on alcoholism. *Psychological Bulletin, 98,* 84–107.

Miller, W. R. (1986/1987). Motivation and treatment goals. *Drugs and Society, 1,* 133–151.

Miller, W. R., & Baca, L. M. (1983). Two-year follow-up of bibliotherapy and therapist-directed controlled drinking training for problem drinkers. *Behavior Therapy, 14,* 441–448.

Miller, W. R., Gribskov, C. J., & Mortell, R. L. (1981). Effectiveness of a self-control manual for problem drinkers with and without therapist contact. *International Journal of the Addictions, 16,* 1247–1254.

Miller, W. R., & Hester, R. K. (1980). Treating the problem drinker: Modern approaches. In W. R. Miller (Ed.), *The addictive behaviors: Treatment of alcoholism, drug abuse, smoking and obesity* (pp. 11–141). New York: Pergamon Press.

Miller, W. R., & Hester, R. K. (1986a). The effectiveness of alcoholism treatment: What research reveals. In W. R. Miller & N. Heather (Eds.), *Treating addictive behaviors: Processes of change* (pp. 121–174). New York: Plenum Press.

Miller, W. R., & Hester, R. K. (1986b). Matching problem drinkers with optimal treatments. In W. R. Miller & N. Heather (Eds.), *Treating addictive behaviors: Processes of change* (pp. 175–203). New York: Plenum Press.

Miller, W. R., & Muñoz, R. F. (1982). *How to control your drinking* (rev. ed.). Albuquerque, NM: University of New Mexico Press.

Miller, W. R., & Rollnick, S. (1991). *Motivational interviewing: Preparing people to change addictive behavior.* New York: Guilford Press.

Miller, W. R., & Sovereign, R. G. (1989). The check-up: A model for early intervention in addictive behaviors. In T. Løberg, W. R. Miller, P. E. Nathan, & G. A. Marlatt (Eds.), *Addictive behaviors: Prevention and early intervention* (pp. 219–231). Amsterdam: Swets & Zeitlinger.

Miller, W. R., Sovereign, R. G., & Krege, B. (1988). Motivational interviewing with problem drinkers: II. The drinkers's check-up as a preventive intervention. *Behavioural Psychotherapy, 16,* 251–268.

Miller, W. R., & Taylor, C. A. (1980). Relative effectiveness of bibliotherapy, individual and group self-control training in the treatment of problem drinkers. *Addictive Behaviors, 5,* 13–24.

Miller, W. R., Taylor, C. A., & West, J. C. (1980). Focused versus broad-spectrum behavior therapy for problem drinkers. *Journal of Consulting and Clinical Psychology, 48,* 590–601.

Moore, M. H., & Gerstein, D. R. (Eds.). (1981). *Alcohol and public policy: Beyond the shadow of prohibition.* Washington, DC: National Academy Press.

Nathan, P. E. (1991). Substance use disorders in DSM-IV. *Journal of Abnormal Psychology, 100,* 356–361.

Nathan, P. E., & McCrady, B. S. (1986/1987). Bases for the use of abstinence as a goal in the behavioral treatment of alcohol abusers. *Drugs and Society, 1,* 109–131.

National Institute on Alcohol Abuse and Alcoholism. (1990). *Seventh special report to the U.S. Congress on alcohol and health* (U.S. Department of Health and Human Services Publication No. ADM 90–1656). Washington, DC: U.S. Government Printing Office.

Nelson, R. O., & Hayes, S. C. (1981). Theoretical explanations for reactivity in self-monitoring. *Behavior Modification, 5,* 3–14.

Niaura, R. S., Rohsenow, D. J., Binkoff, J. A., Monti, P. M., Abrams, D. B., & Pedraza, M. (1988). Relevance of cue reactivity to understanding alcohol and smoking relapse. *Journal of Abnormal Psychology, 97,* 133–152.

Nowinski, J., Baker, S., & Carroll, K. (1992). *Twelve step facilitation therapy manual* (DHHS Publication No. ADM 92–1893). Rockville, MD: National Institute on Alcohol Abuse and Alcoholism.

O'Farrell, T. J., & Maisto, S. A. (1987). The utility of self-report and biological measures of alcohol consumption in alcoholism treatment outcome studies. *Advances in Behaviour Research and Therapy, 9,* 91–125.

Orford, J., & Keddie, A. (1986a). Abstinence or controlled drinking in clinical practice: A test of the dependence and persuasion hypotheses. *British Journal of Addiction, 81,* 495–504.

Orford, J., & Keddie, A. (1986b). Abstinence or controlled drinking in clinical practice: Indications at initial assessment. *Addictive Behaviors, 11,* 71–86.

Orford, J., Oppenheimer, E., & Edwards, G. (1976). Abstinence or control: The outcome for excessive drinkers two years after consultation. *Behaviour Research and Therapy, 14,* 409–418.

Pattison, E. M., Sobell, M. B., & Sobell, L. C. (Eds.). (1977). *Emerging concepts of alcohol dependence.* New York: Springer.

Peele, S. (1989). *Diseasing of America: Addiction treatment out of control.* Lexington, MA: Lexington Books.

Peele, S. (1990). Why and by whom the American alcoholism treatment industry is under siege. *Journal of Psychoactive Drugs, 22,* 1–13.

Persson, J., & Magnusson, P. H. (1989). Early intervention in patients with excessive consumption of alcohol: A controlled study. *Alcohol, 6,* 403–408.

Pittman, D. J., & Tate, R. L. (1969). A comparison of two treatment programs for alcoholics. *Quarterly Journal of Studies on Alcohol, 30,* 888–899.

Polich, J. M. (1981). Epidemiology of alcohol abuse in military and civilian populations. *American Journal of Public Health, 71,* 1125–1132.

Polich, J. M., Armor, D. J., & Braiker, H. B. (1981). *The course of alcoholism: Four years after treatment.* New York: Wiley.

Pomerleau, O., & Adkins, D. (1980). Evaluating behavioral and traditional treatment for problem drinkers. In L. C. Sobell, M. B. Sobell, & E. Ward (Eds.), *Evaluating alcohol and drug abuse treatment effectiveness: Recent advances* (pp. 93–108). New York: Pergamon Press.

Pomerleau, O., Pertschuk, M., Adkins, D., & Brady, J. P. (1978). A comparison of behavioral and traditional treatment for middle income problem drinkers. *Journal of Behavioral Medicine, 1,* 187–200.

Rankin, H. (1990). Validity of self-reports in clinical settings. *Behavioral Assessment, 12,* 107–116.

Robertson, I., Heather, N., Dzialdowski, A., Crawford, J., & Winton, M. (1986). A comparison of minimal versus intensive controlled drinking treatment interventions for problem drinkers. *British Journal of Clinical Psychology, 25,* 185–194.

Roffman, R. A., Stephens, R. S., & Simpson, E. S. (1990, November). *Relapse prevention and the treatment of marijuana dependence: Long-term outcomes.* Paper presented at the meeting of the Association for Advancement of Behavior Therapy, San Francisco.

Roffman, R. A., Stephens, R. S., Simpson, E. E., & Whitaker, D. L. (1988). Treatment of marijuana dependence: Preliminary results. *Journal of Psychoactive Drugs, 20,* 129–137.

Romach, M. K., Sellers, E. M., Toneatto, T., Sobell, L. C., Somer, G. R., & Sobell, M. B. (1991). Ondansetron, a 5-HT$_3$ antagonist, is associated with a reduction in drinking in alcohol abusers. *Serotonin, 185*, 155.

Room, R. (1977). Measurement and distribution of drinking patterns and problems in general populations. In G. Edwards, M. M. Gross, M. Keller, J. Moser, & R. Room (Eds.), *Alcohol-related disabilities* (pp. 62–87). Geneva: World Health Organization.

Room, R. (1980). Treatment-seeking populations in large realities. In G. Edwards & M. Grant (Eds.), *Alcoholism treatment in transition* (pp. 205–224). London: Croom Helm.

Room, R. (1990). Measuring alcohol consumption in the United States: Methods and rationales. In L. T. Kozlowski, H. M. Annis, H. D. Cappell, F. B. Glaser, M. S. Goodstadt, Y. Israel, H. Kalant, E. M. Sellers, & E. R. Vingilis (Eds.), *Research advances in alcohol and drug problems* (Vol. 10, pp. 39–80). New York: Plenum Press.

Russell, M. A. H., Wilson, C., Taylor, C., & Baker, C. D. (1979). Effect of general practitioners' advice against smoking. *British Medical Journal, 2*, 231–235.

Sanchez-Craig, M. (1980). Random assignment to abstinence or controlled drinking in a cognitive-behavioral program: Short-term effects on drinking behavior. *Addictive Behaviors, 5*, 35–39.

Sanchez-Craig, M. (1986). How much is too much? Estimates of hazardous drinking based on clients' self-reports. *British Journal of Addiction, 81*, 251–256.

Sanchez-Craig, M. (1987). *Dealing with drinking: Steps to abstinence or moderate drinking*. Toronto: Addiction Research Foundation.

Sanchez, Craig, M. (1990). Brief didactic treatment for alcohol and drug-related problems: An approach based on client choice. *British Journal of Addiction, 85*, 169–177.

Sanchez, Craig, M., Annis, H. M., Bornet, A. R., & MacDonald, K. R. (1984). Random assignment to abstinence and controlled drinking: Evaluation of a cognitive-behavioral program for problem drinkers. *Journal of Consulting and Clinical Psychology, 52*, 390–403.

Sanchez-Craig, M., & Israel, Y. (1985). Pattern of alcohol use associated with self-identified problem drinking. *American Journal of Public Health, 75*, 178–180.

Sanchez-Craig, M., & Lei, H. (1986). Disadvantages to imposing the goal of abstinence on problem drinkers: An empirical study. *British Journal of Addiction, 81*, 505–512.

Sanchez-Craig, M., Leigh, G., Spivak, K., & Lei, H. (1989). Superior outcome of females over males after brief treatment for the reduction of heavy drinking. *British Journal of Addiction, 84*, 395–404.

Sanchez-Craig, M., Spivak, K., & Davila, R. (1991). Superior outcome of females over males after brief treatment for the reduction of heavy drinking: Replication and report of therapist effects. *British Journal of Addiction, 86*, 867–876.

Sanchez-Craig, M., & Wilkinson, D. A. (1986/1987). Treating problem drinkers who are not severely dependent on alcohol. *Drugs and Society, 1*, 39–67.

Saunders, B., & Allsop, S. (1987). Relapse: A psychological perspective. *British Journal of Addiction, 82*, 417–429.

Saunders, B., & Allsop, S. (1992). Incentives and restraints: Clinical research into problem drug use and self-control. In N. Heather, W. R. Miller, & J. Greeley (Eds.), *Self-control and addictive behaviors* (pp. 283–303). New York: Macmillan.

Saunders, J. B., & Aasland, O. G. (1987). WHO collaborative project on identification and treatment of persons with harmful alcohol consumption (Doc. WHO/ MNH/DAT/86.3). Geneva: World Health Organization.

Scogin, F., Bynum, J., Stephens, G., & Calhoon, S. (1990). Efficacy of self-administered treatment programs: Meta-analytic review. *Professional Psychology: Research and Practice, 21,* 42–47.

Sellers, E. M., Romach, M. K., Toneatto, T., Sobell, L. C., Somer, G. R., & Sobell, M. (1991). Efficacy of Ondansetron, 5-HT$_3$ antagonist, in alcoholism treatment. *Biological Psychiatry, 29* (Suppl.), 495.

Shaffer, H. J. (1985). The disease controversy: Of metaphors, maps and menus. *Journal of Psychoactive Drugs, 17,* 65–76.

Shiffman, S. M. (1982). Relapse following smoking cessation: A situational analysis. *Journal of Clinical and Consulting Psychology, 50,* 71–86.

Sjoberg, L., & Samsonowitz, V. (1985). Coping strategies in alcohol abuse. *Drug and Alcohol Dependence, 15,* 283–301.

Skinner, H. A. (1990). Spectrum of drinkers and intervention opportunities. *Canadian Medical Association Journal, 143,* 1054–1059.

Skinner, H. A., & Allen, B. A. (1982). Alcohol dependence syndrome: Measurement and validation. *Journal of Abnormal Psychology, 91,* 199–209.

Skinner, H. A., & Horn, J. L. (1984). *Alcohol Dependence Scale (ADS) user's guide.* Toronto: Addiction Research Foundation.

Skutle, A., & Berg, G. (1987). Training in controlled drinking for early-stage problem drinkers. *British Journal of Addiction, 82,* 493–501.

Smith, R. E. (1989). Effects of coping skills training on generalized self-efficacy and locus of control. *Journal of Personality and Social Psychology, 56,* 228–233.

Sobell, L. C. (1993). *Motivational interventions with problem drinkers.* Paper presented at the Sixth International Conference on Treatment of Addictive Behaviors, Santa Fe, NM.

Sobell, L. C., & Sobell, M. B. (1973). A self-feedback technique to monitor drinking behavior in alcoholics. *Behaviour Research and Therapy, 11,* 237–238.

Sobell, L. C., & Sobell, M. B. (1983). Behavioral research and therapy: Its impact on the alcohol field. In K. D. Craig & R. J. McMahon (Eds.), *Advances in clinical behavior therapy* (pp. 175–193). New York: Brunner/Mazel.

Sobell, L. C., & Sobell, M. B. (1986). Can we do without alcohol abusers' self-reports? *Behavior Therapist, 7,* 141–146.

Sobell, L. C., & Sobell, M. B. (1990). Self-report issues in alcohol abuse: State of the art and future directions. *Behavioral Assessment, 12,* 91–106.

Sobell, L. C., & Sobell, M. B. (1992a). Spousal social support: A motivational interventional for alcohol abusers. Unpublished data. Toronto, Ont.

Sobell, L. C., & Sobell, M. B. (1992b). Timeline Follow-back: A technique for assessing self-reported ethanol consumption. In J. Allen & R. Z. Litten (Eds.), *Measuring alcohol consumption: Psychosocial and biological methods* (pp. 41–72). Totowa, NJ: Humana Press.

Sobell, L. C., Sobell, M. B., Leo, G. I., & Cancilla, A. (1988). Reliability of a timeline method: Assessing normal drinkers' reports of recent drinking and a comparative evaluation across several populations. *British Journal of Addiction*, 83, 393–402.

Sobell, L. C., Sobell, M. B., & Nirenberg, T. D. (1988). Behavioral assessment and treatment planning with alcohol and drug abusers: A review with an emphasis on clinical application. *Clinical Psychology Review*, 8, 19–54.

Sobell, L. C., Sobell, M. B., Riley, D. M., Schuller, R., Pavan, D. S., Cancilla, A., Klajner, F., & Leo, G. I. (1988). The reliability of alcohol abusers' self-reports of drinking and life events that occurred in the distant past. *Journal of Studies on Alcohol*, 49, 225–232.

Sobell, L. C., Sobell, M. B., & Toneatto, T. (1992). Recovery from alcohol problems without treatment. In N. Heather, W. R. Miller, & J. Greeley (Eds.), *Self-control and the addictive behaviours* (pp. 198–242). New York: Macmillan.

Sobell, L. C., Sobell, M. B., Toneatto, T., & Leo, G. I. (in press). What triggers the resolution of alcohol problems without treatment? *Alcoholism: Clinical and experimental research*.

Sobell, M. B., Bogardis, J., Schuller, R., Leo, G. I., & Sobell, L. C. (1989). Is self-monitoring of alcohol consumption reactive? *Behavioral Assessment*, 11, 447–458.

Sobell, M. B., Sellers, E. M., & Sobell, L. C. (1990, January). *Combining pharmacological and behavioral treatments for enhancing self-control over addictive behaviors*. Paper presented at the Fifth International Conference on Treatment of Addictive Behaviors, Sydney, Australia.

Sobell, M. B., & Sobell, L. C. (1973). Individualized behavior therapy for alcoholics. *Behavior Therapy*, 4, 49–72.

Sobell, M. B., & Sobell, L. C. (1975). A brief technical report on the Mobat: An inexpensive portable test for determining blood alcohol concentration. *Journal of Applied Behavior Analysis*, 8, 117–120.

Sobell, M. B., & Sobell, L. C. (1978). *Behavioral treatment of alcohol problems: Individualized therapy and controlled drinking*. New York: Plenum Press.

Sobell, M. B., & Sobell, L. C. (1986/1987). Conceptual issues regarding goals in the treatment of alcohol problems. *Drugs and Society*, 1, 1–37.

Sobell, M. B., & Sobell, L. C. (1990, January). *Problem drinkers and self-control treatments: A closer look*. Paper presented at the Fifth International Conference on Treatment of Addictive Behaviors, Sydney, Australia.

Sobell, M. B., & Sobell, L. C. (1993). Treatment for problem drinkers: A public health priority. In J. S. Baer, G. A. Marlatt, & R. J. McMahon (Eds.), *Addictive behaviors across the lifespan: Prevention, treatment, and policy issues* (pp. 138–157). Beverly Hills, CA: Sage.

Sobell, M. B., Sobell, L. C., Bogardis, J., Leo, G. I., & Skinner, W. (1992). Problem drinkers' perceptions of whether treatment goals should be self-selected or therapist-selected. *Behavior Therapy*, 23, 43–52.

Sobell, M. B., Sobell, L. C., & Leo, G. I. (1990, November). *Guided self-management for problem drinkers: An evaluation of the unique contribution of a relapse prevention perspective*. Poster session presented at the 24rd Annual Meeting of the Association for Advancement of Behavior Therapy, San Francisco.

Sobell, M. B., Sobell, L. C., & Sheahan, D. B. (1976). Functional analysis of drinking problems as an aid in developing individual treatment strategies. *Addictive Behaviors, 1,* 127–132.

Sobell, M. B., Sobell, L. C., & VanderSpek, R. (1979). Relationships between clinical judgment, self-report and breath analysis measures of intoxication in alcoholics. *Journal of Consulting and Clinical Psychology, 47,* 204–206.

Stein, L. I., Newton, J. R., & Bowman, R. S. (1975). Duration of hospitalization for alcoholism. *Archives of General Psychiatry, 32,* 247–252.

Stewart, J., DeWit, H., & Eikelboom, R. (1984). Role of unconditioned and conditioned drug effects in the self-administration of opiates and stimulants. *Psychological Review, 91,* 251–268.

Stockwell, T., Murphy, D., & Hodgson, R. (1983). The Severity of Alcohol Dependence Questionnaire: Its use, reliability and validity. *British Journal of Addiction, 78,* 145–155.

Thom, B. (1986). Sex differences in help-seeking for alcohol problems: 1. The barriers to help-seeking. *British Journal of Addiction, 81,* 777–788.

Thom, B. (1987). Sex differences in help-seeking for alcohol problems: 2. Entry into treatment. *British Journal of Addiction, 82,* 989–997.

Thorley, A. (1980). Medical response to problem drinking. *Medicine, 35,* 1816–1827.

Tipton, R. M., & Worthington, E. L. Jr. (1984). The measurement of generalized self-efficacy: A study of construct validity. *Journal of Personality Assessment, 48,* 545–548.

Toneatto, T., Romach, M. K., Sobell, L. C., Sobell, M. B., Somer, G. R., & Sellers, E. M. (1991). Ondansetron, a $5\text{-}HT_3$ antagonist, reduces alcohol consumption in alcohol abusers. *Alcoholism: Clinical and Experimental Research, 15,* 382.

Tuchfeld, B. S. (1981). Spontaneous remission in alcoholics: Empirical observations and theoretical implications. *Journal of Studies on Alcohol, 42,* 626–641.

Twentyman, C. T., Greenwald, D. P., Greenwald, M. A., Kloss, J. D., Kovaleski, M. E., & Zibung-Hoffman, P. (1982). An assessment of social skills deficits in alcoholics. *Behavioral Assessment, 4,* 317–326.

Vaillant, G. E., Clark, W., Cyrus, C., Milofsky, E. S., Kopp, J., Wulsin, V. W., & Mogielnicki, N. P. (1983). Prospective study of alcoholism treatment: Eight-year follow-up. *American Journal of Medicine, 75,* 455–463.

Voegtlin, W. L., & Lemere, F. (1942). The treatment of alcohol addiction: A review of the literature. *Quarterly Journal of Studies on Alcohol, 2,* 717–803.

Vogler, R. E., & Bartz, W. R. (1982). *The better way to drink.* New York: Simon and Schuster.

Wallace, P., Cutler, S., & Haines, A. (1988). Randomised controlled trial of general practitioner intervention in patients with excessive alcohol consumption. *British Medical Journal, 297,* 663–668.

Wang, A. Y., & RiCharde, R. S. (1988). Global versus task-specific measures of self-efficacy. *Psychological Record, 38,* 533–541.

Watson, P. E., Watson, I. D., & Batt, R. D. (1980). Total body volume for adult males and females estimated from simple anthropometric measurements. *American Journal of Clinical Nutrition, 33,* 27–39.

Weisner, C., & Room, R. (1984/1985). Financing and ideology in alcohol treatment. *Social Problems, 32,* 167–184.

182   **References**

Wikler, A. (1948). Recent progress in research on the neurophysiologic basis of morphine addiction. *American Journal of Psychiatry, 105,* 329–338.

Wilkinson, D. A., & Carlen, P. L. (1981). Chronic organic brain syndromes associated with alcoholism. In Y. Israel, F. B. Glaser, H. Kalant, R. E. Popham, W. Schmidt, & R. G. Smart (Eds.), *Research advances in alcohol and drug problems* (pp. 107–145). New York: Plenum Press.

Wilson, A., White, J., & Lange, D. E. (1978). Outcome evaluation of a hospital-based alcoholism treatment programme. *British Journal of Addiction, 73,* 39–45.

Wise, R. A., & Bozarth, M. A. (1987). A psychomotor stimulant theory of addiction. *Psychological Review, 94,* 469–492.

Zweben, A., Pearlman, S., & Li, S. (1988). A comparison of brief advice and conjoint therapy in the treatment of alcohol abuse: The results of the marital systems study. *British Journal of Addiction, 83,* 899–916.

Index